The Evolution of Pervasive Information Systems

Manuele Kirsch Pinheiro • Carine Souveyet •
Philippe Roose • Luiz Angelo Steffenel
Editors

The Evolution of Pervasive Information Systems

 Springer

Editors
Manuele Kirsch Pinheiro
Center for Research in Informatics
Pantheon-Sorbonne University
Paris, France

Carine Souveyet
Centre de Recherche en Informatique
Pantheon-Sorbonne University
Paris, France

Philippe Roose
Université de Pau
Anglet, France

Luiz Angelo Steffenel
University of Reims Champagne-Ardenne
Reims, France

ISBN 978-3-031-18178-8   ISBN 978-3-031-18176-4   (eBook)
https://doi.org/10.1007/978-3-031-18176-4

This Springer imprint is published by the registered company Springer Nature Switzerland AG
The registered company address is: Gewerbestrasse 11, 6330 Cham, Switzerland

Preface

The purpose of this book is to combine "state-of-the-art" solutions of various research communities (such as Information Systems Engineering, Cloud Computing, Fog/Edge Computing, Pervasive systems, Distributed systems, Middleware systems) related to the Pervasive Information Systems emergence as a common point of view. Pervasive Information Systems (PIS, for short) are deeply multidisciplinary systems, demanding a holistic view in which multiple domains are invited to contribute.

Indeed, new IT trends have an important impact on IT infrastructures, which become more and more heterogeneous, flexible, and dynamic. For example, IT infrastructures now are supposed to:

- Push the business by supporting alternative pervasive business processes
- Capture data from IoT devices, which can be used to improve business layers

PIS should be aware of the evolution of its real environment and its own execution environment, helping to adapt its behavior at each layer according to the situation at hand.

Therefore, Kirsch Pinheiro et al. introduce in chapter "What is a "Pervasive Information System" (PIS)?" the definition of PIS and present a transversal view of a PIS, its interactions, and the multiple research domain that contribute to this view. This chapter also describes the implications of its adoption on both technical and organizational aspects, identifying a set of requirements for the construction of a PIS and its operation.

In chapter "Design and Modeling in Pervasive Information Systems", Souveyet and Deneckere propose a systematic literature review to analyze how researchers handle the design of PIS. This literature review demonstrates that the requirements identified in chapter "What is a "Pervasive Information System" (PIS)?" remain an open issue for PIS at the design level.

In chapter "The Context Awareness Challenges for PIS", Kirsch Pinheiro discusses the challenges related to context awareness support on PIS. Multiple insights are highlighted from the literature, including the need for an efficient middleware for context awareness support, but also the opportunities that arise with

Edge Computing and Edge Learning technics that are respectively the subject of chapters "Middleware Supporting PIS: Requirements, Solutions, and Challenges" and "Edge Computing and Learning".

In chapter "Middleware Supporting PIS: Requirements, Solutions, and Challenges", Taconet et al. examine challenges related to middleware supporting PIS activities. Several requirements and state of the art of available solutions are discussed, with a particular interest in energy concerns.

In chapter "Edge Computing and Learning", Lalanda expands the vision of PIS toward IoT, Edge Computing, and Edge Learning (Edge AI). By analyzing usages and similarities among these research domains, this chapter tackles the opportunities and challenges for the deployment of PIS.

Looking closer to implementation aspects, Le Moël and Carrilo produce in chapter "IS: IoT & Industry 4.0 Challenges" a detailed panorama of environments, protocols, and standards that enable the implementation of PIS over IoT and Industry 4.0 environments. By observing how context information is handled in these environments, the authors invite a reflection on how to conciliate customer and industry goals with the help of PIS.

Finally, going further on the deployment of PIS aspects, Fernandes et al. produce in chapter "PIS: Interoperability and Decision-Making Process – A Review" a detailed survey on requirements and strategies to ensure the interoperability of PIS. This is indeed a key aspect for the integration of services and the adoption of PIS.

Paris, France   Manuele Kirsch Pinheiro
Paris, France   Carine Souveyet
Anglet, France   Philippe Roose
Reims, France   Luiz Angelo Steffenel

Contents

What Is a "Pervasive Information System" (PIS)?

Manuele Kirsch Pinheiro, Philippe Roose, Luiz Angelo Steffenel, and Carine Souveyet

1 Introduction

The integration of new technologies such as IoT, Big Data, Cloud and Edge Computing, as well as new practices, such as agile and DevOps makes organizations rapidly evolving. Through these technologies and practices, organizations are mainly looking for more flexibility in order to better react to a dynamic business context.

The Information Technologie (IT) domain is gradually embedded in the physical environment and can accommodate the user's requirements and desires when necessary. This evolution significantly changes the way Information Systems handle its infrastructure. The traditional approach in Information Systems Engineering is silo-based, in which the IT business services layer and the IT infrastructure layer are always managed separately, whereas this evolution implies considering Information Systems beyond the organization's physical environment to integrate new technologies in a transparent manner, leading to a pervasive environment whose behavior should be more and more reactive & proactive. It corresponds to an important change for Information Systems Engineering and for IS themselves, which are becoming what we call here Pervasive Information Systems.

M. Kirsch Pinheiro (✉) · C. Souveyet
Centre de Recherche en Informatique, Université Paris 1 Panthéon Sorbonne, Paris, France
e-mail: Manuele.Kirsch-Pinheiro@univ-paris1.fr; Carine.Souveyet@univ-paris1.fr

P. Roose
LIUPPA, E2S, Université de Pau et des Pays de l'Adour, Anglet, France
e-mail: Philippe.Roose@iutbayonne.univ-pau.fr

L. A. Steffenel
LICIIS, Université de Reims Champagne Ardenne, Reims, France
e-mail: Luiz-Angelo.Steffenel@univ-reims.fr

© The Author(s), under exclusive license to Springer Nature Switzerland AG 2023
M. Kirsch Pinheiro et al. (eds.), *The Evolution of Pervaize Information Systems*,
https://doi.org/10.1007/978-3-031-18176-4_1

Pervasive Information Systems (PIS) can be defined as a new class of Information Systems. It can be characterized by an IT that is gradually embedded in the physical environment and can accommodate the user's requirements and desires when necessary. In contrast to traditional Information System, Pervasive Information Systems should be aware of the evolution of its real environment and its own execution environment, requiring a holistic view of them at the design time but also at the execution time. Thanks to these multiple influences that characterize this new generation of Information System, Pervasive Information Systems are deeply multidisciplinary systems, demanding a holistic view in which multiple domains are invited to contribute.

The purpose of this book is to combine "state-of-the-art" from various research communities related to the PIS emergence (such as Information Systems Engineering, Cloud Computing, Fog/Edge Computing, Pervasive systems, Distributed systems, Middleware systems), in order to build such a holistic view. But, before analyzing the different aspects contributing to this view, it is necessary to define what is a Pervasive Information System and what can be its outstanding characteristics. In this first chapter, we tackle this question, abording different definitions found in the literature and proposing a set of requirements and characteristics for those systems.

The remaining of this chapter is organized as follows: Section 2 remind the definitions of traditional Information Systems; Section 3 tries to understand the evolutions leading to emergence of PIS, while Sect. 4 proposes a definition for PIS. Section 5 identifies relevant requirements and additional characteristics for these systems, before concluding on Sect. 6.

2   What Is an Information System (IS)?

Before considering Pervasive Information Systems (PIS), it would be important to consider the notion of Information System (IS) itself.

Several definitions for IS can be found in the literature. For instance, Laudon and Laudon (2013) consider as IS as an interconnected set of resources which are able to gather, to handle, to store and to disseminate information in order to contribute to decision making, coordination, control and management in an organization. Rolland et al. (1988) have defined IS as set formed by: data; rules that define the informational functional; procedures to collect, store, transform, retrieve and communicate information; human resources and technical means that cooperate and contribute to system function and to achieve its purposes.

Carvalho (2000) has underlined that there is more than one possible meaning for the term "Information System". This author has studied multiple definitions, emphasizing common aspects characterizing these definitions (and by extension the IS themselves): all definitions deal with information; they are all related to organizations or to the work carried out in organizations; and they all are related to information technology, either because they can benefit from its use or because they are made with computers and computer-based devices. Most of the definitions cited by Carvalho (2000) mention information that are necessary to and handled by the organizations, as well as the presence of both IT elements and human/manual elements, reveling a complex ecosystem of resources. According to Carvalho (2000), we may see an IS as: (i) an object that deals with/process information, that collects, store, transmit, code/decode, calculate and create information; and/or (ii) an object whose purpose is to inform, to contribute to someone's acquisition of knowledge, which is necessary for executing some action in some context. Through these definitions, it becomes clear that we are facing a complex ecosystem composed of different aspects related to information (production, management and dissemination) in an organization, and of resources (human and IT) necessary to handle it, acting together on the behalf of organization's interest.

In the last decades, Information Systems have become an important aspect for every organization, contributing to its overall performance. This impact can be observed through the last decades of researches on management of IS, as underlined by Desq et al. (2016). However, we could observe in the last years the growing importance of IT aspects on IS. On many organizations, IS is mostly considered as a set of IT resources necessary for the organization's process and global running. In this sense, IS is often perceived as a set of IT resources controlled by the IT department, who masters all its components and whose existence is bounded by the limits of the organization. In this IT-driven perception, an IS is perceived as a complex construct with technologies, information, processes and practices necessary for satisfying stakeholders' needs and reaching organization's goals. The business aspects represent then the guiding line for the management of this construct, which remains stable: every single component is decided and managed according organization's needs. It is precisely this stability and this fined-tuned control that new technologies and practices are bringing into question.

3 Information System Evolution: Towards a Pervasive Information System

The last decades have witnessed several technological evolutions and new uses that have strongly impacted IS. Among the new trends that have emerged in recent years, we may cite BYOD, IoT, Big Data, Cloud Computing and Edge/Fog Computing, and the democratization of Machine Learning.

The introduction of these trends brings profound changes in organizations and in their Information Systems (IS), as they are now facing a pervasive environment. These systems and their users are confronted with a growing heterogeneity that must be managed and understood. In order to better understanding the upheaval motivated by the introduction of those new trends, it is necessary to get a closer look on these trends, which can be organized on four categories: the usage evolution, the barrier with the physical world, the data revolution and the IT infrastructure.

Usage Evolution

The development of mobile technologies, including 4G, has contributed to the democratization of the Internet access with a reasonable bandwidth almost everywhere, which has also contributed to the adoption of the BYOD (Bring Your Own Device) practice. BYOD consists in using one's own personal computer at work. According to this practice, employees use their own personal terminals to work, navigating seamlessly between their private and work spaces, instead of accumulating multiple terminals according to circumstances, location or professional needs (Chang et al. 2014). This mix of personal and professional hardware represents a significant change for organizations IT departments, which traditionally govern, deploy and control all technologies used by employees/collaborators for their professional activities (Earley et al. 2014). Today, it becomes common (or usual) to use your own personal devices (which are no longer limited to laptops) to access your company's information system, wherever you are. A ubiquitous access "Anytime, anywhere" from any kind of terminal has become a reality. According to Andriole and Bojanova (2014), the use of new devices such as Microsoft HoloLens, Apple Watch, and other Bluetooth devices, creates new opportunities for businesses as these new devices are changing the way we browse, search, shop, and even live. It is therefore natural to think that the arrival of these new personal devices into organizations may also change the way we work.

Breaking the Barrier with the Physical World

The introduction of Internet if Things (IoT) technologies on companies offers new opportunities of interacting with the physical environment, and through these new interactions, it brings new business perspectives. According to Sundmaeker et al. (2010), it is expected that IoT objects will become more and more active, participating in different aspects of society, through business, information and social process. The informational aspect remains probably the most prominent one within today's organizations. Thanks to the IoT, it is possible to easily (and even continuously) collect information from the physical environment, but also to act upon this environment through sensors and actuators often connected to networked nano computers with some computing power. The physical environment can then become an integral part of business processes and, consequently, part of the Information System itself, as shown by the recent development of Industry 4.0, which heavily relies on the IoT and on the data coming from it, as observed by Lu (2017). Data can be new collected almost everywhere directly from the physical environment. As a consequence, the Information System is not anymore bounded to a world of virtual/digital objects, it extends its action into the real/physical world.

Data Revolution

The data collected from IoT objects enriches an already large set of available data within organizations. Big Data platforms allow to better control this impressive data volume and to exploit it properly. The recent success of Data Lakes (O'Leary 2014), often built on the top of platforms such as HDFS, is an excellent illustration of the definitive adoption of Big Data into organizations. This massive volume of data is now available to data scientists, who can extract an added value from it, thanks to multiple data analysis techniques, including those derived from Machine Learning, whose success often depends on the availability of such a large volume of data. The growing interest of companies on Machine Learning techniques illustrates the interest of those on exploring this data and on the potential added value it may offer. Nonetheless, the possibility of performing such analysis depends on the availability of an appropriate infrastructure allowing this kind of exploitation, demanding an appropriate infrastructure and (human resource) skills for doing so. The availability of these new sets of IoT data imposes also considering its management, and particularly handling privacy, security and data quality issues, whose impact grows together with volume.

IT Infrastructure Flexibilization

Last but not least, IT infrastructure has significantly changed with the popularization of Cloud Computing platforms. Indeed, the rise of Cloud Computing has enabled many organizations to rationalize their IT infrastructure. Cloud Computing can be seen as the ability to access a pool of resources owned and maintained by a third party via the Internet. It is not a new technology by itself, but a new way of consuming computing resources (Ferguson-Boucher 2011). In the cloud model, the resources no longer belong to the organization, but they are most often "leased" from one or more providers according to the organization's needs. Cloud resources are thus perceived as having a low maintenance cost, switching to an on-demand model in which organizations may adapt their consumption according to their needs and only pay for the resources they actually consume. However, the adoption of the Cloud model is often accompanied by some fears related to the outsourcing of data and data processing. These fears concern in particularly security, confidentiality and network latency issues. The choice between deploying a certain service in an internal organizational resource or outsourcing it into a public Cloud resource becomes now as strategic as technical. Consequently, resources are more and more visible and must now be managed from more than just a technical perspective.

Edge/Fog Computing have reinforced this aspect. Fog computing is an architecture that extends services that the cloud provides to the Edge devices. It can be seen as a new paradigm for disseminating computing, storage and service management closer to the end user, all along the continuum between the cloud, and objects (IoT) and end devices (Atta-ur-Rahman et al. 2021). Cisco was first introducing the term Edge Computing in 2012 as it works at the edge of the network, but it is also called Fog as we use close to the ground services. Thus, thanks to Edge/Fog Computing platforms, it is possible to consider the use of proximity resources for the execution of certain services. This makes it possible to consider the use of resources other than those located in data centers or in Cloud platforms to run services, offering new perspectives for further rationalizing the use of available resources.

Moreover, the current trend towards increased use of micro-services in organizations, which advocate for a finer breakdown of functionalities, is enabling applications to be deployed more easily over differ kind of infrastructures. It is now possible, with the help of micro-services, to envisage an opportunistic use of available resources, as supported by (Mulfari et al. 2015; Villari et al. 2016). All the conditions are thus in place to enable the dynamic deployment of IS services over resources as varied as cloud resources (private or public), traditional data center resources, network devices, IoT, or mobile terminals, in a transparent way. All these developments have transformed the nature of the resources available in Information Systems. These resources have become more distributed, heterogeneous, and organized in an infrastructure that has itself become more dynamic. The placement of services on these resources, which before stated for a "simple" technical problem, becomes a non-trivial problem, with a strategic dimension.

All these new technologies and trends are gradually entering into the composition of Information Systems, leading to their evolution. Today, we are observing the emergence of a new generation of IS that could be called pervasive, both by their distribution beyond the organization's boundaries, and by the pervasive nature of the environment they integrate. Thanks to these new technologies and practices, Information System can extend well beyond the physical limits of the organization. They are now accessible everywhere, they include resources both inside and outside the organization, and they can even integrate the physical environment itself. As pointed out by Castro-Leon (2014), the notions of what is inside or outside an organization have become blurred with processes that use resources other than those within the organization's traditional perimeter. The environment has become more and more heterogeneous, integrating very different devices, which can moreover be mobile, adding dynamism to the heterogeneity. Thus, we have Information Systems and IS users that are increasingly confronted with a heterogeneous and dynamic environment, in terms of resources, services and data. We may expect from these systems more flexibility and a certain "smartness" in order to better carry out the organization's activities and better satisfy user's and organization needs. This expected "smartness" is one of the main points leading to the rise of Pervasive Information System, whose definition is discussed on the next section.

4 Defining Pervasive Information System

In this section, we will try to define what is a Pervasive Information System, based on the literature and on the expectation, one may have about these systems.

Several visions of the term "Pervasive Information Systems" exist. A first trend is summed up by the fact that the keyword "pervasive" is associated with ubiquitous information that is captured anywhere, thanks to sensors scattered around the physical environment. The system, in this case, is designed as a sensor-oriented system to capture information anywhere and anytime. This trend is represented in particular by systems derived from IoT (Xiao et al. 2017; Brahem et al. 2021; Lippi et al. 2021; Kim and Lee 2021). However, even if the data represents an important concern on these systems, notably thanks to IoT and Big Data related technologies, this evolution cannot be reduced to the availability of data everywhere. It is not only a matter of data, it is about a whole Information Systems that can be deployed everywhere, available all the time. In short, it is about the Weiser's (1991) vision of Ubiquitous Computing becoming reality over current Information Systems.

Another trend consists in assimilating these systems to ubiquitous environments, autonomously providing comfort to one or more users. These pervasive systems are often limited to an application, a location and/or a set of intelligent technological devices. However, they are rarely connected to the trades or traditional Information Systems of an organization. We then speak of pervasive systems or rather applications, of which we can cite (Maass and Varshney 2012; Cheraghi et al. 2021; Lalanda et al. 2021; Raychoudhury et al. 2013; Romero et al. 2010). This trend lacks of a business view, which characterizes traditional Information Systems. Besides, as we could observe on Sect. 2, Information Systems cannot be reduced to a simple set of applications, which will be the case if we consider Pervasive Information System only through pervasive systems lens.

Finally, the trend that we consider in this chapter is indeed that of an Information System that is becoming pervasive. It must consider events in physical environments and offer adapted services as close as possible to users. In this trend, we can cite (Kourouthanassis et al. 2010; Najar et al. 2014; Hauser et al. 2017).

For Kourouthanassis and Giaglis (2006), a Pervasive IS can be seen as an emerging class of IS in which IT is gradually embedded in the physical environment, capable of accommodating users' needs and desires when necessary. The term "Pervasive Information Systems" was introduced by Joel Birnbaum (1997). In this article, Birnbaum (1997) considers a technology that becomes pervasive, and thus invisible to the human eyes: "Today's schoolchildren don't think of TVs and telephones as technology-they can't imagine life without them. Tomorrow's children will feel the same way about computers, the networks connecting them, and the services they perform". This corresponds to the "cognitive invisibility" reported by Bell and Dourish (2007). These authors mention a technology that is invisible to us, since we use it continuously without necessarily perceiving it as computers. Birnbaum (1997) talks about an information technology that should become intuitively affordable for everyone and that should bring enough added value to justify the necessary investments. Considering the aforementioned evolutions and trends, as well as the opportunities they offer to the organizations, we may say that this point has been reached. And the consequences for IS are not insignificant. Birnbaum (1997) emphasizes in particular the expectations with regard to the services offered. For this author, in the same way that people expected (in 1997) to have a dial tone when they picked up a telephone handset, people will (nowadays) wait for useful information to be available and ready for use. To sum up, even if Birnbaum (1997) does not precisely define the notion of PIS as Kourouthanassis and Giaglis (2006) do, the elements that he enumerates in his article, *i.e.* the technology that becomes "invisible", the importance of services and the added value of information, the paradigm shift with people paying by use, modifying what was before a capital investment in service, etc., characterize quite well what today's information systems are becoming.

Again, according Kourouthanassis and Giaglis (2006), unlike traditional IS, PIS encompass a more complex and dynamic environment, composed of a multitude of artefacts (and no longer just desktop computers), capable of perceiving the users' context and of managing the mobility of these users. In the literature, the term "mobile" IS (Krogstie et al. 2004) is also employed, with the notion of mobility used in a broad sense: spatial, temporal, but also contextual. Krogstie et al. (2004) refer to systems characterized by their dynamism, by frequent changes of context (spatio-temporal, environmental context, but also relative to users, their tasks and even available information), and thus requiring an important capacity of adaptation from the system to the users. Even if (Krogstie et al. 2004) mention in particular the adaptation of interfaces for a better interactivity with users, whatever the terminals they use, it is easy to imagine that this adaptation should be extended to the proposed services and their implementation.

Therefore, we are confronted with the emergence of Information Systems that extend beyond the physical (and logical) boundaries of the organization, that integrate new technologies and an environment that has itself become pervasive (in a technologically charged sense) in a more or less transparent way, and from which we expect more intelligent behavior, both reactive and proactive.

Pervasive Information Systems are more then never characterized by its complexity, whose management should change when compared to traditional IS. Indeed, traditionally, Information Systems engineering has mastered the complexity of the system by a layered and "silo" view. This traditional compartmentalized view limits interactions between the different levels and does not promote the flow of information between them. However, the introduction of new technologies and new practices has turned this organization upside down. For example, the strategic nature of the choice between an "on-premise" or Cloud deployment, or the migration of systems to a micro-services architecture are all illustrations of these upheavals. The complexity of managing IT infrastructure is no longer just a technical issue but becomes constrained by policies that the business can drive. Likewise, the ubiquitous IT infrastructure in an organization's physical environment enables information to be captured that can influence the business processes supported by the information system and the organization. Nevertheless, when one considers an Information System that becomes pervasive, the synergy between the business layers of the Information System and the distributed, dynamic and heterogeneous IT infrastructure then becomes an essential factor of PISs.

Therefore, this synergy forces us to question the stratum of partitioned layers in which IS engineering was built and to think of the pervasive information system according to its vertical dimension (verticality) from the business to the IT infrastructure in an integrated manner (see Fig. 1).

In order to promote such verticality, several aspects ought to be considered. In the next section, we consider relevant requirements and characteristics that, for us, should designate Pervasive Information Systems.

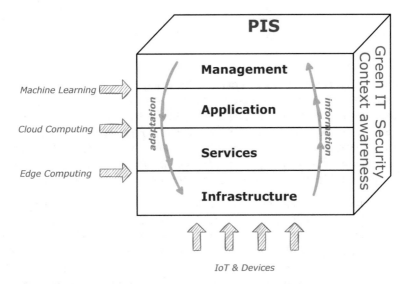

Fig. 1 Schematic view of a Pervasive Information System

5 PIS Requirements and Characteristics

As stated before, Pervasive Information Systems should be aware of the evolution of its real environment and its own execution environment. This will help to adapt the behavior of each system layer according to the situation at hand. This synergy between the layers is materialized in Fig. 1 by the adaptation link coming from the upper layer to the lower layers. Figure 1 illustrates these multiple layers and the influence of several trends mentioned in Sect. 3 on the overall system, *together with transversal concerns such as context-awareness, security, and Green IT.*

Each layer of PIS mentioned in Fig. 1 can be summarized as follows:

- *The "infrastructure" layer* is increasingly complex as it integrates technologies such as Cloud/Edge/Fog computing, and IoT.
- *The "services" layer* represents the application services (or components) deployed and executed on the IT architecture and supporting the user and/or the business. Service orientation is well known in Information Systems and applications. The adoption of a micro-service architecture brings service-oriented architectures back to the fore, not in the sense of technologies like REST and SOAP, but in relation to the principles and qualities expected by these architectures, as pointed out (Shadija et al. 2017).
- *The "application" layer* corresponds to all the applications constituting the Information System. Each application is made up of services interconnected by application rules, which are supposed to translate business needs concerning organization's activities. The siloed operation that IS enjoyed for many years has contributed to the design of applications that are today considered monolithic

and difficult to scale. The transition from these to a micro-services architecture is addressed by many works (Taibi and Systä 2019; Da Silva et al. 2019; Balalaie et al. 2016).

- **The *"management" layer*** provides an overview of the applications at the strategic and business levels. Traditionally, enterprise architecture, governance of IS and business processes are topics of knowledge and skills useful for this layer. This layer will have to integrate the added value of pervasive environments integrated at the layer level: IT infrastructure, services and applications. Once again, the example of the transition to a micro-service architecture clearly illustrates the impact of these transformations, in principle technical, on the enterprise architecture, as underlined, for example (Müssig et al. 2017).

The real challenge of PIS does not lie in adapting each level separately, in an independent way, but in creating a real synergy between the IS levels. Each level should be able to adapt itself according to its own conditions and goals, but also according to observed context information and changes coming from the neighboring levels. It is an entire dynamic between the different levels of an Information System that we are looking for on a Pervasive Information System.

For reaching such a synergy, a set of minimal requirements seems necessary to us. We advocate that such requirements characterize what is essential to a Pervasive Information System. In addition to these requirements, we believe that some extra characteristics may also contribute to lead traditional IS into this PIS vision. We detail such minimal requirements and additional characteristics in the next sections (Sects. 5.1 and 5.2).

5.1   Minimal Requirements

After introducing our vision of the Pervasive Information System, we will discuss the requirements that, we believe, are expected by PISs in order to better identify the problems and issues to be solved. Indeed, various requirements have been put forward in (Najar et al. 2014), some of which seem particularly relevant to the engineering of Pervasive Information Systems. Here we go deeper in this analysis, reviewing these requirements and dividing them in minimal requirements and additional characteristics.

The first expected requirement is "context awareness". Already highlighted by Kourouthanassis et al. (2010) as a central requirement to PIS, this is the capacity of a system to adapt to the environment that surrounds it (Baldauf et al. 2007). As PIS are emerged in a ubiquitous environment, these systems must perceive the evolution of their execution environment and adapt accordingly.

In order to achieve this requirement, PIS must be able to observe its surrounding environment, which means being able to observe context information. Context information correspond to a large concept, that can be seen as "any information that can be used to characterize the situation of an entity. An entity is a person, place, or object that is considered relevant to the interaction between a user and an application, including the user and applications themselves" (Dey 2001). In the case of a PIS, context. Information may refer to multiple things concerning physical environment (e.g. location of people and objects, temperature, humidity, etc.) and infrastructure (e.g. CPU load, network latency and throughput, energy consumption, etc.), but also concerning business and what we may call "organizational context" (Kirsch-Pinheiro et al. 2004) (e.g. user's roles and activities, project status, etc.). All this information may be used for adaptation purposes at different levels on a PIS. The availability of such information and the capability of reacting to changes observed thanks to it represents a key element for reaching the necessary synergy of a PIS.

The second is that of "managing heterogeneity". PIS must support a broad wide variety of technical devices and services offered to the user or executed in these physical environments. Managing heterogeneity is complex but essential.

As we could observe in previous section, we may refer to PIS as an IS particularly characterized by the heterogeneity and the dynamic nature of the environments and resources involved on it. Since these systems are transforming and becoming more and more complex with the arrival of new technologies, it becomes crucial to manage the heterogeneity of these systems and the services in such way users may focus more on the objectives to be achieved rather than on these technologies. Unlike traditional IS, in which the users have often to adapt themselves to the system, PIS must consider this heterogeneity in order to adapt itself and to provide users with the service that best corresponds to their needs and current context. These are systems, whose intention would be to increase the productivity of the users (and infrastructures) by providing them with adapted services, has to consider the heterogeneity of the environment, which turns into a pervasive environment. Accepting and managing such heterogeneity, although its complexity, improves the opportunities of adaptation at different levels: interaction modes, services and information access, but also the infrastructure itself.

The third requirement relates to the "transparency" that should be found in Ubiquitous Computing. As Weiser (1991) has pointed out, Ubiquitous Computing should be invisible to its user, disappear into the environment without being distinguishable from it. PIS, as a ubiquitous system, must hide complexity and heterogeneity from users, becoming transparent. Behind this notion of transparency also hides the ease of use of a system whose manipulation should not require special effort from a cognitive point of view, as underlined by Bell and Dourish (2007).

PIS are characterized by their heterogeneity, which affects both the available services and their implementations as well as the resources used for their execution. The technologies involved are multiple and lead to increased complexity. This complexity makes difficult for both, end-users and those who have to design and manage such systems, to understand and assimilate the system. As Dey (2011) has pointed out, when users experience difficulties in establishing a mental model of how applications work, they are less disposed to adopt and use them. A misunderstanding of a PIS and how it works may affect the acceptance of such a system (entirely or of some of its components), and thus compromise its adoption and the transition from a traditional IS to a PIS. Given the strategic role of Information Systems (and therefore PIS) within organizations as a support to their activities, the consequences of not adopting such a system can be very significant.

Transparency is thus necessary to hide the heterogeneity that characterizes these systems and that affects their resources, infrastructure, services and uses. This transparency is necessary for both: in order to enable users to focus only on the tasks they have to perform and not on the technologies behind those tasks; and in order to make it easier for designers to think about the services that might be offered and under which circumstances, without also having to focus, at a first moment, on the technologies needed for those services. This transparency for end users, as well as for the management of PIS is another key aspect for a successful evolution of IS into PIS.

The fourth requirement concerns "fulfillment of the requirements". PIS as IS must meet the needs of the user or the business anytime, anywhere. It is above all about making the user more productive, offering the most suitable means to meet her/his needs, and focusing more on tasks that generate added value for her/him or the business.

Different from a simple pervasive application, PIS find their foundation on business needs. As IS, they have an important role on the overall performance of organizations. All the adaptation we are looking for on PIS should have a common purpose: to serve organization's business strategy. By proposing a more transparent system, by managing heterogeneity and adapting its behavior to the context at hand, PIS may contribute to the organization's behavior as a whole, by improving to infrastructure use and performance, by freeing users from technological concerns and improving their own activities.

The fifth expected requirement is "adaptation". A PIS must be able to manage the possible variability in the services and technical infrastructures to meet users' and businesses needs in all circumstances. It is about being able to offer a system that can be perceived as "intelligent" by its ability to adapt and to offer "the right service at the right time". It is about offering the right keys to users, about freeing these users from technological constraints so that they could concentrate on tasks with an added value to the organization.

To do this, adaptation and proactivity becomes a necessity. Indeed, users expect an increasingly "intelligent" IS, capable of anticipating their needs and responding to them appropriately. According to Bauer and Dey (2016), we can already witness a move towards increasingly sophisticated systems ("smart", "intelligent", "context-aware", "adaptive", etc.). Here, the notion of context is central as systems become aware of the context in which they are used and intelligently adapt their execution. We believe that the democratization of this kind of behavior that could be considered "intelligent" creates a certain expectation on the users: they now expect that a software and a system will be more intelligent, it will be able to recognize their situation, their behavior, and to adapt itself in a reactive way as well as in a proactive way. Thus, we advocate that Pervasive Information Systems must be able to recognize user's habits and practices in order to be able to anticipate users' needs and proactively adapt themselves, proposing to these users the services that correspond the best to their needs.

5.2 Additional Characteristics

In addition to the minimal requirements discussed above, we strongly believe that some extra characteristics could be observed when considering Pervasive Information Systems.

The first additional characteristic of PIS is to be *"Opportunistic"*. The holistic view of a PIS promoted in this book allows to manage at lower levels a large range of IT resources, a large range of data, and a large range of services. The additional feature to PIS is to apply *opportunistic strategies* to exploit all these items (resources, data, and services) in order to fulfill the business goals in the context at hand in the same organization or among several organizations.

Indeed, environments involved in a PIS contain a varied and variable set of resources, which may include resources ranging from high-performance servers and virtual machines in the cloud to tablets and nanocomputers for the IoT. Many resources are already available and integrated into this environment. They are not necessary placed in a data center. These resources can be disseminated all along the organization, and even beyond, and they can be dedicated (or not) to different uses. Indeed, these resources are not always dedicated exclusively to certain services or tasks, and even if they are not always very powerful, they still offer significant power computing. Unfortunately, except for data center and cloud resources, many of the resources available in a PIS are often underused. It is possible to envision the use of proximity resources for the execution of services on behalf of the PIS.

The second additional characteristic of PIS is *"Determinism"*. This characteristic is related to Information Systems. The PIS must support the user's business needs in a predictable and controlled manner. Organizations lay on IS to keep their activities up and running. Dynamism of pervasive environments adds uncertainty, which must be handled appropriately, since the overall system must by knew and controlled. Behaviors that may lead to undetermined or unexpected results should be avoided since business operations (and goals) might be affected by such results. This tradeoff between having a certain control over environment although its dynamicity makes the determinism an interesting characteristic for PIS.

The third additional characteristic of PIS is *"Automatic"*. The PIS must collect & process heterogeneous data automatically (data management). This automatic capture of data is useful to perform the adaptation requirement and transparency requirement. The capability of automatically acquiring and processing context information is also the basis for context awareness requirement. The main challenge involved in this automatic data acquisition is its scale: it is not only some independent applications that are concerned, but a whole IS. Being able to automatically collect and process important volumes of heterogeneous data becomes a strategic characteristic of PIS.

The fourth additional characteristic of PIS is *"Interactive"*. The PIS must provide various interaction modes to users and can also apply continuous interaction strategies to users. Indeed, PIS are spread over the environment, crossing physical borders of the organization. The integration of physical environment and new devices offers new perspectives of interaction between the system and its users. These new interaction modes may considerably contribute to the transparency requirement and should then be considered as an important additional characteristic for PIS.

6 Final Remarks

In this chapter, we tackled the definition of PIS, from its influences (the notion of IS itself and the evolutions leading to the rise of PIS) till its requirements and characteristics. The main goal is to propose a better understanding of this new generation of IS and to promote a holistic view of those, which we believe is essential for the management and the engineering of such systems.

As we could observe in this chapter, PIS are complex systems from which users expect an "intelligent" behavior. We believe that such behavior will be possible by observing the requirements and characteristics we underlined in this chapter. Besides, even if context information is seen here essentially as a trigger for adaptation purposes, it is not a question of automating everything in a PIS. A PIS is an Information System that evolves, and the very nature of these systems requires them to be predictable and manageable. One must be able to control an IS, its applications, processes, services, infrastructure, etc., in any situation. We must be able to manage a PIS despite the heterogeneity and the dynamism of the involved environment. Adaptation within a PIS can be led automatically, but it can also come from an active management from decision makers. All the requirements and characteristics mentioned earlier in this chapter represents complementary aspects, like facets, that influence each other and that put together may lead IS to their next step: the PIS. However, it is worth noting that this evolution will not be a simple transformation, the path leading to it demands the contribution of multiple domains, considered in the following chapters of this book.

References

Andriole, S.J. & Bojanova, I., (2014): "Optimizing operational and strategic IT", *IEEE IT Professional,* 16(5), September/October 2014, 12–15

Atta-ur-Rahman, Dash S., Ahmad M., Iqbal T. (2021): Mobile Cloud Computing: A Green Perspective. In: Udgata S.K., Sethi S., Srirama S.N. (eds) Intelligent Systems. Lecture Notes in Networks and Systems, vol 185. Springer, Singapore. https://doi.org/10.1007/978-981-33-6081-5_46

Balalaie A., Heydarnoori A. & Jamshidi P. (2016): "Migrating to Cloud-Native Architectures Using Microservices: An Experience Report". In: Celesti A., Leitner P. (eds) Advances in Service-Oriented and Cloud Computing. ESOCC 2015. Communications in Computer and Information Science, vol 567. Springer. https://doi.org/10.1007/978-3-319-33313-7_15

Baldauf, M., Dustdar, S., Rosenberg, F. (2007): A survey on context-aware systems. International Journal of Ad Hoc and Ubiquitous Computing 2(4), 263–277.

Bauer, C. & Dey, A. (2016): "Considering context in the design of intelligent systems: Current practices and suggestions for improvement", *Journal of Systems and Software*, 112, 2016, Elsevier, 26–47

Bell, G. & Dourish, P. (2007): "Yesterday's tomorrows: notes on ubiquitous computing's dominant vision", *Personal and Ubiquitous Computing*, 11 (2), Jan. 2007, 133–143

Birnbaum, J. (1997): "Pervasive information systems", *Communications of the ACM*, 40(2), Feb. 1997, 40–41. https://doi.org/10.1145/253671.253695

Brahem, M., Scerri, G., Anciaux, N., Issarny, V. (2021): Consent-driven data use in crowdsensing platforms: When data reuse meets privacy-preservation. 2021 IEEE International Conference on Pervasive Computing and Communications (PerCom), IEEE, 130–139.

Carvalho, J.A. (2000): Information System? Which One Do You Mean?. In: Falkenberg, E.D., Lyytinen, K., Verrijn-Stuart, A.A. (eds) Information System Concepts: An Integrated Discipline Emerging. IFIP — The International Federation for Information Processing, vol 36. Springer, Boston, MA. https://doi.org/10.1007/978-0-387-35500-9_22

Castro-Leon, E. (2014): "Consumerization in the IT service ecosystem", *IEEE IT Professional*, 16(5), September/October 2014, 20–27

Chang, J.M.; Ho, P.-C. & Chang, T.-C. (2014): "Securing BYOD", *IEEE IT Professional*, 16(5), September/October 2014, 9–11

Cheraghi, S., Namboodiri, V., Arsal, G. (2021): CityGuide: A Seamless Indoor-Outdoor Wayfinding System for People with Vision Impairments. Mobile and Pervasive Assistive Technologies (MPAT 2021), 2021 IEEE Int. Conference on Pervasive Computing and Communications Workshops and other Affiliated Events (PerCom Workshops), 105–110

Da Silva, H.S., Carneiro, G. & Monteiro, M. (2019): "Towards a Roadmap for the Migration of Legacy Software Systems to a Microservice based Architecture", Proceedings of the 9th International Conference on Cloud Computing and Services Science (CLOSER 2019), pp. 37-47. ISBN 978-989-758-365-0

Desq, S., Fallery, B., Reix, R. & Rodhain, F. (2016): "25 ans de recherche en Systèmes d'Information". Systèmes d'information & management, 21(2), 115–141. https://doi.org/10.3917/sim.162.0115

Dey, A.K. (2001): "Understanding and using context", Personal and Ubiquitous Computing, 5(1), 4–7, 2001.

Dey, A.K. (2011): "Intelligibility in ubiquitous computing systems". In: Ferscha, A., *Pervasive Adaptation: Next generation pervasive computing research agenda*, 68–69, 2011. Disponible sur https://www.pervasive.jku.at/Conferences/fet11/RAB.pdf (last access: August 2020).

Earley, S.; Harmon, R.; Lee, M.R. & Mithas, S. (2014): "From BYOD to BYOA, Phishing, and Botnets". *IEEE IT Professional*, 16(5), September/October 2014, 16–18

Ferguson-Boucher, K. (2011): "Cloud Computing: A Records and Information Management Perspective", *IEEE Security & Privacy*, 9(6), Nov.-Dec. 2011, 63–66. https://doi.org/10.1109/MSP.2011.159

Hauser, M., Günther, S. A., Flath, C. M., Thiesse, F. (2017): Designing Pervasive Information Systems: A Fashion Retail Case Study. Proceedings of the 38th International Conference on Information Systems (ICIS 2017)

Kim, H., Lee, D. (2021): TAP: A Transformer based Activity Prediction Exploiting Temporal Relations in Collaborative Tasks. 17th Workshop on Context and Activity Modeling and Recognition (CoMoRea 2021), 2021 IEEE International Conference on Pervasive Computing and Communications Workshops and other Affiliated Events (PerCom Workshops), 20–25

Kirsch-Pinheiro, M.; Gensel, J.; Martin, H. (2004): "Representing Context for an Adaptative Awareness Mechanism", In: de Vreede G.-J.; Guerrero L.A.; Raventos G.M. (Eds.), LNCS 3198 - X International Workshop on Groupware (CRIWG 2004). Springer-Verlag, 339–34, 2004

Kourouthanassis, P. E. & Giaglis, G. M. (2006): "A Design Theory for Pervasive Information Systems". *3rd Int. Workshop on Ubiquitous Computing (IWUC 2006), in conjunction with ICEIS 2006*, May 2006, Paphos, Cyprus, 62–70. https://doi.org/10.5220/0002503700620070. Disponible sur: https://www.scitepress.org/Papers/2006/25037/25037.pdf (Last access: Aout 2020)

Kourouthanassis, P. E., Giaglis, G. M., Karaiskos, D. C. (2010): Delineating 'pervasiveness' in pervasive information systems: a taxonomical framework and design implications. Journal of Information Technology, 25 (3), 273–287.

Krogstie, J.; Lyytinen, K.; Opdahl, A.L.; Pernici, B., Siau, K. & Smolander, K. (2004): "Research areas and challenges for mobile information systems". *International Journal of Mobile Communications*, 2(3), September 2004, 220–234. https://doi.org/10.1504/IJMC.2004.005161

Lalanda, P., Vega, G., Cervantes, H., Morand, D. (2021): Architecture and pervasive platform for machine learning services in Industry 4.0. PerCom Industry Track 2021, 2021 IEEE International Conference on Pervasive Computing and Communications Workshops and other Affiliated Events (PerCom Workshops), 293–298.

Laudon, K.C., Laudon, J.P., (2013): "Management des systèmes d'information", Pearson, 13ème édition, 2013, p. 666. ISBN 978-2-326-00001-8.

Lippi, M., Mariani, S., Zambonelli, F. (2021): Developing a "Sense of Agency" in IoT Systems: Preliminary Experiments in a Smart Home Scenario. 17th Workshop on Context and Activity Modeling and Recognition (CoMoRea 2021), 2021 IEEE International Conference on Pervasive Computing and Communications Workshops and other Affiliated Events (PerCom Workshops), 44–49

Lu, Y. (2017): "Industry 4.0: A survey on technologies, applications and open research issues", *Journal of Industrial Information Integration*, 6, June 2017, 1–10

Maass, W., Varshney, U. (2012): Design and evaluation of Ubiquitous Information Systems and use in healthcare. Decision Support Systems, 54(1), Dec. 2012, 597–609

Mulfari, D.; Fazio, M.; Celesti, A.; Villari, M. & Puliafito, A. (2015): "Design of an IoT cloud system for container virtualization on smart objects". *3rd Workshop on CLoud for IoT (CLIoT 2015), European Conference on Service-Oriented and Cloud Computing (ESOCC 2015), Communications in Computer and Information Science (CCIS)*, vol. 567, 2015, Springer, 33–47

Müssig, D., Stricker, R., Lässig, J., Heider, J. (2017): Highly Scalable Microservice-based Enterprise Architecture for Smart Ecosystems in Hybrid Cloud Environments. Proceedings of the 19th International Conference on Entedrprise Information Systems - Volume 1: ICEIS, 454–459

Najar, S., Kirsch Pinheiro, M., Le Grand, B., Souveyet, C. (2014): A user-centric vision of service-oriented Pervasive Information Systems. 8th International Conference on Research Challenges in Information Science (RCIS 2014), IEEE, 359–370.

O'Leary, D. E. (2014): "Embedding AI and Crowdsourcing in the Big Data Lake", IEEE Intelligent Systems, 29(5), Sept.-Oct. 2014, 70–73. https://doi.org/10.1109/MIS.2014.82

Raychoudhury, V., Cao, J., Kumar, M., Zhang, D. (2013): Middleware for Pervasive Computing: A Survey. Pervasive Mobile Computing, 9 (2), 177–200

Rolland, C., Foucault, O., Benci, G. (1988): "Conception des systems d'information: la méthode Remora », Edition Eyrolles, 1988.

Romero, D., Rouvoy, R., Seinturier, L., Carton, P. (2010): Service Discovery in Ubiquitous Feedback Control Loops. In: Eliassen, F., Kapitza, R. (Eds.), 10th IFIP WG 6.1 International Conference on Distributed Applications and Interoperable Systems (DAIS) /International Federated Conference on Distributed Computing Techniques (DisCoTec), Lecture Notes in Computer Science, 6115, 112–125

Shadija, D.; Rezai, M. & Hill, R. (2017). « Towards an understanding of microservices », 23rd International Conference on Automation and Computing (ICAC 2017), Huddersfield, 2017, pp. 1–6

Sundmaeker, H.; Guillemin, P.; Friess, P. & Woelfflé, S. (2010): "Vision and Challenges for realizing the internet of things". *Cluster of European Research projects on the Internet of Things (CERP-IoT)*, 2010. 10. 2759/26127. Disponible sur: http://www.theinternetofthings.eu/sites/default/files/Rob%20van%20Kranenburg/Clusterbook%202009_0.pdf (Last visit: novembre 2014)

Taibi, D.; Systä, K. (2019). "From Monolithic Systems to Microservices: A Decomposition Framework based on Process Mining", Proceedings of the 9th International Conference on Cloud Computing and Services Science (CLOSER 2019), pp. 153–164. ISBN 978-989-758-365-0

Villari, M.; Fazio, M.; Dustdar, S.; Rana, O. & Ranjan R. (2016): "Osmotic Computing: A New Paradigm for Edge/Cloud Integration", *IEEE Cloud Computing*, 3(6), 2016, 76–83

Weiser, M., "The computer for the 21st century", *Scientific American*, vol. 265, No 3, September 1991, 94–104

Xiao, B., Rahmani, R., Li, Y., Kanter, T. (2017): Edge-based interoperable service-driven information distribution for intelligent pervasive services. Pervasive and Mobile Computing, 40, Sept. 2017, 359–381.

Design and Modeling in Pervasive Information Systems

Carine Souveyet and Rébecca Deneckère

1 Introduction

The previous chapter highlighted the different requirements that a pervasive information system should fulfill, namely Context-awareness, Managing heterogeneity, Transparency, Fulfillment of the requirements and Adaptation.

Despite the numerous works in the pervasive information systems domain, works specifically aiming at its design or modeling seem to be neglected. We decided to study the literature in order to be able to draw some conclusions about this statement. We made a systematic mapping review, specifically addressing design methodology and modelling techniques in pervasive information systems and analyzed the results to draw a panorama of modeling in PIS.

To our knowledge, there is only one existing review about modeling issues in pervasive information systems. In (Ng and Wakenshaw 2017), the authors present four conceptualizations of IoT from the following theoretical constructs: liquification and density of information resources; digital materiality; assemblage and service system; and modularity and transaction network. The paper presents the conceptualizations and implications of IoT, specifically addressing marketing issues. However, this review doesn't give any information on the PIS requirements fulfillments.

According to the PIS vision developed in the first chapter of the book, we would like to see how the requirements are fulfilled in the existing sources in the literature. We also want to know if they either apply traditional design methodology, adapt an existing one or develop a new one for integrating the pervasive aspects in the IS.

C. Souveyet (✉) · R. Deneckère
Centre de Recherche en Informatique, Université Paris 1 Panthéon Sorbonne, Paris, France
e-mail: Carine.Souveyet@univ-paris1.fr; Rebecca.Deneckere@univ-paris1.fr

© The Author(s), under exclusive license to Springer Nature Switzerland AG 2023   19
M. Kirsch Pinheiro et al. (eds.), *The Evolution of Pervasive Information Systems*,
https://doi.org/10.1007/978-3-031-18176-4_2

The remaining of this chapter is organized as follows: Sect. 2 explain the SMS research methodology used in this work, while Sect. 3 analyze the results, before concluding on Sect. 4.

2 Research Approach

We used a systematic mapping design (Petersen et al. 2008) to study the field of research. Systematic Mapping Studies (SMS) are similar to other systematic reviews, except that they employ broader inclusion criteria to select a wider range of research papers and are intended to map out topics with field classification rather than synthesize study results. The study presented here covers the existing work in the field of design methodologies and modeling techniques in pervasive information systems. We followed the process presented in (Petersen et al. 2008) which includes five steps: definition of research questions, conducting search for primary studies, screening of papers, keywording of abstract and data extraction and mapping of studies. Based on (Petersen et al. 2008), we followed the procedure on SMS. We named differently the Steps 2 and 4 as more compliant with our research process (see Fig. 1).

Step 1: Definition of Research Questions
The main goals of this SMS are to define:

- *RQ1*. What is the distribution evolution of the sources?
- *RQ2*. How is addressed the design and modeling of pervasive information systems in research proposals (which strategies are applied in design-dedicated research proposals)?
- *RQ3*. How are met the PIS requirements presented in the first chapter of the book in these design-dedicated research proposals?

Fig. 1 Research process

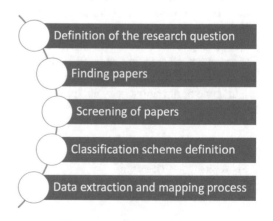

- Definition of the research question
- Finding papers
- Screening of papers
- Classification scheme definition
- Data extraction and mapping process

Step 2: Finding Papers This step aims at identifying a set of papers based on a relevant search string. We searched and selected papers in the SCOPUS scientific database using the SCOPUS Search API. We restricted our search to sources published after 2015. To identify all existing works about design-dedicated research proposals, we used the keywords Design (we search design proposals), Method (these proposals can address methodology issues) and Model (these works can define models or modeling techniques). As we focus on PIS, we used the keywords Information System and Pervasive, but also IoT (pervasive systems often use IoT technologies) and Service (these IS may be defined as service oriented). Our search string was then the following: *(TITLE-ABS-KEY(IoT) or TITLE-ABS-KEY(pervasive)) and (TITLE-ABS-KEY(model) or TITLE-ABS-KEY(method) or TITLE-ABS-KEY(design)) and TITLE-ABS-KEY(service) and TITLE-ABS-KEY("information system") AND PUBYEAR > 2015*. We obtained 333 sources with DOIs. The inclusion criterion related to the search string is given in Table 1.

Step 3: Screening of Papers We analyzed the titles and, if needed the abstract and the papers content, to exclude 288 sources, not representing a research paper or not relevant to modelling in pervasive information systems. We obtained 45 papers. In Table 1 we summarize the exclusion criteria used to obtain the list of relevant papers.

Step 4: Classification Scheme Definition The goal of this step of SMS is to identify the classification scheme to be applied to the obtained results. To answer the defined research questions, we classified all relevant papers accordingly to the

Table 1 Inclusion/exclusion criteria for the study on Smart Topics

Selection criteria	Criteria description
Inclusion criteria (333 sources identified)	The paper contains a set of terms like "IoT" or "Pervasive", concerns either "model" or "method" or "design", "service" and "information system". The paper is published after 2015. From the abstract it is clear that a contribution towards modeling on pervasive system is made. Search string: (TITLE-ABS-KEY(IoT) or TITLE-ABS-KEY(pervasive)) and (TITLE-ABS-KEY(model) or TITLE-ABS-KEY(method) or TITLE-ABS-KEY(design)) and TITLE-ABS-KEY(service) and TITLE-ABS-KEY("information system") AND PUBYEAR >2015
Exclusion criteria	The source is not a research paper (erratum, retracted, etc.).
(TTT sources selected)	The source is not in English or in French. The source is secondary. The source does not concern modelling in pervasive information systems.

Table 2 Classification criteria

Selection criteria	Criteria description
Criteria related to publication evolution	Year Type of venues
Criteria related to the proposal	Type Nature Added value Usage of the IoT based system Application domain
Criteria related to PIS requirements	Context awareness Managing heterogeneity Transparency Fulfillment of the requirements Adaptation

criteria detailed in Table 2. For RQ2 (strategies applied to build PIS), we studied several criteria: the nature of the proposal, its added value, the usage of the IoT system and its application domain.

Step 5: Data Extraction and Mapping Process For RQ1, we studied the publication year and issue to identify the publications evolution, tried to identify which of the PIS requirements stated in chapter "What Is a "Pervasive Information System" (PIS)?" were fulfilled by the selected papers. For the cloud we deleted the stop words, the numbers, and the special characters. For RQ2, we looked deeper into the papers to identify the exact type, nature, added value and usage of the proposal. We used an existing taxonomy of smart life applications to identify the scope of the diverse applications domains of the selected papers. For RQ3, we identified if the proposal was fulfilling the PIS requirements defined in chapter "What Is a "Pervasive Information System" (PIS)?".

Validity Threats Qualitative research is based on subjective, interpretive, and contextual data. Thus, we analyzed the potential biases, which could threaten the validity of our research. (Thomson 2011) proposes five categories of validity. To minimize the impact of the validity threats that could affect our study, we present them with the corresponding mitigation actions in Table 3.

3 Results of the Systematic Mapping Study

In this section, we sum up the results obtained during our SMS. Very few papers are really concerned about design and modelling in pervasive information systems.

Table 3 Validity threats

Validity	Actions
Descriptive validity refers to the accuracy of the data	We unified the concepts and criteria used in the study and structured the information to be collected with a data extraction form to support a uniform recording of data.
Theoretical validity depends on the ability to get the information that it is intended to capture.	We used a search string and applied it on a library including the most popular digital libraries on computer sciences and software engineering. A set of inclusion and exclusion criteria have been defined. We combined two different search methods: an automatic search and a manual search (backward and forward snowballing), to diminish the risk of not finding all the available evidence. The choice of English and French sources should be of minimal impact concerning the discard of other languages.
Generalization validity is concerned with the ability to generalize the results.	Our set of research questions is general enough to identify and classify the findings on modelling on pervasive systems.
Evaluative validity is achieved when the conclusions are reasonable given the data.	Two researchers studied the papers, working independently but with an overlap of studies to identify potential analysis differences. At least two researchers validated every conclusion.
Transparency validity refers to the repeatability of the research protocol.	The research process protocol is detailed enough to ensure it can be exhaustively repeated.

Fig. 2 Growth of the number of papers on modelling on pervasive information systems

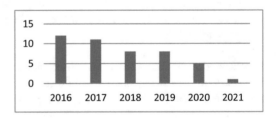

3.1 RQ1. What Is the Distribution Evolution of the Sources?

We studied the evolution of the sources through time and publication venues. We also looked at word frequencies in the papers metadata (titles, abstract and keywords).

Distribution over time Figure 2 shows the appearance of the papers on our topic through time.

Designing a PIS is not an area that is widely studied and we can even see a decreasing of the number of papers allocated to this specific notion over time. It is known for a long time that design and modeling is an important part of an information system development. In (Borgida 1986), the authors state that modeling

Fig. 3 Papers distribution by publication type

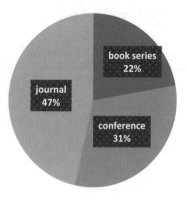

allows to develop information systems in an easier way because of focusing on the application domains semantics. However, here as in most proposals, the need for conceptual schemas in the development of information systems is often overlooked or simply disregarded (Olivé 2007).

Sources of Papers Publishing on Design and Modelling on Pervasive Systems
One of our goals is to analyze the venues of papers publishing on this specific topic. This question leads us to study the distribution of publications by type of venue: conferences, journals, or workshops, resulting on the distribution presented in Fig. 3. Half of the papers are journal papers, a quarter are conference ones and the other quarter are papers in book series. There is a quite a good distribution of publication issues and there is no specific issue which can be identified as 'the' issue to publish on modeling in PIS.

Cloud words We used the titles, abstracts and keywords of the selected papers to look about word frequencies. We deleted the stop words, the numbers, and the special characters. Moreover, we made a pre-processing of the data to change plural nouns into singular ones if the two forms were present in the dataset. We created a word cloud (see Fig. 4) to illustrate the distribution of these words (the size of the word in the cloud indicates its frequency in the dataset).

The papers titles, abstracts and keywords contain 195 occurrences of the word "IoT" or "Internet of Things", which put it in the first place before the others. Table 4 shows the frequencies of the most popular words (over 40 occurrences). When looking to less popular words, we can find "design" (28 occurrences) and "modeling" (19 occurrences). "Pervasive" is only present 24 times in the dataset, which means that this specific term is not so used in the literature.

Fig. 4 Word cloud

Table 4 Popular words frequency in the titles, abstracts and keywords

Word	Frequency	Word	Frequency	Word	Frequency
IoT	195	Model	86	Technology	46
System	179	Cloud	53	Sensor	42
Service	135	Management	49	Device	41
Information	111	Smart	49		
Data	94	Architecture	48		

3.2 RQ2. How Is Addressed the Design and Modeling of Pervasive Information Systems in Research Proposals?

In this section, we looked about the type, nature, added value, usage and application domain of the strategies applied in the design-dedicated research proposals.

3.2.1 Paper Type

We categorized these papers according to the type of research approaches introduced by Wieringa et al. (2006). The research approach applied in all the selected papers is "solution proposal". The authors propose a solution proposal improving the design of pervasive information system or handling a specific aspect of the pervasive systems such as security, access control at the design level. Most of the papers illustrate their proposition on an example but they cannot be qualified as experience papers.

Table 5 Nature of the proposal

Nature	Number	Percentage	References
Framework	21	46.66%	Zschörnig et al. (2018), Zimmermann et al. (2018), Shang et al. (2016), Tai et al. (2019), Qu and Hou (2017), Wang et al. (2018), Thangaraj et al. (2016), Nespoli et al. (2019), Mongiello et al. (2016), Mingozzi et al. (2016), Lyu et al. (2021), Li et al. (2017), Korzun (2016), Howell et al. (2017), Gkioulos et al. (2019), Triantafyllidis et al. (2016), Kashmar et al. (2021), Donnal (2020), Dave et al. (2018), AlSuwaidan (2019), Santiago et al. (2019)
Framework on specific domain	11	24.44%	Xu et al. (2017), Songsom et al. (2020), Razzaq et al. (2020), Li (2016), Gill et al. (2017), Bottaccioli et al. (2017), Tahmasbi et al. (2016), Herrera-Quintero et al. (2016), Chen and Lin (2019), Celesti et al. (2019), Guo et al. (2020)
Model modification	5	11.11%	Zimmermann et al. (2017), Schirmer et al. (2016), Kirchhof et al. (2020), Kayes et al. (2018), Aimene and Rassoul (2017)
New model	8	17.77%	Zúñiga-Prieto et al. (2018), Zhang et al. (2016), Nebhani et al. (2017), Liu et al. (2018), Jin et al. (2017), Feng et al. (2017), Fatma et al. (2016), Hussain and Wu (2018)

3.2.2 Nature of the Proposal

The proposal given in the selected papers can be of a different nature.

- **Framework.** The paper offers a new architecture or framework to design systems using IoT.
- **Framework on Specific Domain.** The paper proposes a new architecture or framework using IoT on a specific domain.
- **Model modification.** The paper uses an existing model and offers some improvement to take into account IoT data.
- **New model.** The proposal offers a new model to take into account IoT data in systems.

Table 5 shows the distribution of the selected papers following the nature of their proposal.

Most of the selected papers (32) are proposing a framework or an architecture, either generic or for a specific domain.

Proposition of a **"New model"** at the design phase is the output of eight papers. It could be used to enhance an aspect of a PIS (for example – access control), to describe the interaction between service layer and physical layer or to integrate the semantic dimension to improve the data reasoning embedded in the PIS.

"Model modification" is associated to only five papers. It can be concerned by a modification of a product model such as state transition diagram, a standard description language to orchestrate services or a model process of an existing design methodology.

3.2.3 Added Value of the Proposal

Each proposal has a specific added value. We identify four possible types of value the proposals can offer. Table 6 indicates the repartition of the papers following the added value specificities.

- **Product model.** The proposal offers a specific product model to describe the concepts of the system.
- **Way of Working.** The source describes a set of steps to design the system.
- **Specific localization of the IoT use – domain specific.** The selected papers promote an architectural framework specific to a domain. The added value of these papers is to envision where the IoT services can be located in a specific application domain.
- **Quality aspect enhancement of the IoT based system.** The authors focus on a specific aspect of the system to develop and discuss it at the design step.

Sometimes, papers have a combination of added values, as they propose way of working and models. It happens when the papers promote an architectural framework based on several layers and provide specific concepts for each of them. In this case, they use layers to organize the design process in steps and for each step they propose a specific concept to model or design the system.

A main part of the works proposes some design or modeling part, either as a product model (7 papers), a way of working (12 papers) or both (14 papers). Seven sources are helping to see where the IoT services can be localized for a specific domain, like the system ports or the digital footprint for instance. Seven papers propose an enhancement of a quality aspect of the IoT system, like the confidentiality, the user authentication and profiling or even access control services.

3.2.4 Usage of the IoT Based System

Pervasive information systems are usually seen, in the literature, as IoT Systems. We studied the different sources to identify the purpose of the IoT systems to design.

- **Data-oriented system.** This type means that the pervasive systems are only viewed to capture, manage and organize the pervasive information. It means that IoT devices are only considered as sensors.
- **Monitor & control systems.** This type is used when the pervasive systems are used to implement a smart monitor and control systems such as in smart cities, smart home, smart health care system, etc.
- **Business improvement**. This type is used when the IoT systems are used as a way to improve the business processes of the organization by adding IoT devices in a physical environment to capture data as well as to change the enactment of business processes.
- **Adaptation of service.** This type focuses only to adapt or recommend services according to the user's context.

Table 6 Added value of the proposal

Added value	Number	Percentage	References
Product model	21	46.66%	Zúñiga-Prieto et al. (2018), Zschörnig et al. (2018), Zhang et al. (2016), Shang et al. (2016), Nebhani et al. (2017), Zimmermann et al. (2017), Schirmer et al. (2016), Liu et al. (2018), Li et al. (2017), Korzun (2016), Jin et al. (2017), Triantafyllidis et al. (2016), Tahmasbi et al. (2016), Kirchhof et al. (2020), Herrera-Quintero et al. (2016), Feng et al. (2017), Fatma et al. (2016), Dave et al. (2018), Celesti et al. (2019), Hussain and Wu (2018), Kayes et al. (2018)
Way of working	26	57.77%	Zúñiga-Prieto et al. (2018), Zschörnig et al. (2018), Zimmermann et al. (2018), Zhang et al. (2016), Shang et al. (2016), Xu et al. (2017), Wang et al. (2018), Thangaraj et al. (2016), Liu et al. (2018), Li et al. (2017), Korzun (2016), Howell et al. (2017), Gill et al. (2017), Bottaccioli et al. (2017), Triantafyllidis et al. (2016), Tahmasbi et al. (2016), Kirchhof et al. (2020), Herrera-Quintero et al. (2016), Donnal (2020), Dave et al. (2018), Celesti et al. (2019), AlSuwaidan (2019), Guo et al. (2020), Hussain and Wu (2018), Santiago et al. (2019), Aimene and Rassoul (2017)
Specific localization of the IoT use – domain specific	5	11.11%	Qu and Hou (2017), Songsom et al. (2020), Razzaq et al. (2020), Li (2016), Chen and Lin (2019)
Quality aspect enhancement of the IoT based system	7	15.55%	Tai et al. (2019), Nespoli et al. (2019), Mongiello et al. (2016), Mingozzi et al. (2016), Lyu et al. (2021), Gkioulos et al. (2019), Kashmar et al. (2021)

- **Technical improvement.** Some articles are not dealing with the designing of the whole pervasive systems but only focusing on improving a technical aspect of such systems.

    Table 7 shows the distribution of the usages over the selected papers.

"Data-oriented system" usage:

- The main part of the selected papers focusses on how to design systems dealing with "pervasive information" in a generic manner (Zimmermann et al. 2018; Zhang et al. 2016; Shang et al. 2016; Schirmer et al. 2016; Korzun 2016; Donnal 2020; AlSuwaidan 2019; Santiago et al. 2019) or in a more specific domain (Xu et al. 2017; Tai et al. 2019; Qu and Hou 2017; Songsom et al. 2020; Razzaq et al. 2020; Thangaraj et al. 2016; Li et al. 2017; Howell et al. 2017; Gill et al.

Table 7 Usage of the IoT system

Nature	Number	Percentage	References
Data-oriented system	26	57.77%	Zimmermann et al. (2018), Zhang et al. (2016), Shang et al. (2016), Xu et al. (2017), Tai et al. (2019), Qu and Hou (2017), Songsom et al. (2020), Razzaq et al. (2020), Thangaraj et al. (2016), Schirmer et al. (2016), Li et al. (2017), Korzun (2016), Howell et al. (2017), Gill et al. (2017), Bottaccioli et al. (2017), Triantafyllidis et al. (2016), Herrera-Quintero et al. (2016), Donnal (2020), Dave et al. (2018), Chen and Lin (2019), Celesti et al. (2019), AlSuwaidan (2019), Guo et al. (2020), Hussain and Wu (2018), Santiago et al. (2019), Kayes et al. (2018)
Technical improvement	11	24.4%	Zúñiga-Prieto et al. (2018), Zimmermann et al. (2017), Nespoli et al. (2019), Mongiello et al. (2016), Mingozzi et al. (2016), Lyu et al. (2021), Liu et al. (2018), Jin et al. (2017), Gkioulos et al. (2019), Kashmar et al. (2021), Fatma et al. (2016)
Monitor and control system	3	6.67%	Wang et al. (2018), Kirchhof et al. (2020), Feng et al. (2017)
Business improvement	4	8.88%	Zschörnig et al. (2018), Li (2016), Tahmasbi et al. (2016), Aimene and Rassoul (2017)
Adaptation of services	1	2.22%	Nebhani et al. (2017)

2017; Bottaccioli et al. 2017; Triantafyllidis et al. 2016; Herrera-Quintero et al. 2016; Dave et al. 2018; Chen and Lin 2019; Celesti et al. 2019; Guo et al. 2020; Hussain and Wu 2018; Kayes et al. 2018).

- Four papers (Qu and Hou 2017; Songsom et al. 2020; Razzaq et al. 2020; Chen and Lin 2019) propose a framework to deal with IoT sensors-based systems without other added value than helping to understand where to locate the pervasive information in that domain (Framework on Specific Domain – Specific, localization of the IoT use – domain specific).
- Six papers provide an architectural framework for IoT sensors-based systems specific to an application domain with a way of working (Gill et al. 2017; Bottaccioli et al. 2017; Guo et al. 2020) and with models (Xu et al. 2017; Celesti et al. 2019; Herrera-Quintero et al. 2016).
- Eleven papers provide an architectural framework for IoT sensors-based systems with a way of working (Xu et al. 2017; Howell et al. 2017; Donnal 2020; AlSuwaidan 2019; Santiago et al. 2019) and with models (Shang et al. 2016; Thangaraj et al. 2016; Li et al. 2017; Korzun 2016; Triantafyllidis et al. 2016; Dave et al. 2018).
- Two papers (Zhang et al. 2016; Hussain and Wu 2018) propose a new model and a way of working for IoT sensors based systems. (Zhang et al. 2016)

proposes a modeling technique for the interactions between the sensor and the geographic environment in emerging sensor, whereas (Hussain and Wu 2018) defines semantic annotations in a model to maintain the comprehension between the application layer and the physical layer.

The three remaining papers are:

- Tai et al. (2019) propose an authentication framework to ensure reliable and anonymous data-oriented services with anonymity, availability and security (*architectural framework – quality aspect enhancement of the IoT based system*).
- Kayes et al. (2018) modifies a traditional state-transition-diagrams to specify the dynamic state change of a context (*Model modification, Product Model*)
- Schirmer et al. (2016) proposes to extend enterprise architectures for the "smart Port" application domain (*model modification, Product model*).

In the "**monitor & control systems**" usage, the aim of the pervasive information system is to monitor and control activities performed in a physical environment. It is handled by only three papers and it concerns smart building (Wang et al. 2018), smart home (Kirchhof et al. 2020) and smart industry (Feng et al. 2017). In more details:

- Wang et al. (2018) proposes an architectural framework to build an operation management of cloud ecosystem IoT platform for smart home device level, networking level, IoT platform level and operation management applications level (*way of working & models*).
- Kirchhof et al. (2020) promotes at the design stage a model-driven digital twin construction for synthesizing the integration of cyber-physical systems with their information systems. Authors propose a *modified existing model* to handle specifically a "Smart home" system.
- Feng et al. (2017) targets a context-aware supervision for logistics asset management in the smart industry field. The authors propose concepts (*new model*) at the design level to the system implementation.

The "**Business improvement**" usage is the category we are interested in because it considered the information systems can be improved or extended by "pervasive services" which are related to IoT sensors and IoT actuators. This category is covered by only four papers where three are specific to a domain (smart energy (Zschörnig et al. 2018), smart logistics (Li 2016) and Smart patient care (Tahmasbi et al. 2016)) and only one is generic (Aimene and Rassoul 2017). In more details,

- Li (2016) promotes an architectural framework at the design level to improve the supply-chain business systems by using a RFID technology to track the circulation of the product. The added value of this proposition is to help the user to understand where the pervasive services are located and the impact at the business level (*Localized the use of IoT – domain specific*).
- Zschörnig et al. (2018) provides an architectural framework including concepts specifics to pervasive IS and models at three levels: *integration layer, data & analytics layer and IoT aware process layer*. It is used to propose a way of

working at the design phase as well as models to use to specify each layer (*Way of Working & model*).

- Tahmasbi et al. (2016) promotes an architectural framework for a pervasive healthcare system focused on availability, interoperability, and performance, wherein components, their relationships and the necessary constraints are defined to contribute to easier implementation of these systems. At the design phase, it proposes *a way of working and models* to specify the pervasive healthcare system.
- Aimene and Rassoul (2017) proposes to extend Booch's design methodology[1] to handle ubiquitous specification in a generic manner. The specificity of the PIS is proposed by adding to the traditional way of working two early steps to deal with ubiquitous requirements specification and context specification (*Way of working*).

The **"Adaptation of service"** usage is covered by only 1 paper (Nebhani et al. 2017) proposing a formal Context-awareness model at the design phase based on an ontology traceability to provide adaptive services to accomplish a specific goal at any moment and any place (*new model – Product model*). The IoT system is user-centric and focusing on mobile devices.

The **"technical improvement"** category concerns 11 papers where only one is specific to a domain (*smart water management* (Liu et al. 2018)). The aspects of the PIS targeted by these papers are the following.

- Three papers are dealing with *access control aspect* of the PIS at the design phase by providing specific framework (Zimmermann et al. 2017; Nespoli et al. 2019; Kashmar et al. 2021).
- Two papers add *semantic facility with ontologies to context* at the design phase (Mingozzi et al. 2016; Fatma et al. 2016),
- Three papers deal with the *interaction between IoT physical layer to the service layer* with specific models at the design phase (Zúñiga-Prieto et al. 2018; Zimmermann et al. 2017; Liu et al. 2018) but (Zimmermann et al. 2017) extends the TOSCA standard to automate orchestration of services.
- One paper (Lyu et al. 2021) proposes a *support control aspect* in PIS as a service with a framework at the design phase including a hierarchy of ontologies.
- One paper (Mongiello et al. 2016) targets the *reflexivity capability* required in PIS to integrate it in context-aware design of reflective middleware.

3.2.5 Application Domain

One of our goals is to analyze the impacted domains. Over our 45 papers, 19 papers are completely generic and don't address a particular domain. On the remaining 26 papers, 20 are concerned about a specific application domain, whereas the

---

[1] Booch's design method: Grady Booch published in 1992 and revised in 1994 an object-oriented design method called OMT. It was widely used in software engineering for object-oriented analysis and design.

Table 8 Application domains

Application domain	Number	Main domain	Case study
Smart applications for persons	**12**		
Smart healthcare	8	Smart healthcare monitoring (Xu et al. 2017) Smart patient healthcare (Triantafyllidis et al. 2016; Celesti et al. 2019; Tai et al. 2019; Thangaraj et al. 2016; Tahmasbi et al. 2016)	Hussain and Wu (2018), Kayes et al. (2018)
Smart home	4	Smart home building (Wang et al. 2018; Bottaccioli et al. 2017)	Mingozzi et al. (2016), Kirchhof et al. (2020)
Smart applications for environment	**2**		
Smart natural resource management	2	Smart water management (Liu et al. 2018; Howell et al. 2017)	
Smart applications for society	**4**		
Smart city	2	Smart urbanism (Chen and Lin 2019; Guo et al. 2020)	
Smart education	2	Smart campus (Dave et al. 2018) Smart university (Songsom et al. 2020)	
Smart applications for enterprises	**8**		
Smart agriculture	1	(Gill et al. 2017)	
Smart business management	2	(Li et al. 2017)	Lyu et al. (2021)
Smart industry	3	Smart energy (Zschörnig et al. 2018) Smart logistics (Li 2016)	Smart logistics (Feng et al. 2017)
Smart transportation	2	(Razzaq et al. 2020; Herrera-Quintero et al. 2016)	

other 6 gives some generic solution illustrated on a domain case study. For the 26 papers either specific or illustrating their generic solution on a specific domain, we refer to the smart applications taxonomy defined in (Kornyshova et al. 2022) to characterize the domain. The following table shows the number of each paper for each represented domain (Table 8).

We can conclude that the selected papers cover a large panel of smart applications domains. This means that any domain can be concerned and impacted by design and modeling in pervasive information systems.

3.2.6 Discussion

The analysis of the selected papers shows that only seven papers (Wang et al. 2018; Kirchhof et al. 2020; Feng et al. 2017; Zschörnig et al. 2018; Li 2016; Tahmasbi et al. 2016; Aimene and Rassoul 2017) deal with a PIS compliant with the definition detailed in chapter "What Is a "Pervasive Information System" (PIS)?". The "Business improvement" and "control & monitor system" are the usage types compliant with our PIS definition. More than half of the papers twenty-six aim at designing a system to manage "pervasive information" from IoT-sensors based systems and less than a quarter of the papers concern an improvement of a technical aspect of a PIS.

The PIS vision, developed in chapter "What Is a "Pervasive Information System" (PIS)?", is structured by a set of layers from the infrastructure layer to the application or business process layer. In addition, it includes two main flows across layers – the bottom-up one corresponding to the data flow whereas the top-down one represents the adaptation flow. The bottom-up data flow represents the way of managing "pervasive information" from the lower layer to the upper layer. This flow is tackled by most of the research works. However, the top-down flow for adaption purpose is not handled explicitly in the selected papers on IoT or pervasive systems.

The seven papers compliant to our PIS definition deal with (1) an architectural framework connecting the lower layers (infrastructure or physical) to the upper layers (application or business processes) and (2) deal with the bottom-up data flow across layers. However, they are not mentioned explicitly the top-down adaptation flow. The architecture layers are used by four papers (Zschörnig et al. 2018; Wang et al. 2018; Tahmasbi et al. 2016; Feng et al. 2017) to structure the way of working at the design phase and only one (Aimene and Rassoul 2017) extends a traditional Information system design method (Booch's design methodology). (Kirchhof et al. 2020) adapts the "digital twin" approach to integrate the cyber-physical systems with their information systems. Five papers (Zschörnig et al. 2018; Wang et al. 2018; Tahmasbi et al. 2016; Kirchhof et al. 2020; Feng et al. 2017) propose at the design phase at least one modelling technique adapted to the PIS.

Beside these seven papers, we would like to underline the fact that (Schirmer et al. 2016) extends existing enterprise architectures approaches for building IoT-based systems.

Before concluding on RQ2, we can highlight some research works that are based on new trends for sharing on the cloud "pervasive information" such as:

- Razzaq et al. (2020) is related to the Cloud of Thing (CoT). Cloud computing, coupled with IoT, gathers data from remote areas with wireless sensors and organizes them in an added-value service facility for a specific domain.
- Korzun (2016) uses the "smart space approach". Smart spaces define a software development approach that enables creating service-oriented information systems for emerging computing environments of the Internet of Things (IoT). Such environments follow the paradigms of ubiquitous and pervasive computing

and provide a growing multitude of digital networked devices surrounding their human users.

- AlSuwaidan (2019) handles the data management on Internet of Everything (IoE). The IoE is defined on top of the IoT by adding the human element to the IoT network. In particular, the IoE can improve quality of lives via smart connection between people, processes, data, and things. The ITU Telecommunication Standardization Sector characterizes the IoE as "*a worldwide base for the data society, empowering propelled administrations by interconnecting (physical and virtual) things taking into account existing and advancing interoperable data and correspondence innovations*" (Majeed 2017).

In addition, two papers address a relevant point for designing and developing a PIS:

- Dave et al. (2018) emphasizes the fact that pervasive information systems dealing with real space like a building or a University, an Airport, a station, etc. needs to integrate a "Building Information Modelling" (BIM) to at least the physical infrastructure IoT layer to be able to reason on it at the application layer.
- The top-down adaptation flow mentioned in our PIS vision can be handled with a reflexivity capability we can at least develop at the physical layer by a context-aware design of reflective middleware (Mongiello et al. 2016).

As it is stated in (Schirmer et al. 2016), "Today, many companies use models and tools that are based on enterprise architecture approaches for improving the alignment between business and IT. For managing the enterprise architecture, appropriate models need to be built, kept up-to-date and should be taken as a basis for decision making regarding issues that affect the relation between business and IT." That's why existing enterprise architecture (EA) models have to be extended or rethink to handle our PIS vison.

The research works exposed by the selected papers proposes an architectural framework, ways of working or/and models for a specific domain, a specific aspect of a PIS in order to connect the physical layer to the application layer. Only one paper (Aimene and Rassoul 2017) refers to a traditional Information system design methodology or modelling techniques (Booch's design methodology). However, the extension which could be in (Aimene and Rassoul 2017) but also external sources such as in (Zimmermann et al. 2015) and (Bassi et al. 2013) do not help stakeholders to envision the use of the IoT to improve business processes, it is why a domain-dependent approach could be more efficient to guide stakeholders to build PIS.

3.3 RQ3. How Are Met the PIS Requirements in These Design-Dedicated Research Proposals?

One of our main goals is to analyze the fulfilling of the PIS requirements defined in chapter "What Is a "Pervasive Information System" (PIS)?". Table 9 shows the fulfilled PIS requirements (with an X in the cell) for each selected paper. Sometimes,

Table 9 Requirements

Article	Context awareness	Heterogeneity	Transparency	Requirements satisfaction	Adaptation
Zúñiga-Prieto et al. (2018)	n/a	X	X	X	n/a
Zschörnig et al. (2018)	X	X	X	X	X
Zimmermann et al. (2018)		X	X	n/a	n/a
Zhang et al. (2016)	n/a	X	X	X	n/a
Shang et al. (2016)	n/a	X	X	X	n/a
Xu et al. (2017)		X	n/a	n/a	n/a
Tai et al. (2019)		X	n/a	X	n/a
Qu &and Hou (2017)		X	X	X	n/a
Songsom et al. (2020)	n/a	X	n/a	X	n/a
Razzaq et al. (2020)	X	X	X	X	X
Nebhani et al. (2017)	X		X	X	X
Zimmermann et al. (2017)	n/a	X	n/a	X	n/a
Wang et al. (2018)	X	X	X	X	X
Thangaraj et al. (2016)	n/a	X	X	X	n/a
Schirmer et al. (2016)		X	X	X	n/a
Nespoli et al. (2019)	X	X	n/a	n/a	n/a
Mongiello et al. (2016)	X	X	n/a	X	X
Mingozzi et al. (2016)	X	X	n/a	n/a	X
Lyu et al. (2021)	X	X	n/a	X	n/a
Liu et al. (2018)	n/a	X	n/a	X	n/a
Li (2016)			n/a	X	n/a
Li et al. (2017)	n/a	X	X	X	n/a
Korzun (2016)	n/a	X	X	X	n/a
Jin et al. (2017)	n/a	X		X	X
Howell et al. (2017)	X	n/a	n/a	X	n/a
Gkioulos et al. (2019)	n/a	X	n/a	X	n/a
Gill et al. (2017)	n/a	X	n/a	X	n/a
Bottaccioli et al. (2017)	X	X	n/a	X	n/a
Triantafyllidis et al. (2016)	X	X		X	n/a
Tahmasbi et al. (2016)	X	X	X	X	n/a
Kirchhof et al. (2020)	X	X	n/a	X	
Kashmar et al. (2021)	X	X	n/a	n/a	n/a
Herrera-Quintero et al. (2016)	n/a	X	n/a	n/a	n/a
Feng et al. (2017)	X	X	n/a	X	
Fatma et al. (2016)	X	n/a	X	X	X
Donnal (2020)	X	X	n/a	X	n/a
Dave et al. (2018)	X	X	n/a	X	n/a
Chen and Lin (2019)	X	X	n/a	X	n/a
Celesti et al. (2019)	X	X	n/a	X	n/a
AlSuwaidan (2019)	X	X	n/a	X	n/a
Guo et al. (2020)	X	X	n/a	X	n/a
Hussain and Wu (2018)	X	X	n/a	X	n/a
Santiago et al. (2019)	X	X	n/a	X	n/a
Kayes et al. (2018)	X	X	n/a	n/a	n/a
Aimene and Rassoul (2017)	X	n/a	n/a	X	n/a

the proposal does not give enough information to be able to decide and, in this case, a non-applicable sign (n/a) was put in the corresponding cell. Empty cells mean that the PIS requirement is not fulfilled.

- **Heterogeneity.** This requirement is present in 88.9% of the sources (fourty papers) as it is quite usual to manage several kind of IoT devices at the physical layer for a PIS. Two papers do not satisfy this requirement (empty cell) because at the physical level they choose to integrate only one technology ((Nebhani et al. 2017) with mobile phone technology and (Li 2016) with RFID technology). Three papers are not concerned ("n/a" cell) by the requirement because their proposal does not manage or are not concerned by the physical layer (Howell et al. 2017; Fatma et al. 2016; Aimene and Rassoul 2017).

- **Requirements satisfaction.** 88.44% of the sources are concerned about meeting the user needs or the purpose of the IoT based systems to improve the overall performance of the organization (thirty-eight papers). They meet this requirement when the proposal includes the application or business process layers in the architectural framework. Six papers are not concerned by this requirement ("n/a" cell) because they are only tackling in their proposal the data access control (Nespoli et al. 2019; Kashmar et al. 2021; Kayes et al. 2018) or are dedicated only to share or gather data (Xu et al. 2017; Zimmermann et al. 2018; Herrera-Quintero et al. 2016) without referring to the PIS at the designing phase.

- **Context awareness.** It is considered in 57.8% of the sources (twenty-six papers). This requirement is satisfied by the research works where data are captured in the environment and also identified by the authors as a context information of entities and not only raw data. Twelve papers are not concerned by this requirement ("n/a" cell) because they are related to build a data-oriented IoT systems (IoT sensors-based systems) but they are concerned about capturing, sharing and distributing data without using them (Zhang et al. 2016; Shang et al. 2016; Songsom et al. 2020; Li et al. 2017; Gill et al. 2017; Herrera-Quintero et al. 2016) or because their proposal is to improve a technical aspect which is not related to context information and management (Zúñiga-Prieto et al. 2018; Zimmermann et al. 2017; Thangaraj et al. 2016; Liu et al. 2018; Jin et al. 2017; Gkioulos et al. 2019). Seven papers do not meet this requirement because they are related to the building of a data-oriented systems (Zimmermann et al. 2018; Xu et al. 2017; Tai et al. 2019; Qu and Hou 2017; Schirmer et al. 2016; Li 2016; Korzun 2016), which observe and use data without considering these as context information of entities.

- **Transparency.** This requirement is not a relevant characteristic for this bunch of sources as only fifteen papers are concerned about it. The purpose of this requirement is mainly to hide the heterogeneity of the IoT devices at the physical layer (Zúñiga-Prieto et al. 2018; Zschörnig et al. 2018; Zimmermann et al. 2018; Zhang et al. 2016; Shang et al. 2016; Qu and Hou 2017; Razzaq et al. 2020; Wang et al. 2018; Thangaraj et al. 2016; Schirmer et al. 2016; Li et al. 2017; Korzun 2016; Tahmasbi et al. 2016) or to hide the complexity of the adaptation process (Nebhani et al. 2017; Fatma et al. 2016). The proposal of the two papers (Jin et al. 2017) and (Triantafyllidis et al. 2016) do not meet this requirement as the former paper proposes a model helping to choose the selected service without hiddening the heterogeneity and the adaptation process whereas in the latter the heterogeneity is not handled at all. Twenty eight papers are not concerned by this requirement (n/a cells) either because their proposal aim at designing data-oriented system or monitor & control system and they do not hide the heterogeneity or because their proposal is a technical improvement which is not concerned by heterogeneity or which do not hide at all the heterogeneity.

- **Adaptation**. Not a lot of sources are taking this particular requirement into account. Only 15.56% of the proposals (Mingozzi et al. 2016; Jin et al. 2017; Fatma et al. 2016; Mongiello et al. 2016; Wang et al. 2018; Zimmermann et al. 2017; Nebhani et al. 2017) meet this requirement as they handle the selection and/or the adaptation of services according to quality criteria or context information. Two papers (Kirchhof et al. 2020; Feng et al. 2017) do not satisfied this requirement because the monitor & control systems they target does not include the selection or adaptation of services. Thirty six papers are not concerned by this requirement because they are targeting a data-oriented system or technical improvement without relation with adaptation.

Only two papers fulfill all the PIS requirements as defined in the first chapter.

- Zschörnig et al. (2018) proposes an architectural concept, divided into three technical layers (integration, data and analytics, and IoT-aware processes) and a software prototype called SEPL. This proposal also fulfill two of the additional characteristics: it support the user's business needs in a predictable and controlled manner (Determinism) and collect and process heterogeneous data automatically (Automatic).
- In Wang et al. (2018), the authors propose a building operation management cloud ecosystem for smart buildings, containing several levels, namely the building operation management application level, the IoT platform, networking level and the device level. However, it is difficult to determine if the proposal fulfills some additional characteristics.

Three papers fulfill 4/5 of the PIS requirements.

- Razzaq et al. (2020) introduced an edge information system for intelligent Internet of Vehicle, including edge caching, edge computing, and edge AI. Authors present platforms, design methodologies, and key use cases. It satisfies Context awareness, Heterogeneity, Transparency and Requirements satisfaction. It is difficult to determine if this proposal fulfill additional characteristics. However, if only one of them has to be fulfilled, it can only be the "Automatic" one.
- Tahmasbi et al. (2016) propose a software architecture for a cloud-based healthcare system for mobile patients. It is focused on non-functional require-ments including availability, interoperability, and performance. The cloud major component is designed in the form of multiple independent clouds and also makes use of virtualization concept. The proposal satisfies Context awareness, Heterogeneity, Transparency and Requirements satisfaction. It is difficult to determine if the proposal fulfills some additional characteristics.
- Fatma et al. (2016) adds contextual information to the semantic web service description to ensure the pervasive system adaptation and to change the web service behavior depending on the contextual information categories. Authors propose a methodological approach to assist the designers to develop PIS

instances based on semantic web services and to adapt these instances to the user's need in a specific contextual situation. This work satisfies Context awareness, Transparency, Requirements satisfaction and Adaptation. However it is difficult to determine if it fulfills some additional characteristics.

Twenty-four sources fulfill 3/5 of the PIS requirements, each of them satisfying at least Heterogeneity and Requirement satisfaction. On this subset, 62% satisfy Context awareness, 33% Transparency and 8% Adaptation.

4   Conclusion and Open Issues

We conducted a systematic mapping study on papers addressing design and modeling in pervasive information systems. We had three research questions.

- To answer to *RQ1* (What is the distribution evolution of the sources?), we studied the distribution of the selected papers over time and issues and identified the most frequent words present in the selected sources.
- To answer *RQ2* (How is addressed the design and modeling of pervasive information systems in research proposals?), we then characterized the selected papers following the type, nature of the proposal, usage of the IoT system and application domain. It gave us some insight about the proposals in each of the sources.
- To answer to *RQ3* (How are met the PIS requirements presented in the first chapter of the book in these design-dedicated research proposals?) we finally looked if the proposal were fulfilling the requirements identified for pervasive information systems. Only two papers were fulfilling 100% of the PIS requirements and three papers 4/5 of them.

This literature review leads us to draw some conclusions. There are works in the literature which propose some interesting value about design and modeling in PIS but a common terminology is required in the field to be able to compare and link all the existing proposals on a more efficient way.

Our PIS vision uses a two-way flow between the layers: the data flow from the infrastructure layer to the management layer – bottom-up flow – and the adaptation flow the other way around – top-down flow (see chapter "What Is a "Pervasive Information System" (PIS)?"). The bottom-up flow is mostly taken into account in the selected works of our dataset, whereas the top-down one is usually ignored. The reflexivity capability and the context-awareness in middleware are important elements but are not usual in information system development method. New methodologies must be defined to handle correctly adaptative systems. We also highlighted that a domain-dependent approach could be more efficient to guide stakeholders to build PIS and to help them to envision the use of the IoT to improve business processes. Moreover, existing enterprise architecture (EA) models have to be extended or redesigned to handle our PIS vison and to take into account the two-way flows of the PIS dynamics. Information about building (BIM) and physical environment should be integrated in the design methodology for domain-specific PIS like smart university, smart airport, and so on.

The majority of the systems used in the selected works can't be qualified as pervasive information system as we have defined it earlier as they mostly have a pervasive information vision (they use only the bottom-up flow). They do not fulfill all of the five requirements stated in chapter one and usually don't give any information about the additional characteristics.

References

Bassi, A. et al.: Enabling things to talk. Springer, New York (2013).

Borgida, A. Conceptual Modeling of Information Systems. In: Brodie, M.L., Mylopoulos, J. (eds) On Knowledge Base Management Systems. Topics in Information Systems. Springer, New York, NY (1986)

Kornyshova E., Deneckere, R., Sadouki K., Gressier-Soudan E., Brinkkemper S., Smart Life: Review of the Contemporary Smart Applications, 16th International Conference on Research Challenges in Information Science (RCIS 2022), May 2022, Barcelona, Spain (2022)

Majeed, A.: Developing countries and internet-of-everything (IoE). In: 2017 IEEE 7th Annual Computing and Communication Workshop and Conference (CCWC), pp. 1–4. IEEE (2017)

Ng I. C.L, Wakenshaw S. Y.L, The Internet-of-Things: Review and research directions, International Journal of Research in Marketing, Volume 34, Issue 1, March 2017, Pages 3–21

Olivé A. Conceptual Modeling of Information Systems, Springer (2007)

Petersen, K., Feldt, R., Mujtaba, S., and Mattsson, M.: Systematic mapping studies in software engineering. In 12th Intl Conference on Evaluation and Assessment in Software Engineering, volume 17 (2008)

Thomson, S. B.. Qualitative Research: Validity. JOAAG, Vol. 6. No 1 (2011)

Wieringa, R., Maiden, N. A. M., Mead, N. R. & Rolland, C.: Requirements engineering paper classification and evaluation criteria: a proposal and a discussion, Requir. Eng. 11(1), 102–107 (2006).

Zimmermann, A. et al.: Digital Enterprise Architecture – Transformation for the Internet of Things. In: IEEE EDOCW 2015, pp. 130–138 (2015).

SMS References

Aimene, S. & Rassoul, I. Integration of ubiquitous specifications in the lifecycle of design object oriented. *Adv. Intell. Syst. Comput.***612**, 513–519 (2017).

AlSuwaidan, L. Data Management Model for Internet of Everything. Lect. Notes Comput. Sci. (including Subser. Lect. Notes Artif. Intell. Lect. Notes Bioinformatics) **11673 LNCS**, 331–341 (2019).

Bottaccioli, L. *et al.* Building Energy Modelling and Monitoring by Integration of IoT Devices and Building Information Models. *Proc. - Int. Comput. Softw. Appl. Conf.***1**, 914–922 (2017).

Celesti, A. *et al.* How to develop IoT cloud e-health systems based on fiware: A lesson learnt. *J. Sens. Actuator Networks***8**, (2019).

Chen, M. & Lin, Y. Exploration and implementation of intelligent park information system based on cloud computing and Internet of Things. *Int. J. online Biomed. Eng.***15**, 115–128 (2019).

Dave, B., Buda, A., Nurminen, A. & Främling, K. A framework for integrating BIM and IoT through open standards. *Autom. Constr.***95**, 35–45 (2018).

Donnal, J. S. Wattsworth: An Open-Source Platform for Decentralized Sensor Networks. *IEEE Internet Things J.***7**, 189–196 (2020).

Fatma, A., Jedidi, A. & Gargouri, F. Semantic Web service and pervasive information system conceptual adaptation. *Int. J. Pervasive Comput. Commun.***12**, 466–502 (2016).

Feng, F., Pang, Y. & Lodewijks, G. Towards context-aware supervision for logistics asset management: Concept design and system implementation. *Lect. Notes Bus. Inf. Process.***277**, 3–19 (2017).

Gill, S. S., Buyya, R. & Chana, I. IoT based agriculture as a cloud and big data service: The beginning of digital India. *J. Organ. End User Comput.***29**, 1–23 (2017).

Gkioulos, V., Rizos, A., Michailidou, C., Mori, P. & Saracino, A. Enhancing usage control for performance: An architecture for systems of systems. *Lect. Notes Comput. Sci. (including Subser. Lect. Notes Artif. Intell. Lect. Notes Bioinformatics)***11387 LNCS**, 69–84 (2019).

Guo, H., Petersen, S. A., Gao, S., Li, J. & Bokolo, A. J. Embracing modern technologies and urban development trends: Initial evaluation of a smart city enterprise architecture frameworks. *Lect. Notes Bus. Inf. Process.***381 LNBIP**, 247–257 (2020).

Herrera-Quintero, L. F., Banse, K., Vega-Alfonso, J. & Venegas-Sanchez, A. Smart ITS sensor for the transportation planning using the IoT and Bigdata approaches to produce ITS cloud services. *2016 8th Euro Am. Conf. Telemat. Inf. Syst. EATIS 2016* (2016) https://doi.org/ 10.1109/EATIS.2016.7520096.

Howell, S., Rezgui, Y. & Beach, T. Integrating building and urban semantics to empower smart water solutions. *Autom. Constr.***81**, 434–448 (2017).

Hussain, A. & Wu, W. Sustainable interoperability and data integration for the IoT-based information systems. Proc. - 2017 IEEE Int. Conf. Internet Things, IEEE Green Comput. Commun. IEEE Cyber, Phys. Soc. Comput. IEEE Smart Data, iThings-GreenCom-CPSCom-SmartData 2017 **2018-Janua**, 824–829 (2018).

Jin, X., Chun, S., Jung, J. & Lee, K. H. A fast and scalable approach for IoT service selection based on a physical service model. *Inf. Syst. Front.***19**, 1357–1372 (2017).

Kashmar, N., Adda, M., Atieh, M. & Ibrahim, H. Access control metamodel for policy specification and enforcement: From conception to formalization. *Procedia Comput. Sci.***184**, 887–892 (2021).

Kayes, A. S. M. *et al.* Dynamic Transitions of States for Context-Sensitive Access Control Decision. *Lect. Notes Comput. Sci. (including Subser. Lect. Notes Artif. Intell. Lect. Notes Bioinformatics)***11233 LNCS**, 127–142 (2018).

Kirchhof, J. C., Michael, J., Rumpe, B., Varga, S. & Wortmann, A. Model-driven digital twin construction: Synthesizing the integration of cyber-physical systems with their information systems. *Proc. - 23rd ACM/IEEE Int. Conf. Model Driven Eng. Lang. Syst. Model. 2020* 90–101 (2020) https://doi.org/10.1145/3365438.3410941.

Korzun, D. On the smart spaces approach to semantic-driven design of service-oriented information systems. *Commun. Comput. Inf. Sci.***615**, 181–195 (2016).

Li, Z. A study of agricultural products distribution using the internet of things. *Int. J. Simul. Syst. Sci. Technol.***17**, 13.1–13.5 (2016).

Li, M., Xu, G., Shao, S., Lin, P. & Huang, G. Q. Ubiquitous cloud object for fine-grained resource management in e-commerce logistics. *Adv. Transdiscipl. Eng.***5**, 1049–1056 (2017).

Liu, Z. *et al.* A Case Study of Service-Centric IoT Model for Rural Sewage Disposal. *Proc. - 2018 IEEE 15th Int. Conf. E-bus. Eng. ICEBE 2018*, 133–138 (2018) https://doi.org/10.1109/ ICEBE.2018.00029.

Lyu, M., Biennier, F. & Ghodous, P. Integration of ontologies to support Control as a Service in an Industry 4.0 context. *Serv. Oriented Comput. Appl.***15**, 127–140 (2021).

Mingozzi, E. *et al.* Semantic-based context modeling for quality of service support in IoT platforms. *WoWMoM 2016 - 17th Int. Symp. a World Wireless, Mob. Multimed. Networks* (2016) https://doi.org/10.1109/WoWMoM.2016.7523563.

Mongiello, M., di Noia, T., Nocera, F., di Sciascio, E. & Parchitelli, A. Context-aware design of reflective middleware in the internet of everything. *Lect. Notes Comput. Sci. (including Subser. Lect. Notes Artif. Intell. Lect. Notes Bioinformatics)***9946 LNCS**, 423–435 (2016).

Nebhani, N., Lapayre, J. C. & Bouhlel, M. S. Ontology traceability for the adaptation of services in pervasive environment. *2016 IEEE Int. Conf. Syst. Man, Cybern. SMC 2016 - Conf. Proc.* 4543–4548 (2017) https://doi.org/10.1109/SMC.2016.7844947.

Nespoli, P. *et al.* PALOT: Profiling and authenticating users leveraging internet of things. *Sensors (Switzerland)***19**, (2019).

Qu, L. & Hou, J. H. Port information platform service design based on internet of things technologies. *ACM Int. Conf. Proceeding Ser.* 164–169 (2017) https://doi.org/10.1145/3158233.3159309.

Razzaq, N. *et al.* Cloud of things (CoT) based parking prediction. *Int. J. Adv. Comput. Sci. Appl.***11**, 645–654 (2020).

Santiago, A. R., Antunes, M., Barraca, J. P., Gomes, D. & Aguiar, R. L. SCoTv2: Large scale data acquisition, processing, and visualization platform. *Proc. - 2019 Int. Conf. Futur. Internet Things Cloud, FiCloud 2019* 318–323 (2019) https://doi.org/10.1109/FiCloud.2019.00053.

Schirmer, I., Drews, P., Saxe, S., Baldauf, U. & Tesse, J. Extending enterprise architectures for adopting the internet of things – Lessons learned from the smartPORT projects in Hamburg. *Lect. Notes Bus. Inf. Process.***255**, 169–180 (2016).

Shang, X., Zhang, R., Zhu, X. & Zhou, Q. Design theory, modelling and the application for the Internet of Things service. *Enterp. Inf. Syst.***10**, 249–267 (2016).

Songsom, N., Nilsook, P., Wannapiroon, P., Fung, L. C. C. & Wong, K. W. System design of a student relationship management system using the internet of things to collect the digital footprint. *Int. J. Inf. Educ. Technol.***10**, 222–226 (2020).

Tahmasbi, A., Adabi, S. & Rezaee, A. Behavioral Reference Model for Pervasive Healthcare Systems. *J. Med. Syst.***40**, (2016).

Tai, W. L., Chang, Y. F. & Lo, Y. L. An Anonymity, Availability and Security-Ensured Authentication Model of the IoT Control System for Reliable and Anonymous eHealth Services. *J. Med. Biol. Eng.***39**, 443–455 (2019).

Thangaraj, M., Ponmalar, P. P. & Anuradha, S. Internet of Things (IOT) enabled smart autonomous hospital management system - A real world health care use case with the technology drivers. *2015 IEEE Int. Conf. Comput. Intell. Comput. Res. ICCIC 2015* (2016) https://doi.org/10.1109/ICCIC.2015.7435678.

Triantafyllidis, A. K. *et al.* Framework of sensor-based monitoring for pervasive patient care. *Healthc. Technol. Lett.***3**, 153–158 (2016).

Wang, M., Qiu, S., Zhang, G., Yu, J. & Wang, Y. An Operation Management Cloud Ecosystem for Smart Buildings Based on Internet of Things. *2017 IEEE 7th Annu. Int. Conf. CYBER Technol. Autom. Control. Intell. Syst. CYBER 2017* 1627–1630 (2018) https://doi.org/10.1109/CYBER.2017.8446174.

Xu, B. *et al.* The design of an m-Health monitoring system based on a cloud computing platform. *Enterp. Inf. Syst.***11**, 17–36 (2017).

Zhang, F., Xu, Y. & Chou, J. A novel Petri nets-based modeling method for the interaction between the sensor and the geographic environment in emerging sensor networks. *Sensors (Switzerland)***16**, (2016).

Zimmermann, M., Breitenbücher, U. & Leymann, F. A TOSCA-based programming model for interacting components of automatically deployed cloud and IoT applications. *ICEIS 2017 - Proc. 19th Int. Conf. Enterp. Inf. Syst.***2**, 121–131 (2017).

Zimmermann, A. *et al.* Decision-controlled digitization architecture for internet of things and microservices. *Smart Innov. Syst. Technol.***73**, 82–92 (2018).

Zschörnig, T., Wehlitz, R., Rößner, I. & Franczyk, B. SEPL: An IoT platform for value-added services in the energy domain: Architectural concept and software prototype. *ICEIS 2018 - Proc. 20th Int. Conf. Enterp. Inf. Syst.***1**, 593–600 (2018).

Zúñiga-Prieto, M. *et al.* IOT-ADL: An ADL for describing cloud IoT applications. *J. Comput.***29**, 264–273 (2018).

The Context Awareness Challenges for PIS

Manuele Kirsch-Pinheiro

1   Introduction

New technologies, such as IoT, Cloud, and Fog/Edge Computing, are bringing more dynamism to Information Systems and are enabling more flexible IT systems that can be potentially better adapted to changes in their execution environment. The recent availability of sensors that can capture a wide range of physical phenomena in real-time has triggered the curiosity of developers to explore what type of services they can create based on sensing (and actuation) (Augusto et al. 2017). Indeed, such sensor data represents an interesting input for adapting services and applications behavior, offering the possibility of having a "smarter" system. According to Bauer and Dey (2016), we can already witness a move towards increasingly sophisticated systems ("smart", "intelligent", "context-aware", "adaptive", etc.). Information System users are not an exception, they expect an increasingly "intelligent" system capable of anticipating their needs and responding to them appropriately. Besides, developers are mainly interested in the contexts the system can "perceive" and what that can enable a system to do. The ability to learn behavior patterns becomes essential for the successful implementation of intelligent environments because knowing such patterns allows the environment to act intelligently and pro-actively when it matters (Augusto et al. 2017).

In order to provide such kind of "intelligent" behavior that is expected from them, Pervasive Information System (PIS) must become aware of the context in which they are used and intelligently adapt their execution. In other words, PIS must integrate *context-awareness* properties in their behavior, and they should behave as context-aware systems. The notion of context becomes central to PIS since it may

M. Kirsch-Pinheiro (✉)
Centre de Recherche en Informatique, Université Paris 1 Panthéon Sorbonne, Paris, France
e-mail: Manuele.Kirsch-Pinheiro@univ-paris1.fr

© The Author(s), under exclusive license to Springer Nature Switzerland AG 2023
M. Kirsch Pinheiro et al. (eds.), *The Evolution of Pervasive Information Systems*,
https://doi.org/10.1007/978-3-031-18176-4_3

contribute to achieving the flexibility necessary for PIS to better account for the dynamic environment in which Information Systems are gradually moving towards.

The notion of context can be defined as any piece of information that characterizes the situation of an entity, whether it is a person, a place, or another object (user, application, etc.), considered relevant for the interaction between the user and the application (Dey 2001). Context-awareness can be roughly seen as the capability a software system has to adapt its behavior according to changes observed in its execution context (Dey 2001; Baldauf et al. 2007; Bauer and Dey 2016).

From its beginning, in the early'90s (Schilit and Theimer 1994; Schilit et al. 1994; Brown et al. 1997, just to name a few) till nowadays, Context-Aware Computing has received much attention in the literature (Alegre et al. 2016; Augusto et al. 2017; Baldauf et al. 2007; Bauer et al. 2014; Kirsch-Pinheiro and Souveyet 2018). Among the challenges underlined by the literature, the acquisition of context information itself is not a challenge anymore, thanks to technologies such as IoT and smartphones. As pointed out by Sarker (2019), smartphones can collect and process raw context data about users' surrounding environment and their corresponding behavioral activities with their phones. According to this author, such data offers an understanding of users' behavioral activity patterns in different contexts and to derive useful information.

Context information can thus be captured and used for adaptation purposes on PIS. It may influence PIS behavior at all levels. It may be acquired and, theoretically, fed back up, level by level, like events, in order to contribute to the adaptation of each level and, consequently, of the system as a whole.

However, considering context awareness for an entire PIS represents an important shift in context management approaches. These approaches operate habitually in an application scale, but when considering PIS, a system scale must be considered. This is because PIS can be seen as a complex ecosystem of dynamic and heterogeneous resources, including not only software applications and IT resources and infrastructures but also business processes and human resources. Therefore, bringing context-awareness to this new generation of Information Systems means making it available to all system components. In other words, context management features cannot be limited to single context-aware applications, but they should be generalized to the whole system, which implies considering context management as a "facility", a service proposed to all components of the PIS. This notion of a "context facility" brings to light several challenges related notably to this change of scale on context management, from an application scale to a system scale.

This chapter focuses on this vision of "context facility" as a means of supporting context awareness on an entire PIS. Starting by considering lessons learned from Context-Aware Computing, we will present this vision, the challenges it brings, and possible solution insights.

This chapter is organized as follows: Section 2 highlights important features for context management discussed in the literature; Section 3 details the vision of a "context facility", while Sect. 4 discusses the impact of this vision on context management; Finally, Sect. 5 discusses possible insights for realizing this vision, before concluding in Sect. 6.

2   Literature Review

The notion of context is becoming more and more used today within applications that could be called "intelligent" because they are able to observe elements from the environment, such as the location of the user, his physical activity, etc., and to react accordingly. Context information appears here essentially as a trigger for adaptation purposes. This observation of the environment is now possible thanks notably to the development of smartphones, but also sensors, actuators, nanocomputers, and other low-cost technologies related to the Internet of Things (IoT), which allows developers to easily propose applications that observe and interact with the physical environment.

This kind of application is already part of our daily life, but, in most cases, their development is still carried out in an ad hoc way, despite all the research that has been done on the notion of context and Context-aware Computing. Context-aware applications can be defined as applications capable of observing changes in context and adapting their behavior accordingly (Baldauf et al. 2007; Bauer and Dey 2016).

Context-aware computing literature stressed the importance of an efficient context management. Indeed, there is a significant contrast between the development needs of applications presenting some context-awareness behavior compared to the traditional ones (Alegre et al. 2016). Context-aware applications have the ambition "to create computational systems that are able to understand not only simple contexts, but others such as their environment, the person that is using the device, or the social context in which they are executing services" (Alegre et al. 2016). However, realizing such ambition implies considering multiple issues, from the environment observation to the reaction to changes observed on it.

From a practical point of view, supporting the notion of context in a computer application raises several challenges ranging from identifying relevant context information, acquiring and modeling it, to its interpretation and exploitation for different purposes (Baldauf et al. 2007; Bettini et al. 2010; Kirsch-Pinheiro et al. 2016; Kirsch-Pinheiro and Souveyet 2018).

Several works such as Perera et al. (2014), Alegre et al. (2016), Baldauf et al. (2007), and Greenberg (2001) have underlined multiple challenges in the design and development of context-aware applications, as well as different phases and issues on context management life cycle. Based on this literature, we have identified on Kirsch-Pinheiro et al. (2016) and Kirsch-Pinheiro and Souveyet (2018) multiple dimensions allowing considering common context management issues. The dimensions represented in the "roadmap", illustrated in Fig. 1, let us foresee the hardness of designing context-aware applications.

Compared to traditional applications, context-aware applications can be considered more complex because they have to cope with the so-called pervasive environments. Indeed, these environments are characterized by their heterogeneity, including devices as varied as network equipment (router, switch, etc.), "traditional" personal computers (fixed or portable), smartphones and tablets, and even devices used for IoT (*e.g.*, RaspberryPI, Arduino). As underlined by Lalanda and Hamon

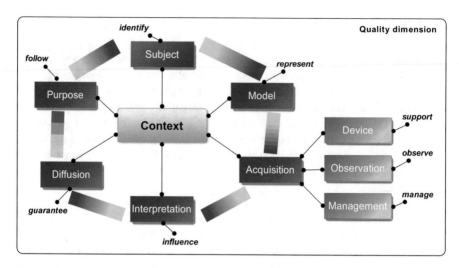

Fig. 1 Context management dimensions (Kirsch-Pinheiro and Souveyet 2018)

(2020), pervasive environments are highly dynamic and volatile. Devices can connect and disconnect without warning, the quality of the network connectivity can dramatically vary, and failures can happen anytime on various system levels. This dynamicity and unpredictability of daily life situations can partially explain the hardness of designing context-aware applications. According to Augusto et al. (2017), "it is difficult to program systems which can take every possibility into account and have a pre-planned specific reaction, but we can at least highlight which are some of the situations of interest we can aim to react to appropriately".

Context-aware applications must operate, often continuously, under these changing conditions. They need to observe different elements of the environment and react to their changes, often using very limited computing platforms (*e.g.*, nanocomputers or smartphones with battery and connectivity limitations). Such a dynamic and constrained execution environment significantly impacts the architecture and development of such software, particularly in terms of modularity, integration, interoperability, and a growing number of non-functional constraints (*e.g.*, robustness and scalability). Under these conditions, the qualities traditionally expected from software, such as flexibility, dynamics, modularity, and scalability, become difficult to meet, especially with the ad hoc development processes that are often adopted when developing context-aware applications, as observed in (Bauer and Dey 2016; Bauer et al. 2014).

All these characteristics of pervasive environments have a strong impact on context information itself. Context information is naturally uncertain and incomplete. It may contain errors and be very dynamic. It is often heterogeneous, including different formats. It may be observed using different frequencies or be pushed up by its different sources (*i.e.*, sensors). These sources may also vary since new sources can potentially integrate the application, and others may disappear (temporarily or definitely) (Bettini et al. 2010; Chalmers et al. 2004; Kirsch-Pinheiro and Souveyet 2018).

All these characteristics inherent to context information challenges the identification of possible context sources (represented through the "acquisition" dimension in Fig. 1), the representation of such information ("model" dimension), as well as its interpretation through appropriate reasoning methods ("interpretation" dimension).

Previous works on context-aware computing have considered the evolution of context sources through middleware and context models allowing new sources, data types, and formats to be easily added (Bettini et al. 2010; Wagner et al. 2011; Paspallis and Papadopoulos 2014; Vahdat-Nejad 2014; Pradeep and Krishnamoorthy 2019). According to Alegre et al. (2016), middleware is the most used structure to collect context information, support sensor deployment, and hide heterogeneity. According to these authors, separating how context is used from how it is acquired eases the development of a generic set of applications by reusing and customizing the necessary structure for context manipulation. Nevertheless, according to these authors, once the context is modeled, there is a need to create new knowledge and have a better understanding based on the currently sensed context.

This need of creating new knowledge corresponds to what we call in Kirsch-Pinheiro and Souveyet (2018) the "interpretation" dimension (see Fig. 1). It refers to different interpretation techniques for context information, from simple adaptation mechanisms, such as rule-based systems, to advanced reasoning mechanisms. When considering tendencies on context reasoning, an important one that can be observed in the literature is the use of Machine Learning (ML) techniques for reasoning or "mining" context data and to extract meaningful information from these data. Several machine learning and data mining techniques, such as data clustering, feature optimization and selection, rule-based classification and association analysis, incremental learning for dynamic updating and management, and corresponding rule-based prediction model can be designed to provide smartphone data analytic solutions (Sarker 2019). The same can be said about IoT and other sensor data. For example, reasoning mechanisms may allow applications to detect or anticipate particular situations and to adapt their behavior accordingly (Mayrhofer 2005; Sigg et al. 2010; Ameyed et al. 2015; Ramakrishnan 2016). Mining context data may have multiple uses: adaptation of applications (or processes) behavior, recommendation of actions, data prediction, the anticipation of user's needs, and decision making (*e.g.*, Najar et al. 2015; Maio et al. 2016; Mokhtari et al. 2017).

The use of such techniques presupposes the identification at design time of relevant context elements to be observed at run time. This is one of the most important challenges in the design of context-aware applications (represented by the "subject" dimension in Fig. 1): the identification of relevant context information that should be observed in order to obtain a significant behavior from the application. Furthermore, identifying such data leads mechanically to selecting appropriate sensors and acquiring methods, models for representing it, and reasoning methods for exploring such information.

This particularly important challenge has been highlighted by several authors (Bauer and Dey 2016; Dey 2001; Greenberg 2001; Grudin 2001). For example, it has been summarized by Bauer and Dey (2016) as follows: since context information is a key element for controlling the behavior of these applications, the identification of the relevant elements for these applications becomes a crucial task in their development, forcing the designers of these applications to anticipate their combinations and their relevant characteristics before implementation.

The literature has tackled all these challenges through an "application-based" focus. Indeed, the focus is always on developing independent applications that can be complex but that present few cooperative aspects with other applications, like sharing context data and models or even reasoning models. The focus remains mainly on single "applications", and no systemic view is considered. At the maximum, we have middleware and similar constructs, but applications and models are mainly built independently from each other, working in silos. Nevertheless, considering the generalization of context-awareness capabilities into a whole Pervasive Information System (PIS) means considering context management issues on a system scale. This represents a key requirement for the evolution of traditional Information Systems into Pervasive Information Systems, which cannot become real without context awareness. In other words, in order to become a reality, PIS should assimilate context management to a "service" that should be available for all components in the system, similar to a "facility" in a city. In the next section, we present this vision of a "context facility", which we consider a key element for satisfying context awareness requirements of PIS.

3 Towards a Context Facility

A PIS is an Information System that evolves. This evolution is guided by many factors, including a need for more flexibility from the organizations, but also the opportunity of obtaining a "smarter" behavior thanks to new technologies, thanks to a more context-aware behavior. In order to become more flexible, each level of a PIS, represented in Fig. 2, may use context information to adapt its behavior: from its infrastructure till management and decision making, passing to proposed services, applications, and business processes. The most important challenge of this evolution does not lie in adapting each level composing such systems separately, in an independent way, but in creating a real synergy between the IS levels. Each level should be able to adapt itself according to its own conditions and goals, but also according to observed context information and changes coming from the neighboring levels. All of this leads almost inevitably to the generalization of the context support to the entire system. This means considering this context support as a "facility" available to all PIS components. Figure 2 illustrates this idea of synergy among all PIS levels. In the lower part of the picture, we may observe different elements acting as a source of context information and feeding this "facility", which in its turn makes this information available to all levels of the system. At each level, this information can trigger changes, which will feed back to this facility new information, thus improving a dynamic interaction among PIS levels.

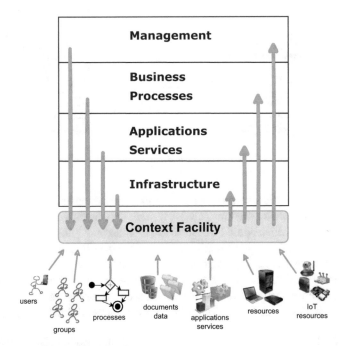

Fig. 2 Overview of a context facility on a PIS

Behind the idea of such a "context facility" lies the idea of proposing context management as a service, which will be available to all elements in every level of a PIS. Thus, if we see a PIS as a city, context management should be like a "facility" integrated into the city, such as water or electricity, a service available to all community members. Thinking of context management as a "context facility" implies generalizing this notion to the entire system. Everything may become observable. Each element in a PIS could thus be observed, become a source of context information, and at the same time, a consumer of this kind of information for different uses, from adaptation to decision-making.

Through this idea of a "*context facility*", everything becomes a possible source of context information. This information can thus be fed back to all levels of a PIS and launch reactions on these levels, from adaptation to decision-making, reactions that may, in their turn, trigger new changes. It is through this "facility" that the synergy between all levels of a PIS can be created. This synergy could provide Pervasive Information Systems with the flexibility they will need to better take advantage of the opportunities offered by the new technologies and by the environment's dynamics, whether physical, logical, or organizational.

In Ben Rabah et al. (2020), we have first introduced with other researchers a vision of a "context mining facility", i.e., context mining functionalities proposed as a service offered by an IS for all its applications. Such a "context mining facility" would open up new application perspectives within IS (adaptation to the

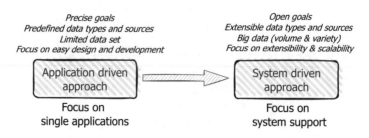

Precise goals
Predefined data types and sources
Limited data set
Focus on easy design and development

Open goals
Extensible data types and sources
Big data (volume & variety)
Focus on extensibility & scalability

Application driven approach → System driven approach

Focus on
single applications

Focus on
system support

Fig. 3 Change of scale on context management when considering a context facility

context, recommendation of services or content, prediction/anticipation of user's needs or actions, decision-making, etc.). We may thus envisage the generalization of these behaviors, which could be described as "smart" or "intelligent", by offering appropriate support for context mining as a service specific to an IS. Nevertheless, the idea of "context facility" should not be reduced to only the mining of context information, even if this mining, seen as part of reasoning mechanisms, represents a major challenge for this vision. Moreover, as we will discuss in the next section, many other challenges follow this view since it embraces all dimensions of context management.

Indeed, this vision of a "context facility", available for an entire PIS, raises several challenges, particularly related to the scale that this vision implies, as illustrated by Fig. 3: it is no longer a particular application or service that benefits from such a platform, but potentially all the elements of a PIS, whatever their level. Context information is no longer captured for a specific use but for many different uses, even future ones. This raises the question of how to model this information, store it, and process it on a large scale.

Considering context management as a system "facility" implies an important shift in the way this management is currently handled since the scale changes drastically. As illustrated in Fig. 3, we no longer consider single applications with precise goals and data but a service that is available for an entire ecosystem of users (stakeholders, employees, customers, etc.), services, and applications supporting different business processes. When considering a given application, its developers/designers may define precisely what context data will be considered, the processing steps these data will need, the storage and distribution mechanisms that might be necessary, and the Quality of Context (QoC) (Marie et al. 2014) metrics that should be considered, and even the most adapted reasoning mechanism to apply considering these data and the application's purposes. If we consider a service at the PIS scale, we can neither focus on a single purpose nor predefine a specific set of context data or an appropriated reasoning technique to be used by all since the same service is supposed to be available to many different applications. The same service is supposed to satisfy the needs of multiple existing applications, considering currently available sources of context data, but also consider the needs of future applications and users. Besides, we are confronted with a different volume of data, passing from a potentially limited data set to a data set that can be characterized as Big Data, both by its volume and variety. Finally, the design concerns for such a facility will not be the same that traditional middleware or frameworks for Context-Aware Computing. Traditionally, those focus on proposing a more straightforward design and the development of new context-aware applications. The goal is to allow developers to quickly produce new context-aware applications by freeing such developers from several context management concerns. A context facility should do the same, but at the system scale, which means that it should focus not only on these "easy to use" design concerns but also (and mainly) focus on extensibility and scalability since it should be available at run time to a dynamic set of multiple applications and services.

This change in scale has an important impact on several context management dimensions. We will discuss this impact in the next section.

4 Impact of a Context Facility Vision on Context Management

A PIS is not a simple set of applications. It implies data, technical and human resources, and business processes, all acting together to help the organization fulfill its strategic goals. We can see these systems as living organisms that must evolve with the organization, whose goals and needs are constantly evolving. In order to support this evolution appropriately, PIS must behave as context-aware systems to adapt their behavior to an evolving environment. Context awareness becomes then an important requirement for supporting this evolution, bringing us to the idea of "context facility" presented in the previous section. We believe that such a context facility may play a significant role in this evolution precisely because it is intended to support PIS elements in their needs for context awareness.

The generalization of a context-aware behavior to an entire Information System implies delegating issues related to context management to this context facility, freeing application developers from these concerns and consequently, allowing those developers to focus on the "smart behavior" they are looking for. However, for the context facility itself, this means offering high levels of customization to satisfy multiple system components. This is probably the main challenge when considering a system scale: the fact of supporting multiple purpose applications, including current applications and context sources, but also future ones. Figure 4 summarizes the main challenges raised by this context facility vision. We discuss those in the following paragraphs.

As illustrated in Fig. 4, having multiple purposes applications has an important impact on context management decisions since the purpose of an application will often guide many other decisions related to context management, illustrated by the dimensions presented in Fig. 1, like subject, model, and acquisition dimensions. Indeed, as with any software application, context-aware applications must match

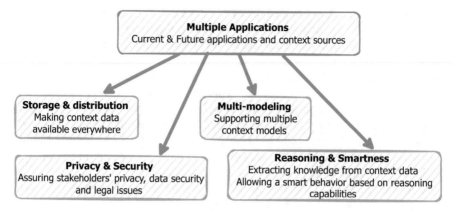

Fig. 4 Most relevant issues when considering context support for multiple applications on a PIS scale

precise requirements defined for them. Furthermore, when integrated into a PIS, such applications must also be aligned with the organization's goals and expectations. As underlined by Alegre et al. (2016), if the proper requirements are not well defined prior to the development of the system, it will be more likely to fail to meet the user and other stakeholders' expectations. It is then imperative for a context facility to allow applications to explore context information according to their own requirements.

As Coutaz et al. (2005) point out, it is commonly accepted that context concerns the evolution of a structured and shared information space and that this space is designed to serve a particular purpose. Whatever information is considered as context depends profoundly on the system in question and its objectives. Whatever this information is, it needs to be managed appropriately in order to realize its full potential. This requires an understanding of the challenges involved in using this notion and the main characteristics of context information, such as its heterogeneity, dynamism, and uncertainty. The main benefits for an application of disposing of a context facility lie mainly in these characteristics, since such facility may include different mechanisms for handling different context sources and Quality of Context metrics, freeing the application developers of thinking on those, while allowing sharing those among multiple applications. This facility should then appear as a building block flexible enough to allow the design and the development of different independent applications with their own requirements. This implies allowing to identify and to add extra context information to be observed and handled through the facility. Furthermore, every new application should be able to add new context sources that, once integrated, will be available for any other PIS component.

This sharing of context sources and data at a system level represents an interesting gain of energy for the whole system: instead of gradually multiplying sensors and other data sources across the Information System with the growing number of smart applications and services, the facility could allow a sensor introduced by one application to be used by many others, including, for instance, reporting applications for decision-making and the system management.

However, this context sharing raises another challenge: the one of making available a massive set of context information everywhere in a PIS. Indeed, a PIS goes far beyond the LAN perspective usually considered by context-aware applications, which traditionally consider locally available data. In this sense, the context facility may be compared to a data lake (Giebler et al. 2019) of context data. As with any data lake, it is concerned with storage and distribution issues. The first concerns how to store a high volume of available data time enough to extract an added value from it, while the latter concerns how to convey data from the data sources until the data lake. However, more than any other "normal" enterprise data, context data is subject to several important and inherent quality issues, like freshness and uncertainty, that should also be considered during storage and transfer. Unfortunately, on the one side, more complex context distribution mechanisms (Bellavista et al. 2013) do not receive much attention in Context-Aware Computing literature. Conversely, current IoT solutions often rely on simple cloud-based solutions (Gubbi et al. 2013; Elazhary 2019), whose centrality and latency might represent a problem in different scenarios.

Besides, such availability of context information leads to other concerns: privacy and security. As underlined by Alegre et al. (2016), context information will inherently contain important data related to the users, which raises some privacy issues. Moreover, privacy concerns may differ from user to user and may also be dynamically changing over time. Therefore, the balance between privacy and system potential is delicate. Similarly, context-aware applications must consider data security and privacy aspects, providing the right balance between privacy and system potential (Munoz-Arcentales et al. 2021). This leads to an important concern that must be considered not only from an application point of view but also from an institutional point of view. Indeed, context information must be considered by the organization's Data Protection Offices, like any other organization's data. Inversely, the context facility must integrate not only security rules from individual applications or context sources but also privacy and security policies defined by the organization itself.

Having multiple purpose applications to satisfy also leads to a context facility's modeling challenge. This facility must be able to handle multiple context models, or, at least, a very extensible one. In such a way, application developers could easily add new concepts corresponding to new context sources and information. This leads us back to the context identification issues mentioned in Sect. 2. Certainly, a context facility must handle multiple models, but the availability of such models and multiple sources might also offer interesting insights for developers (and potentially stakeholders) that must identify relevant context information for their own applications (and business processes). According to Alegre et al. (2016), the potential of context-aware applications remains limited to the context that developers are able to encode and foresee. The problem is that developers must know beforehand the context they need to program, but they might not be able to foresee some situations. Some situations can also be specific to some users or may not be useful enough to justify the effort of implementing them. In other words, if developers cannot determine all that can be affected by an action, it will be very difficult to write a closed and comprehensive set of actions to take in those cases. The availability of a large amount of context information shared through the context facility may contribute to this issue thanks to the possibility of promoting context mining mechanisms. For instance, Jaffal et al. (2014) promote the idea of identifying relevant context information from previously observed data. This corresponds to what we call "context mining". Mining available context information may enable the identification of complex situations and reveal relevant context elements that otherwise could remain unknown to stakeholders and application developers. However, this implies analyzing a large amount of heterogeneous data, which can be particularly challenging considering current data analysis techniques.

It becomes then clear that only making context data available for the applications composing a PIS is not enough since the cornerstone of this context facility vision is the expected smart behavior, which lies mainly on the capability of reasoning and mining context data. We believe that the democratization of this kind of behavior that could be considered "intelligent" creates an expectation on the users: they now expect that software and systems will be more intelligent, able to recognize their situation and their behavior and adapt in a reactive way as well as in a proactive way. Such smart behavior is also important for assuring the transparency of these systems, which is a key requirement of PIS. Hiding the technological complexity that characterizes PIS from end-users is essential in order to relieve users and stakeholders from technological constraints so that they can concentrate their effort on tasks with an added value to the organization.

To do this, Pervasive Information Systems must be able to recognize users' habits and practices in order to be able to anticipate users' needs and proactively propose to these users the services that correspond the best to their needs. The added value of context data relies on the capability of the context facility to allow applications and stakeholders to extract knowledge from this data by mining it according to applications, organizations, and individuals' needs.

Thinking of context as a facility implies collecting data not only for a specific application but for several potential consumers, including future ones. Therefore, different approaches can be considered to address the various uses of such a context facility. For example, Sarker (2019) has analyzed different strategies, notably based on time series and rule-based reasoning. He underlines some limitations of these techniques with context data, such as the mapping between patterns of usage defined by these models and actual users' behavior, since the users behave differently in different contexts, which also may vary from user-to-user in the real world. Similarly, Miranda et al. (2022) have studied the use of multiple Machine Learning (ML) techniques applied to Human Activity Recognition (which is essentially based on context data) and underlined multiple limitations concerning notably data stream management and model evolution.

Variability in reasoning techniques appears then as a necessity for a context facility since applications and stakeholders' needs will significantly vary on a system scale. For instance, extracting indicators (KPI) and tendencies for stakeholders in business organizations will not necessarily be achieved the same way as providing context reasoning to applications for runtime adaptation. Therefore, different approaches are required, and it is important to understand their strengths and drawbacks in view of handling such evolutive, uncertain and heterogeneous context data at a large scale.

Nevertheless, the heterogeneity and other characteristics of the context data appear to be a major obstacle to a generalized and fully automated analysis of these data. Therefore, data analysis methods are often applied to specific "categories" of data. For example, the FFT (Fast Fourier Transformation) used in Ramakrishnan (2016) is particularly adapted to numerical data, whereas the FCA (Formal Concept Analysis) applied by Jaffal et al. (2014) is more adapted to symbolic data (*i.e.*, labels). Data concerning GPS location illustrates quite well this issue since very often a preprocessing is necessary in order to translate GPS coordinates into "labels" ("localization_1", "home", "office", etc.) or "ids" that could be more easily exploited by the different data analysis techniques such as, for example, FCA.

Therefore, given the heterogeneity that characterizes context data, it is difficult to imagine the application of a single technique for data analysis regardless of the context element considered. At the same time, it is difficult not to consider the risk of losing information on the possible links between the different context elements by splitting the data set according to their nature. This leads to the necessity of supporting multiple reasoning models and techniques at the context facility level.

However, the scale in which a context facility should operate may represent a significant issue for some data analysis techniques. In Ben Rabah et al. (2020), we have analyzed how Machine Learning (ML) approaches are used for context mining and the conditions necessary for this analysis considering the specificities of context information. The limitations we have underlined in this paper suggest an issue when considering the use of ML techniques on a context facility scale. It seems clear that current data mining techniques are not sufficiently adapted to manage the heterogeneity of context data without a significant preprocessing phase. Whatever the adopted paradigm (supervised, unsupervised, semi-supervised, or reinforcement learning), ML is about selecting an algorithm and training it on some data. The effectiveness of a given method depends on various factors, such as the quality of the training data, the chosen algorithm, and its hyperparameters. Low-quality data may compromise the success of the most powerful ML algorithms (García et al. 2016; Ramırez-Gallego et al. 2017). Unfortunately, characteristics inherent to context data, such as its heterogeneity and uncertainty, may lead to problems such as higher model complexity and overfitting decrease, decreasing ML performance and quality of results. In order to address these problems, preprocessing steps are often considered, including *data cleaning* techniques for identifying and correcting noisy data (Mokhtari et al. 2017; Rueda et al. 2019), processing missing values or detecting outliers (Lork et al. 2017); *data transformation*, proposing, for instance, digitalization and normalization of raw data; and *data augmentation*, including methods create additional training samples (Grzeszick et al. 2017).

Such preprocessing steps are possible thanks to the "application" focus adopted by those approaches. Indeed, when focusing on a single application with precise goals, it becomes possible to consider these phases since data types and formats are known in advance. However, when considering a context facility and its "system" perspective, such narrowed vision becomes quite difficult to assume. Not only the goals are not necessarily the same between applications, processes, and stakeholders supported by the context facility, but also new context data sources and formats may join the system at any moment. This represents a significant issue since, on the one side, if these phases are not reconsidered, new relevant data may remain ignored and context data unexplored. On the other side, stopping the facility from re-executing those phases may also negatively affect critical applications that may depend on it. To sum up, although ML algorithms have proven to be useful for mining specific context data, the overall process can be challenging when considering a context facility scale. Both supervised and unsupervised approaches require preprocessing phases and often human intervention during the pipeline, and considering a system scale, even a minimal human intervention may be complex.

5   Discussion

The previous section has discussed multiple challenges that characterize context-awareness support on PIS through the idea of a context facility offering context-awareness capabilities for the whole system. Most of these challenges are related to scalability issues and the generalization of reasoning techniques to a whole system. Although PIS do not represent (yet) a common reality in most organizations nowadays, several insights can be considered from the literature, notably in terms of architecture and reasoning.

Indeed, it is worth noting that scalability is not a concern only for PIS, smart-cities scenarios (*e.g.*, Zappatore et al. 2016; Arasteh et al. 2016) are also concerned by scalability, as well as the heterogeneity of devices and protocols, often leading incompatibility issues. Similarly, in large IoT-based smart environment scenarios, the need for providing and capturing context data but also processing it efficiently must be considered. These challenges are followed by the need for unifying the way to capture and store the data since many compatibility issues can be derived from this in the case that many applications need to share data or coordinate between them (Munoz-Arcentales et al. 2021). This is the case of PIS, in which many different applications and processes must share context information. Although some initiatives exist in the literature, Munoz-Arcentales et al. (2021) underline that many proposals still fail to provide an architecture for collaborative scopes, in which several systems can exchange relevant contextual information based on detected complex events, due to the lack of data standardization or harmonization process for exchanging the data. These authors propose instead a common semantic model and data structure predefined for each application domain (agriculture, health, airports, etc.), using a service-oriented model, which allows increasing or decreasing resources according to the demand.

Besides, issues related to storage and availability of context information can be assimilated to Big Data issues, notably in IoT-based applications. Today's availability of an unprecedented mass of data, including data from the IoT, combined with the available computing offer (whether on Cloud or Fog/Edge Computing platforms), opens up new application perspectives, especially regarding data analysis. These technologies may constitute the basis of a context facility.

In the first place, cloud-based solutions are often considered in IoT-based environments, such as smart-home (*e.g.*, Zdankin et al. 2020) and smart-health (*e.g.*, Rangarajan et al. 2022) scenarios. According to Lalanda and Hamon (2020), the attractiveness of this approach in such scenarios can be explained in several ways: the availability of a large volume of data that must be stored and accessed quickly and easily; the presence of data analytics services, which are often very greedy in terms of computing power and time; as well as the administration simplicity. The same can be said about Information Systems, in which cloud-based approaches are largely adopted for different business applications (*e.g.*, cloud-based CRM such as Salesforce,[1] or ERP such as SAP S/4HANA[2]).

However, some cloud concerns may limit its use in certain cases. Lalanda and Hamon (2020) underline, for instance, time-critical applications that can suffer from network delay and limited bandwidth. These authors also underline security concerns, since some users may not feel comfortable with the idea of personal data being stored in clouds or data centers they do not trust, as well as economic and ecological concerns, since transport and storage of large amounts of data in the cloud may appear as inopportune, particularly when it could be processed in gateways located close to data sources. For these authors (Lalanda and Hamon 2020), "pervasive services should make use of edge infrastructures as much as possible and, thus, place some computing, control, and storage functions close to devices. This appears to be necessary to deal with stringent requirements related to latency, privacy, or security".

The adoption of edge-based solutions, such as Lalanda and Hamon (2020), Peng et al. (2018), or Villari et al. (2016), appears as an interesting approach for the deployment of a context facility on PIS. In fact, the scale involved in a context facility leads naturally to consider a distribution of resources all around the PIS and, consequently, to favor distributed solutions, such as edge-based ones. Instead of centralizing all context data and processing on data centers or cloud platforms, these data and processing may be spread all over the PIS, being then nearest the users and their applications.

The distribution of computing tasks on the network edge promoted by Fog/Edge Computing brings several advantages when considering a context facility. First, pushing the context facility into the network edge promotes the distribution of context management capabilities nearest to context sources and to users and applications interested in consuming context information. It may also contribute

---

[1] https://www.salesforce.com/

[2] https://www.sap.com/products/s4hana-erp.html

to managing privacy concerns since it limits or reduces context data distribution. Finally, such distribution can also benefit the organization since it allows fully exploiting resources already available inside the organization and its PIS.

Pushing context facility into PIS edge may also contribute to promoting a better distribution of context reasoning capabilities all around the Information System. We are talking here about what some people call "Edge AI" or the use of edge platforms, in association with cloud platforms, for the application of Artificial Intelligence techniques, and in particular Deep Learning, on data mostly from the IoT (Zhou et al. 2019; Deng et al. 2020; Ding et al. 2022). The "Edge AI" represents a new field of application for resources already available in a Pervasive Information Systems, which could benefit a wide range of sectors: Industry 4.0, logistics, but also Human Resources, financial, among many others.

Different learning techniques can be deployed using Edge AI. Among them, we may cite Federated Learning (Presotto et al. 2022; Ek et al. 2021) and Opportunistic Learning (Lee et al. 2021; Yu et al. 2022; Lee et al. 2022). Indeed, current developments in Federated Learning and Opportunistic Learning open interesting perspectives when considering the Edge AI horizon. On the one hand, Federated Learning is pointed out as an interesting solution for privacy concerns (*e.g.*, Kumar et al. 2022) since data is processed locally, on the network edge, and only model fragments are shared. On the other hand, Opportunistic Learning (*e.g.*, Lee et al. 2021; Lee et al. 2022; Yu et al. 2022) is based on the principle, but it allows applications with slightly different goals to share model fragments. This opens the possibility of cooperation between applications with similar goals (or common sub-goals) to share model fragments, improving their local knowledge about a given community, which may be related to a locality or to a traditional Information System domain or application silo.

Still, concerning context reasoning, another tendency can be highlighted: the use of hybrid methods, combining different reasoning techniques. For instance, Sarker (2019) considers applying multiple time series analyses and rule-based techniques in a single framework. Similarly, we believe that context management on PIS should follow the same principle of combining different reasoning methods, which could be distributed all along with the Information System thanks to edge and cloud facilities.

Finally, it is worth noting that only distributing reasoning models and engines do not solve all reasoning issues underlined in the previous section (cf. Sect. 4). Issues related to preprocessing and human intervention remain open. We strongly believe that Machine Learning practices should still evolve towards more powerful tools that gradually remove the human from the loop. We can already observe this tendency through initiatives such as automated ML (AutoML) frameworks and initiatives (Feurer et al. 2015; Hutter et al. 2019), which aim at automating the entire ML pipeline. This automatization of preprocessing phases and the development of configurable frameworks constitute a key aspect of developing a context facility on PIS since they could reduce the need for human intervention on the ML pipeline and allow customizing the framework according to applications and organizations' needs.

Last but not least, the context facility scale also raises the question of allowing multiple and federated context models to co-exist in a PIS. A similar issue has been tackled in some IoT-based proposals, which are confronted with interoperability issues among multiple data types from IoT sensors. Solutions based on extensible semantic models, such as Mormul and Stach (2020), Munoz-Arcentales et al. (2021), and Guennouni et al. (2022), appear to us as the most promising ones, allowing us to consider in the future a possible cooperation between multiple context models that can be understood by different applications and business process all over the system.

6 Conclusion

Context awareness represents a main requirement for Pervasive Information Systems. In order to reach such a requirement, it is necessary to generalize context management support to all PIS components, which corresponds to the idea of a "context facility" we advocate in this chapter.

Many challenges follow this vision of a context facility. However, these challenges are mostly related to the generalization of context management capabilities to the scale of a whole Information System. We have discussed in this chapter the challenges that arise from this scale change in context management and some insights from possible solutions found in the literature. Among these challenges, the generalization of context reasoning capabilities is probably the most ambitious one. In this sense, the recent developments concerning Edge AI represent an interesting perspective for transforming reasoning in a context facility scale into a reality.

However, other challenges should also be considered, notably the energetic consumption of such a facility. Green IT concerns should now be integrated into every IT project, and this during all its life cycle, from its design to its execution. Context facility is not an exception. It should be designed considering Green IT design principles and consider energy conception as an important parameter for adaptation purposes during its own execution. Additionally, this context facility may also contribute to Green IT goals from the organization itself by supplying appropriate context information to PIS components, and notably applications, that may use such information for reaching their own energy consumption goals. Energy-aware middleware and platforms represent the first step in this sense.

Finally, PIS and this vision of a "context facility" also raise questions concerning social and human acceptance levels. Are we ready to accept such a high level of observation of our daily business life? Will we be able to accept the increasing automation of our work environment? Like any new technology, like any change, all these upheavals bring with them hope and fear, which we, as a society, should learn to balance.

Bibliography

Alegre, U.; Augusto, J. C. & Clark, T. "Engineering context-aware systems and applications: A survey", *Journal of Systems and Software*, 117, **2016**, 55–83, Elsevier. https://doi.org/10.1016/j.jss.2016.02.010

Ameyed, D.; Miraoui, M. & Tadj, C. "A survey of prediction approach in pervasive computing," International Journal of Scientific & Engineering Research, 6, 306–316, **2015**.

Arasteh, H.; Hosseinnezhad, V.; Loia, V.; Tommasetti, A.; Troisi, O.; Shafie-khah, M. & Siano, P. "Iot-Based Smart Cities: A Survey". *2016 IEEE 16th International Conference on Environment and Electrical Engineering (EEEIC)*, IEEE, **2016**, 1–6. https://doi.org/10.1109/EEEIC.2016.7555867.

Augusto, J.; Aztiria, A.; Kramer D. & Alegre U. "A Survey on the Evolution of the Notion of Context-Awareness", *Applied Artificial Intelligence*, 31(7–8), 613–642, **2017**, https://doi.org/10.1080/08839514.2018.1428490

Baldauf, M.; Dustdar, S. & Rosenberg, F., "A survey on context-aware systems", *International Journal of Ad Hoc and Ubiquitous Computing*, 2 (4), **2007**, 263–277

Bauer, C. & Dey, A., "Considering context in the design of intelligent systems: Current practices and suggestions for improvement", *Journal of Systems and Software*, 112, **2016**, 26–47, Elsevier

Bauer, J. S.; Newman, M. W. & Kientz, J. A., "Thinking About Context: Design Practices for Information Architecture with Context-Aware Systems", *iConference 2014 Proceedings*, **2014**, 398–411. https://doi.org/10.9776/14116.

Ben Rabah, N., Kirsch Pinheiro, M., Le Grand, B., Jaffal, A., Souveyet, C.: Machine Learning for a Context Mining Facility, 16th Workshop on Context and Activity Modeling and Recognition, 2020 IEEE International Conference on Pervasive Computing and Communications Workshops (PerCom Workshops), (2020), pp. 1-7. https://doi.org/10.1109/PerComWorkshops48775.2020.9156134

Bellavista, P.; Corradi, A.; Fanelli, M. & Foschini, L. "A survey of context data distribution for mobile ubiquitous systems", *ACM Computing Survey*, **2013**, 45 (1), 1–49

Bettini, C.; Brdiczka, O.; Henricksen, K.; Indulska, J.; Nicklas, D.; Ranganathan, A. & Riboni, D., "A survey of context modelling and reasoning techniques", *Pervasive and Mobile Computing*, 6(2), Apr **2010**, 161–180.

Brown, P.; Bovey, J. & Chen, X. "Context-aware applications: from the laboratory to the marketplace ", *IEEE Personal Communications,* 4(5), **1997**, 58–64

Chalmers, D.; Dulay, N. & Sloman, M. "Towards Reasoning About Context in the Presence of Uncertainty", *1st international workshop on advanced context modelling, reasoning and management*, Nottingham, UK, September **2004**.

Coutaz, J.; Crowley, J.; Dobson, S. & Garlan, D., "Context is the key", *Communications of the ACM*, 48 (3), **2005**, 49–53.

Deng, S.; Zhao, H.; Fang, W.; Yin, J.; Dustdar, S. & Zomaya, A. Y. "Edge Intelligence: The Confluence of Edge Computing and Artificial Intelligence". *IEEE Internet Things Journal*, 7 (8), **2020**, 7457–7469. https://doi.org/10.1109/JIOT.2020.2984887.

Dey, A. K., "Understanding and using context", *Personal and Ubiquitous Computing*, 5(1), **2001**, 4–7.

Ding, A. Y.; Peltonen, E.; Meuser, T.; Aral, A.; Becker, C.; Dustdar, S.; Hiessl, T.; Kranzlmüller, D.; Liyanage, M.; Maghsudi, S.; Mohan, N.; Ott, J.; Rellermeyer, J. S.; Schulte, S.; Schulzrinne, H.; Solmaz, G.; Tarkoma, S.; Varghese, B. & Wolf, L. "Roadmap for Edge AI: A Dagstuhl Perspective". *SIGCOMM Computer Communication Review*, 52 (1), **2022**, 28–33. https://doi.org/10.1145/3523230.3523235.

Ek, S.; Portet, F.; Lalanda, P. & Vega, G. "A Federated Learning Aggregation Algorithm for Pervasive Computing: Evaluation and Comparison". *2021 IEEE International Conference on Pervasive Computing and Communications (PerCom 2021),***2021**; 1–10. https://doi.org/10.1109/PERCOM50583.2021.9439129.

Elazhary, H. "Internet of Things (IoT), mobile cloud, cloudlet, mobile IoT, IoT cloud, fog, mobile edge, and edge emerging computing paradigms: Disambiguation and research directions", *Journal of Network and Computer Applications*, 128, **2019**, 105–140.

Feurer, M.; Klein, A.; Eggensperger, K.; Springenberg, J.; Blum M. & Hutter, F. "Efficient and Robust Automated Machine Learning," in *Advances in Neural Information Processing Systems* 28, C. Cortes, N. D. Lawrence, D. D. Lee, M. Sugiyama and R. Garnett, Eds., Curran Associates Inc., **2015**, 2962–2970

Garcıa, S.; Luengo J. & Herrera, F. "Tutorial on practical tips of the most influential data preprocessing algorithms in data mining," *Knowledge-Based Systems*, 98, **2016**, 1–29

Giebler, C.; Gröger, C.; Hoos, E.; Schwarz, H. & Mitschang, B. "Leveraging the Data Lake: Current State and Challenges". In: Ordonez, C., Song, IY., Anderst-Kotsis, G., Tjoa, A. & Khalil, I. (eds), *Big Data Analytics and Knowledge Discovery (DaWaK 2019)*, Lecture Notes in Computer Science, 11708, **2019**, 179–188. Springer. https://doi.org/10.1007/978-3-030-27520-4_13

Greenberg, S., "Context as a dynamic construct", *Human-Computing Interaction*, 16(2–4), **2001**, 257–268

Grudin, J., "Desituating action: digital representation of context", *Human-Computing Interaction*, 16(2–4), **2001**, 269–286

Grzeszick, R.; Lenk, J. M.; Rueda, F. M.; Fink, G. A.; Feldhorst S. & Hompel, M. "Deep neural network based human activity recognition for the order picking process," *4th Int. Workshop on Sensor-based Activity Recognition and Interaction*, **2017**

Gubbi, J.; Buyya, R.; Marusic, S. & Palaniswami, M., "Internet of Things (IoT): A vision, architectural elements, and future directions", *Future Generation Computer Systems*, 29 (7), **2013**, 1645–1660.

Guennouni, N.; Laborie, S.; Sallaberry, C.; Chbeir, R. & Mansour, E. "ISEEapp: An Event Explanation Prototype bridging the gap between sensor network and document corpora data", *18th International Conference on Intelligent Environments (IE2022)*, Biarritz, France, **2022**.

Hutter, F.; Kotthoff L. & Vanschoren, J. "Automated Machine Learning-Methods", *Systems, Challenges*, Springer, **2019**

Jaffal, A.; Kirsch-Pinheiro, M. & Le Grand, B., "Unified and Conceptual Context Analysis in Ubiquitous Environments", In: Jaime Lloret Mauri, Christoph Steup & Sönke Knoch (Eds.), *8th International Conference on Mobile Ubiquitous Computing, Systems, Services and Technologies (UBICOMM 2014)*, August 24–28, 2014, ISBN 978-1-61208-353-7, IARIA, **2014**, 48–55

Kirsch-Pinheiro, M., Mazo, R., Souveyet, C. & Sprovieri, D., "Requirements Analysis for Context-oriented Systems", *7th Int. Conf. on Ambient Systems, Networks and Technologies (ANT 2016)*, *Procedia Computer Science*, 83, **2016**, 253–261

Kirsch-Pinheiro, M. & Souveyet, C. "Supporting context on software applications: a survey on context engineering", *Modélisation et utilisation du contexte*, 2(1), **2018**, ISTE OpenScience. Disponible sur: https://www.openscience.fr/Le-support-applicatif-a-la-notion-de-contexte-revue-de-la-litterature-en/ (Last visit: août 2020)

Kumar, A.; Tourani, R.; Vij, M. & Srikanteswara, S. "SCLERA: A Framework for Privacy-Preserving MLaaS at the Pervasive Edge". *2022 IEEE International Conference on Pervasive Computing and Communications Workshops and other Affiliated Events (PerCom Workshops): Industry Track*, 2022, 175–180. https://doi.org/10.1109/PerComWorkshops53856.2022.9767528.

Lalanda, P. & Hamon, C. "A service-oriented edge platform for cyber-physical systems", *CCF Transactions on Pervasive Computing and Interaction*, 2 (3), **2020**, 206–217, Springer Science and Business Media LLC. https://doi.org/10.1007/s42486-020-00046-y

Lee, S.; Zheng, X.; Hua, J.; Vikalo, H. & Julien, C. "Opportunistic Federated Learning: An Exploration of Egocentric Collaboration for Pervasive Computing Applications". *2021 IEEE International Conference on Pervasive Computing and Communications (PerCom 2021)*, **2021**; 1–8. https://doi.org/10.1109/PERCOM50583.2021.9439130.

Lee, S.; Julien, C. & Zheng, X. "Facilitating Decentralized and Opportunistic Learning in Pervasive Computing". *2022 IEEE International Conference on Pervasive Computing and Communications Workshops and other Affiliated Events (PerCom Workshops): PhD Forum*, **2022**; 144–145. https://doi.org/10.1109/PerComWorkshops53856.2022.9767211.

Lork, C.; Rajasekhar, B.; Yuen C. & Pindoriya, N. M. "How many watts: A data driven approach to aggregated residential air- conditioning load forecasting," *CoMoRea 2017, IEEE International Conference on Pervasive Computing and Communications Workshops (PerCom Workshops)*, **2017**

Maio, C. D.; Fenza, G.; Loia, V.; Orciuoli F. & Herrera- Viedma, E. "A framework for context-aware heterogeneous group decision making in business processes," *Knowledge-Based Systems*, 102, **2016**, 39–50

Marie, P.; Desprats, T.; Chabridon, S. & Sibilla, M., "The QoCIM Framework: Concepts and Tools for Quality of Context Management". In: Brézillon, P. & Gonzalez, A. J. (Eds.), *Context in Computing: A Cross-Disciplinary Approach for Modeling the Real World*, Springer New York, **2014**, 155–172

Mayrhofer, R. "Context Prediction based on Context Histories: Expected Benefits, Issues and Current State-of-the-Art," *in 1st International Workshop on Exploiting Context Histories in Smart Environments (ECHISE 2005), 3rd International Conference on Pervasive Computing (PERVASIVE 2005)*, **2005**.

Miranda, L.; Viterbo, J. & Bernardini, F. "A Survey on the Use of Machine Learning Methods in Context-Aware Middlewares for Human Activity Recognition". *Artificial Intelligence Review*, 55 (4), **2022**, 3369–3400. https://doi.org/10.1007/s10462-021-10094-0.

Mokhtari, G.; Zhang, Q. & Fazlollahi, A. "Non-wearable UWB sensor to detect falls in smart home environment," in *CoMoRea 2017, IEEE International Conference on Pervasive Computing and Communications Workshops (PerCom Workshops)*, **2017.**

Mormul, M. & Stach, C. "A Context Model for Holistic Monitoring and Management of Complex IT Environments". *16th Workshop on Context and Activity Modeling and Recognition (CoMoRea 2020), IEEE International Conference on Pervasive Computing and Communications Workshops (PerCom Workshops)*, **2020**, 1–6. https://doi.org/10.1109/PerComWorkshops48775.2020.9156101.

Munoz-Arcentales, A.; López-Pernas, S.; Conde, J.; Alonso, Á.; Salvachúa, J. & Hierro, J. J. "Enabling Context-Aware Data Analytics in Smart Environments: An Open Source Reference Implementation", *Sensors*, 21 (21), 7095, MDPI AG, **2021**. https://doi.org/10.3390/s21217095

Najar, S.; Kirsch-Pinheiro, M. & Souveyet, C. "Service discovery and prediction on Pervasive Information System," *J. of Ambient Intelligence and Humanized Comp.*, 6(4), pp. 407–423, **2015**

Paspallis N. & Papadopoulos, G. A. "A Pluggable Middleware Architecture for Developing Context-aware Mobile Applications," *Personal Ubiquitous Comp.*, 18(5), **2014**, 1099–1116

Peng, L.; Dhaini, A. R. & Ho, P.-H. "Toward Integrated Cloud–Fog Networks for Efficient IoT Provisioning: Key Challenges and Solutions". *Future Generation Computer Systems*, 88, **2018**, 606–613. https://doi.org/10.1016/j.future.2018.05.015.

Perera, C.; Zaslavsky, A. B.; Christen, P. & Georgakopoulos, D. "Context Aware Computing for The Internet of Things: A Survey", *IEEE Communications Surveys & Tutorials*, 16 (1), **2014**, 414–454

Pradeep, P. & Krishnamoorthy, S. "The MOM of context-aware systems: A survey", *Computer Communications*, 137, **2019**, 44–69

Presotto, R.; Civitarese, G. & Bettini, C. "FedCLAR: Federated Clustering for Personalized Sensor-Based Human Activity Recognition". *2022 IEEE International Conference on Pervasive Computing and Communications (PerCom 2022)*, **2022**; 227–236. https://doi.org/10.1109/PerCom53586.2022.9762352.

Ramakrishnan, A.K., "Support for Data-driven Context Awareness in Smart Mobile and IoT Applications: Resource Efficient Probabilistic Models and a Quality-aware Middleware Architecture" (Ondersteuning voor data-gedreven context-bewustzijn in intelligente mobiele en IoT applicaties: Hulpbronnenefficiënte probabilistische modellen en een kwaliteit-aware middleware architectuur), PhD thesis, Katholieke Universiteit Leuven, Belgium **2016**

Ramırez-Gallego, S.; Krawczyk, B.; Garcıa, S.; Woźniak, M. & Herrera, F. "A survey on data preprocessing for data stream mining: Current status and future directions," *Neurocomputing*, 239, **2017**, 39–57

Rangarajan, S.; Lee, Y.; Johnson, V.; Schorger, K.; Lee, H.; Nguyen, D.; Behfar, M. H.; Jansson, E.; Rekila, J.; Hiltunen, J.; Vin, E. & Obraczka, K. "A Novel IoT System For Patient-Centric Pressure Ulcer Prevention Using Sensor Embedded Dressings". 2022 IEEE International Conference on Pervasive Computing and Communications Workshops and other Affiliated Events (PerCom Workshops): Work in Progress, IEEE, **2022**; 42–45. https://doi.org/10.1109/PerComWorkshops53856.2022.9767294

Rueda, F. M.; Lüdtke, S.; Schröder, M.; Yordanova, K.; Kirste T. & Fink, G. A. "Combining Symbolic Reasoning and Deep Learning for Human Activity Recognition," in *CoMoRea 2019, IEEE International Conference on Pervasive Computing and Communications Workshops (PerCom Workshops)*, **2019**

Sarker, I. H. "Context-aware rule learning from smartphone data: survey, challenges and future directions", *Journal of Big Data*, 6 (1), **2019**, Springer Science and Business Media LLC. https://doi.org/10.1186/s40537-019-0258-4

Schilit, B.; Adams, N. & Want, R. "Context-Aware Computing Applications", *Proceedings of the IEEE Workshop on Mobile Computing Systems and Applications*, **1994**, 85–90.

Schilit, B. & Theimer, M. "Disseminating active map information to mobile hosts", *IEEE Network*, 8(5), **1994**, 22–32

Sigg, S.; Haseloff S. & David, K. "An alignment approach for context prediction tasks in ubicomp environments," *IEEE Pervasive Computing*, 9(4), **2010**, 90–97.

Vahdat-Nejad, H. "Context-Aware Middleware: A Review", *Context in Computing*, Springer New York, **2014**, 83–96.

Villari, M.; Fazio, M.; Dustdar, S.; Rana, O. & Ranjan R. "Osmotic Computing: A New Paradigm for Edge/Cloud Integration". *IEEE Cloud Computing*, 3(6), November **2016**, 76–83. https://doi.org/10.1109/MCC.2016.124.

Wagner, M.; Reichle R. & Geihs, K. "Context as a service - Requirements, design and middleware support," in *IEEE International Conference on Pervasive Computing and Communications Workshops* (PERCOM Workshops), **2011**.

Yu, H.; Chen, H.-Y.; Lee, S.; Zheng, X. & Julien, C. "Prototyping Opportunistic Learning in Resource Constrained Mobile Devices". *First Workshop on Pervasive and Resource-Constrained Artificial Intelligence (PeRConAI 2022), IEEE International Conference on Pervasive Computing and Communications Workshops and other Affiliated Events (PerCom Workshops)*, **2022**, IEEE, 521–526. https://doi.org/10.1109/PerComWorkshops53856.2022.9767493.

Zappatore, M.; Longo, A.; Bochicchio, M. A.; Zappatore, D.; Morrone, A. A. & De Mitri, G. "Towards Urban Mobile Sensing as a Service: An Experience from Southern Italy". In: Mandler, B., Marquez-Barja, J., Mitre Campista, M. E., Cagáňová, D., Chaouchi, H., Zeadally, S., Badra, M., Giordano, S., Fazio, M., Somov, A. & Vieriu, R.-L. (Eds), *Internet of Things: IoT Infrastructures. 2nd Int. Summit, IoT 360° 2015, Revised Selected Papers, Part I*, Springer, **2016**; 377–387

Zdankin, P.; Waltereit, M.; Matkovic, V. & Weis, T. "Towards Longevity of Smart Home Systems", *4th International Workshop on Mobile and Pervasive Internet of Things (PerIoT 2020), 2020 IEEE International Conference on Pervasive Computing and Communications Workshops (PerCom Workshops)*, **2020**, 1–6. https://doi.org/10.1109/PerComWorkshops48775.2020.9156165.

Zhou, Z.; Chen, X.; Li, E.; Zeng, L.; Luo, K. & Zhang, J. "Edge Intelligence: Paving the Last Mile of Artificial Intelligence with Edge Computing". Proceedings of the IEEE, 107 (8), Aug. **2019**, 1738–1762. https://doi.org/10.1109/JPROC.2019.2918951.

Middleware Supporting PIS: Requirements, Solutions, and Challenges

Chantal Taconet, Thais Batista, Pedro Borges, Georgios Bouloukakis, Everton Cavalcante, Sophie Chabridon, Denis Conan, Thierry Desprats, and Denisse Muñante

1 Introduction

Pervasive computing, the computing that disappears, has been introduced by Weiser (1991). It has been followed by ubiquitous computing, the computing appearing everywhere and anytime introduced by Satyanarayanan (2001a). They both have profoundly changed Information Systems (IS[1]) in the three last decades. Those IS are sometimes qualified as *Pervasive Information Systems* (PIS[2]) (Kourouthanassis and Giaglis 2007). With PIS, IS features are enriched while their architecture becomes more and more distributed. In addition to the traditional databases they

---

[1] The term IS will be herein interchangeably used to express both singular and plural.

[2] The term PIS will be herein interchangeably used to express both singular and plural.

C. Taconet (✉) · P. Borges · G. Bouloukakis · S. Chabridon · D. Conan
SAMOVAR, Télécom SudParis, Institut Polytechnique de Paris, Évry and Palaiseau, France
e-mail: chantal.taconet@telecom-sudparis.eu; pedro.borges@telecom-sudparis.eu;
georgios.bouloukakis@telecom-sudparis.eu; sophie.chabridon@telecom-sudparis.eu;
denis.conan@telecom-sudparis.eu

T. Batista · E. Cavalcante
Federal University of Rio Grande do Norte, Natal, Brazil
e-mail: thais@dimap.ufrn.br; everton.cavalcante@ufrn.br

T. Desprats
IRIT, Université de Toulouse, CNRS, Toulouse, France
e-mail: Thierry.Desprats@irit.fr

D. Muñante
SAMOVAR, ENSIIE, Évry, France
e-mail: denisse.munantearzapalo@ensiie.fr

© The Author(s), under exclusive license to Springer Nature Switzerland AG 2023
M. Kirsch Pinheiro et al. (eds.), *The Evolution of Pervasive Information Systems*,
https://doi.org/10.1007/978-3-031-18176-4_4

were built upon, they include data coming from the physical environment and should be accessible anytime and from any (mobile) device.

To illustrate the complexity of PIS throughout this chapter, we consider the case of a logistic chain traceability system related to the transport operations of shipments (Ahmed et al. 2021). Each shipment transport involves at least three types of stakeholders: (1) *the shipper* at the origin of the transport request; (2) *the carriers* in charge of transport operations; and (3) *the consignee* that receives the transported shipment. Other stakeholders can also be involved in this process, e.g., logistic service providers, customs, insurance companies, and banks. These traceability IS were centralized in the past, but next-generation IS in this domain are going to be more and more distributed. The system is deployed at each stakeholder infrastructure locally and in the cloud. IS includes data collected from the Internet of Things (IoT) with wireless connected devices (such as a temperature sensor) deployed on the shipment and in the stakeholders' infrastructures. Furthermore, traceability data may be used dynamically for decision-making purposes, e.g., a change in a transport company, notification of transport delays to the consignee and the carriers, and the early identification of transport default such as the non-respect of temperature conditions.

PIS software architecture comprises several layers: a *business layer*, a *service/middleware layer*, and *context-management data layer* (a.k.a. IoT layer). Each layer might be composed of several software components provided by different organizations and deployed on a large-scale, heterogeneous, and distributed infrastructure. A PIS may be abstracted by a distributed software architecture in which data and actions are transmitted among components, both inside and between layers. The so-called *middleware* is an essential part of the design and execution of this software architecture.

In a distributed computing system, middleware is defined as the software layer that lies between the operating system and the applications on each site of the system. Its role is to make application development easier, by providing common programming abstractions, by masking the heterogeneity and the distribution of the underlying hardware and operating systems, and by hiding low-level programming details (Krakowiak 2009). Middleware has provided a key set of features enabling distributed architectures to expand. In the 1990s, middleware started by offering the basic client-server model that has been extensively used by IS. Since then, there have been extensive innovations in middleware capabilities. We can mention the persistence capability that enables transparent interactions between applications and databases and the publish-subscribe interaction pattern that enables designers to decouple system components.

PIS have specific requirements concerning middleware. Biegel and Cahill (2007) have identified some of these requirements, such as loosely coupled communication and sensor and actuator abstractions. Raychoudhury et al. (2013) surveyed the literature on middleware for pervasive systems and highlighted new requirements for PIS, such as context management, i.e., how to consume high-level context information obtained after processing, fusing, and filtering a large amount of low-level context data collected from the environment. They also draw attention to the service-oriented paradigm, the common middleware abstraction in this decade, which comes with service discovery and service composition issues. In this chapter, we focus on presenting the state of the art on requirements concerning middleware for PIS in the context of the IoT, i.e., the integration of connected devices that interact with the environment into the Internet. As stated by Blair et al. (2016), the IoT ensues with new requirements and challenges for PIS middleware such as scalability and heterogeneity.

At the same time, as PIS grow in terms of complexity and distribution and become ubiquitous, they raise a new concern in terms of energy consumption. According to Ferreboeuf et al. (2021), the energy demand of Information Technology (IT) in 2019 was estimated to be 4184 TWh (IT represents 4.2% of the energy consumption and 3.5% of greenhouse gas in the world). If the energy consumption continues to rise by 6.2% by year as it has had since 2015, both energy and greenhouse gas could double in 10 years, a non-sustainable scenario. As middleware has a central position in IS and as it is used by many of them, middleware platforms might play a key role in making systems developed atop of them become energy-aware and energy-efficient. These requirements are even more relevant considering that programmers often have limited knowledge on how much energy their software consumes and which parts use most energy (Pang et al. 2016). Consequently, energy consumption is a first-class concern for PIS middleware that we address in this chapter.

The remainder of this chapter is organized as follows. Section 2 describes the requirements imposed by PIS to middleware. Section 3 presents how some of those requirements are handled by middleware in the literature. Section 4 details how platforms proposed in our research respond to some of the identified requirements concerning PIS middleware. Next, Sect. 5 draws open challenges to be handled in the future. Section 6 concludes the chapter with final remarks.

2 Requirements for PIS Middleware

This section gives an overview of the requirements for PIS middleware in the context of the IoT. As the aim of a middleware layer is to bridge the gap between the pervasive elements spread over the physical environment and the applications, the requirements for PIS middleware include the provision of several services to allow applications to gather contextual information from heterogeneous distributed devices. We present the main functional requirements (i.e., driven by application constraints such as interacting with a given sensor or defining application adaptation rules) and non-functional requirements essential in a PIS scenario (such as handling interoperability, scalability, and the need for supporting energy-efficiency). Table 1 summarizes the presented requirements by organizing them in three categories: requirements necessary for *Context data management in the IoT*, *Application support*, and requirements *Exacerbated in IoT systems*. Table 1 also maps the

Table 1 Requirements for PIS in the context of the IoT

Requirement	Type	SotA[a]	Proposals
Context data management			
2.1 Sensing and actuation support	FR[b]		IoTvar (4.5)
2.2 Context-awareness	FR		
2.3 Dynamic adaptation capabilities	FR		
2.4 Quality of Context management	NFR[c]	3.1	QoCIM (4.1), QoDisco (4.4)
Application support			
2.5 Application development support	FR		IoTvar (4.5)
2.6 Support for multiple interaction patterns	FR	3.2	
Exacerbated in IoT systems			
2.7 Enabling interoperability	NFR	3.3	DeX Mediators (4.3), QoDisco (4.4), IoTvar (4.5)
2.8 Security and privacy	FR/NFR	3.4	MUDEBS (4.2), QoCIM (4.1)
2.9 Scalability	NFR	3.5	MUDEBS (4.2)
2.10 Energy efficiency and energy-awareness	FR/NFR	3.6	

[a] SotA = State of the art
[b] FR = Functional requirement
[c] NFR = Non-functional requirement

middleware proposals that will be presented in Sect. 4 with the requirements they tackle and for which we discuss the state of the art in Sect. 3.

2.1 Sensing and Actuation Support

PIS middleware needs to deal with small, often battery-powered devices such as sensors and actuators, the physical elements that the system needs to interact with the environment. Sensors typically obtain information from entities of interest or their environment, whereas actuators act on an entity or the environment or provide feedback to the user. A relevant requirement for PIS middleware is to provide programming abstractions that enable event-driven programming at a high level, thereby significantly simplifying the use of sensors and actuators by hiding the complexity of accessing heterogeneous devices that use different communication protocols.

In the example of the logistic chain traceability related to the transport operations of shipments, all the data collected by sensors providing the temperature in the compartments of a ship during the transportation need to be received by the application. Similarly, the application needs to set the desired temperature remotely by sending a message to some temperature actuators. The middleware layer should provide programming abstractions for the communication with heterogeneous sensors and actuators to support high-level interaction with them.

2.2 Context-Awareness

Several works have defined the terms *context* and *context-awareness*. In this chapter, we rely on a generic, well-known definition from Dey and Abowd (2000): *Context is any information that can be used to characterize the situation of an entity. An entity is a person, place, or object that is considered relevant to the interaction between a user and an application, including the user and applications themselves.* Context-awareness is one of the most notorious characteristics of PIS as it is related to the pervasive capability of collecting, processing, storing, and reasoning about environmental information on a real-time basis. This requirement is essential to support PIS self-adaptation to any environmental condition. For instance, users' mobility, or any environmental disruption, such as temperature increase, that can impact the quality of the application.

In essence, middleware should provide a well-defined interface to generic context management solutions to prevent PIS from dealing with the burden of context-awareness management. Middleware for PIS typically should offer system-level services to deal with context data acquisition, storage, reasoning, discovery, and query processing, as well as automated context-aware adaptation.

In the logistic chain traceability system example, context-awareness is essential to provide specific information to the different stakeholders involved. For instance, the insurance companies do not need to receive the same information as the customs services. Insurance companies are often interested only in information important to the insurance context, which differs from the information of interest to the customs services. Another example of context-awareness, is to automatically trigger alert and reconfiguration in case of an inappropriate temperature detection.

2.3 Dynamic Adaptation Capabilities

PIS have to be dynamic for diverse reasons, such as failure management, energy budget, network unavailability, user mobility, and unpredictable interactions. In the face of these situations, PIS middleware should hence provide dynamic adaptation capabilities to ensure the quality and availability of applications at runtime. Dynamic adaptation means the ability of an application to reconfigure its structure, behavior, protocols, etc. without interrupting its execution, ideally with minimal or no human intervention or disruption.

PIS should possess inherent characteristics that make dynamic adaptation particularly relevant. Context-awareness is related to the ability of a system to perceive information about the context where it is inserted into. By sensing environmental conditions, the system can recognize the current context and adapt itself according to changes in it. Another sort of dynamic adaptation in PIS is device mobility, e.g., a user with a mobile device in the environment at a given moment and leaving that location at another, so that PIS needs to transparently discover and (un)link participating devices into the network. Kourouthanassis and Giaglis (2015) also raises opportunistic user interaction as a challenge to the development of PIS, in the sense that it may not be possible to know in advance the users who will interact with the system or the frequency of such interactions. All these features need to be adequately supported by PIS middleware components to enable building applications atop them that can have their structure and behavior adapted at runtime while maintaining their availability and quality.

In the logistic chain traceability system example, dynamic adaptations may be required due to communication latency issues (e.g., changing protocols for the sake of reliability and performance), anomalous operation, unavailability of connected devices due to a low power level or even failure, or measures to improve the accuracy of gathered data. These scenarios point out PIS middleware to maintain availability and work properly in such a dynamic environment while collecting, analyzing, planning and reacting to changes.

2.4 Quality of Context Management

An important requirement concerns monitoring and managing the quality of the context information received by applications. International standardization bodies underline the importance of uncertainty in metrology (Joint Committee for Guides in Metrology 2008). When reporting the result of a measurement of a physical quantity, some quantitative indication of the quality of the result should be given so that those who use it can assess its reliability.

Regarding context information, Henricksen and Indulska (2004) acknowledge that it may be inherently *ambiguous*, when two different sources provide contradictory information, *inaccurate*, when too little information is available about a situation, or even *erroneous* when it does not reflect reality. For information provided by open data or human beings, e.g., data from social networks, the latter may be incomplete or erroneous, whether voluntarily or not. In general, context information sources are numerous and diverse. They do not all share the same formats or units of measurement, which means that conversion operations are necessary and potentially add new errors.

Quality of Context (QoC) has first been defined by Buchholz et al. (2003) as *any information that describes the quality of information that is used as context information* and can be represented as a set of parameters that reflects the quality of context data (Bellavista et al. 2012). We consider that QoC parameters, such as accuracy or currentness as defined in ISO/IEC 25012 (2008), should therefore be associated with context information in the form of metadata and be used to compute the quality level of context information.

In the case of logistic chains, at least four quality parameters should be considered in these metadata (Ahmed et al. 2021): (1) the *accuracy*, to ensure that the collected data represent the reality of the shipment conditions, (2) the *completeness*, to ensure that there is no gap in the collected data, (3) the *consistency*, to ensure the users' agreement on the traceability data collected from multiple sources, and (4) the *currentness*, to ensure that the collected data are timely valid.

Information provided to context-aware applications is derived through analysis operations and various transformations. However, if these operations are performed on erroneous information, the new information produced is also erroneous. QoC management must hence be carried out throughout the entire information life cycle, from its collection to its dissemination to the applications through all the intermediate transformation steps. Middleware should enable applications to become QoC-aware and provide PIS developers with QoC management facilities.

2.5 Application Development Support

Middleware platforms are a key element in leveraging application development by abstracting away the specificities of the underlying distributed components from users and exposing valuable reusable services to applications. Besides an accessible programming model that adequately supports application developers by taking advantage of abstractions exposed by PIS middleware, it is relevant to come up with interoperable environments that could assist those developers to effortlessly build their applications while orchestrating the diversity of existing devices, platforms, and services. Inspired by a cloud-based IoT scenario (Truong and Dustdar 2015), the life cycle of developing a PIS may comprise (1) selecting, composing, and integrating components across the system for specifying and developing possible governance and control operations, (2) deploying several types of software components at different levels of abstraction and capabilities to configure deployments and continuous resource provisioning, and (3) capabilities to monitor end-to-end metrics and perform governance processes across the system. Transversally, it is necessary to provide environments supporting the development of applications based on data streams generated by devices and available through the underlying deployment infrastructure (i.e., cloud, edge).

2.6 Support for Multiple Interaction Patterns

To facilitate the development of applications that exchange data between devices and services, PIS middleware platforms rely on IP-based protocols. These protocols abstract distributed peers that interact with each other based on different interaction patterns, such as request-reply, publish-subscribe and event-based. Middleware protocols are typically available through an API, and each protocol supports several characteristics (synchronous/asynchronous interactions, QoS guarantees, etc.). In general, each interaction pattern can be characterized by (1) its semantics, which expresses the different dimensions of coupling among interacting peers, and (2) its API, with a set of primitives expressed as functions provided by the middleware.

The *request-reply* pattern is commonly used for Web Services and followed by popular middleware protocols such as HTTP, XMPP, etc. A client interacts directly (without intermediate components) with a server either by direct messaging (one-way) or through remote procedure calls (RPC). Request-reply protocols usually support both synchronous and asynchronous interactions. In turn, the *publish-subscribe* pattern is commonly used for content broadcasting. Middleware protocols such as MQTT and AMQP, APIs (e.g., JMS) and message brokers such as RabbitMQ, EMQx, and Mosquitto follow this pattern. Multiple publisher-consumer peers interact via an intermediate broker. Consumers subscribe to a specific filter (e.g., topic-based filters) on the broker while publishers produce events to that filter, whereas consumers receive events in a FIFO order. Publish-subscribe protocols commonly support asynchronous interactions. In Sect. 3.2, we provide an overview of existing protocols that can be classified into the request-reply and publish-subscribe patterns.

PIS are characterized by diverse entities (devices, systems, users, etc.) that are pervasively inserted into the environment and provide context information about this environment. These entities are also inherently mobile, i.e., they may be present in the surroundings at a given instant of time and no longer be there at another one, and they may be unknown a priori at design time. Such characteristics lead the communication in a PIS to be preferably loosely coupled due to the inherent dynamicity of interaction among the system constituents and scale well upon the many entities envisioned in PIS environments. In this perspective, Biegel and Cahill (2015) especially advocate using an *event-based pattern* (Bacon et al. 2000) in PIS middleware as a means of providing asynchronous communication in a many-to-many, loosely-coupled interaction among the distributed application components.

2.7   Enabling Interoperability

It is essential to tackle heterogeneity across multiple layers to enable interoperability between IoT devices and other PIS components. For instance, in the logistic chain traceability scenario, a shipment may provide information regarding its state through the following application layer operation: `get_shipment_state (id)`. However, a carrier may require the shipment status via `query_shipment (shipment_id, state)`. Such issues at the application layer can be qualified as semantic heterogeneity issues. Ensuring end-to-end data consistency is one of the goals of semantic interoperability. There are two basic solutions for achieving semantic interoperability between two IoT devices. The first solution is a one-to-one model mapping. Another more suitable approach is to use shared data meta-models that can be used to unambiguously define the meaning of terms in existing models, such as ontologies. In Sect. 3.3, we discuss some existing semantic interoperability approaches in the literature.

Semantic interoperability ensures mapping between diverse data models employed by IoT systems. However, this alone does not make the interacting devices fully interoperable. Different APIs and data representations and primitives used by IoT devices must be mapped with each other at the middleware layer. Solving the middleware interoperability issue is challenging, mainly due to the fast development of protocols and APIs. Existing efforts address the middleware interoperability issue by relying on service-oriented architectures (SOA), IoT gateways, cloud computing platforms, and model-driven engineering. In Sect. 3.3, we discuss some middleware interoperability approaches in the literature.

2.8 Security and Privacy

To promote the user acceptability of new IoT-enabled PIS applications, it is essential to provide mechanisms to ensure the privacy of users and the protection of the handled data. With the heterogeneity and amount of connected things and the unprecedented amount of collected data, security and privacy are no longer an option in PIS. They should be enforced throughout the entire software life cycle. PIS middleware is the right layer to intercept the information flow of applications and integrate security and privacy mechanisms. Such mechanisms can then benefit all applications by default, with the possibility to configure some specific business rules to take into account applications needs.

Security corresponds to *the degree to which a product or system protects information and data so that persons or other products or systems have the degree of data access appropriate to their types and levels of authorization* (ISO/IEC 25010 2011). More specifically, cybersecurity is about ensuring three properties of information, services, and systems, namely confidentiality, integrity, and availability. Securing an information system means preventing an unauthorized entity from accessing information, services, and systems, modifying them, or making them unavailable. *Privacy* can be thought of as the confidentiality of the relationship between people and data. Therefore, it is important to notice that privacy can be guaranteed only when a security strategy is enforced in an end-to-end way. While relying on cryptographic primitives and protocols, privacy protection involves its own properties, techniques, and methodologies.

Cavoukian and Dixon (2013) recommend aligning seven principles for both security-by-design and privacy-by-design. These principles are: (1) proactive and preventative, not reactive and remedial, to anticipate and prevent invasive events before they happen; (2) default setting as no action should be required on the part of individuals for their protection; (3) embedded into the design, not bolt after the fact; (4) a positive-sum, not zero-sum but full functionality by accommodating all legitimate interests and objectives; (5) an end-to-end approach, by ensuring secure life-cycle management of information with confidentiality, integrity, and availability of all information for all stakeholders; (6) visibility and transparency, by keeping IT systems' internal parts transparent to users and providers and by following open standards; and (7) respect for the user in a user-centric approach to protecting the interests of all information owners.

PIS technology is still in its infancy and does not have utterly standardized security and privacy requirements (Chaudhuri and Cavoukian 2018). Alhirabi et al. (2020) recommend using threat modelling techniques during the design stage, like STRIDE for security threats and LINDDUN for privacy threats. The STRIDE framework (Howard and Lipner 2006) is an acronym for *Spoofing, Tampering, Repudiation, Information Disclosure, Denial of Service,* and *Elevation of Privilege.* The LINDDUN framework (Deng et al. 2011) is an acronym for *Linkability, Identifiability, Non-repudiation, Detectability, information Disclosure, content Unawareness,* and *policy and consent Non-compliance.*

Even though PIS mainly rely on an event-driven data reporting method (see Sect. 2.6), there may be situations when a query-driven approach is more relevant to get insights about some phenomenon at a given time. For instance, a query would get a particular set of sensor readings satisfying some condition. Data query privacy (López et al. 2017) is hence an important requirement of PIS in order to reduce the risk of exposing sensitive information to attackers when issuing queries.

In the logistic chain traceability system example, the collected data should be kept confidential and not be transferred to or stored by untrustworthy third parties. Anonymity or pseudonymity should also be enforced so that untrustworthy third parties can distinguish location information from fake locations. These are just examples of some issues. Many more security and privacy aspects should be considered in a PIS middleware all along the data life cycle and at all the system architecture.

2.9 Scalability

The IoT paradigm calls for exchanging data among dynamic, heterogeneous sensors and client applications at unprecedented scales. We follow the framework from Duboc et al. (2007) for characterizing the scalability of PIS middleware. For instance, when considering an IoT-based solution, the scaling dimensions, which represent the scaling aspects, are the number of queries per second and the number of machines in the cluster. The non-scaling variables are the network conditions (e.g., available bandwidth). The dependent variables, which represent the aspects of the system behavior affected by changes in the scaling dimensions, are the response time for a query, bandwidth usage, and cluster load. In this first example, the requirement can then be formulated as follows: "the studied system shall scale with respect to latency" because it can maintain a maximum given response time as the number of requests per second scales by varying the number of machines in the cluster. In another architectural style, such as a highly-distributed publish-subscribe system for the PIS middleware, the scaling dimensions shall include the number of intermediary entities (i.e., brokers of the overlay network) that route data from sensors to client applications. We shall then measure the total resource consumption for filtering data records through the multiple brokers from the sensor to the client application.

When considering the logistic chain traceability illustrative application domain, architects may differentiate PIS systems deployed in relatively small areas mainly managed by one administrative entity, such as merchandise warehouses or ocean liners, from more extensive areas with many stakeholders, e.g., in port cities. In the former scenario, IoT solutions, including ones enhanced with cloud computing, may be appropriate. In the latter configuration, more distributed, decoupled solutions involving several brokers along with distributed routing and filtering might be required.

2.10   Energy Efficiency and Energy-Awareness

Penzenstadler (2015) point out that new quality attributes have recently been studied by the research community in the objective to keep systems sustainable. In the past, resource utilization mainly referred to the efficiency of the use of the available processing, storage, and network. For energy-efficiency purposes, the resource to be monitored is the energy consumption.

While *energy efficiency* means using less energy to perform a given task, *energy-awareness* represents knowing the energy consumption for a given task. The middleware can use energy-awareness to reduce energy consumption through energy-saving strategies, e.g., protocol, scheduling and the volume of exchanged data. Energy-awareness can also be shared with upper layers of applications. Applications may adjust their behavior for energy-saving purposes, e.g., reducing some requirements to remain within the limits of a given energy budget. Applications can also share energy consumption reports with end-users who could adapt their usage based on energy consumption knowledge. Indeed, energy-awareness is expected to have a positive impact in terms of energy efficiency (Hassan et al. 2009).

In the logistic chain traceability system example, to achieve energy efficiency, the PIS middleware could: (1) at design time, choose the most energy-efficient consensus algorithm for sharing securely and transparently data between the stakeholders (Sedlmeir et al. 2020); (2) at runtime, reduce the volume of exchanged data by filtering data based on their content or minimizing the frequency of data transmissions (de Oliveira et al. 2020). For energy-awareness, the middleware could adapt the frequency of data transmissions to keep energy consumption above a certain level of energy budget or transmit energy consumption information to the application level, for example, to inform the end-user about the consumption of the energy budget.

PIS middleware should integrate architectural tactics for energy efficiency, e.g., energy monitoring, resource allocation, and resource adaptation (Paradis et al. 2021). It is reasonable seeing middleware as the good level for integrating energy management strategies due to its operation at the protocol level and high reusability (Noureddine et al. 2013). Additionally, middleware should provide energy-awareness mechanisms (Verdecchia et al. 2021) that allow future PIS providers to master energy consumption.

3   State of the Art on Middleware Supporting PIS Requirements

In Sect. 2, we have identified and defined the requirements for PIS middleware in the context of the IoT. Context-awareness state-of-the-art is covered in chapter "The Context Awareness Challenges for PIS" of this book. In this section, we present only the state of the art concerning the most pregnant requirements in the context of the IoT.

3.1   QoC Management

Even though the management of the quality of context data has long been recognized as a requirement of PIS and context-aware applications (Buchholz et al. 2003), only a few middleware actually provide the necessary support for QoC. We herein present some recent initiatives and summarize the provided mechanisms.

The ContextNet middleware (Endler and Silva 2018) integrates QoC management through the Context Data Distribution Layer (CDDL) (Gomes et al. 2017a). A set of QoC parameters is available, including accuracy, measurement time, age, completeness, and numeric resolution. ContextNet targets the Internet of Mobile Things (IoMT) and takes dynamicity into account at different levels. QoC parameters may also exhibit dynamic variability (they oscillate over time), and CDDL can monitor the variation of a given QoC parameter. CDDL also offers filtering based on context data and their QoC metadata.

The LAURA architecture (Teixeira et al. 2020) was designed to support the deployment of decoupled IoT applications. LAURA provides a fog layer that plays the role of an intermediate between applications and the network or sensor nodes and can be regarded as a middleware. This fog layer, still under development, is designed to filter or aggregate data received from the physical layer to prevent unnecessary or poor quality data from being sent to upper layers. QoC parameters are associated with the sensed data, allowing user applications to verify the context data's usefulness or temporal relevance. QoC-based filtering and aggregation are seen as important features of LAURA.

Jagarlamudi et al. (2021) proposed a Service Level Agreement (SLA) template integrating a QoC-aware mechanism, called the Relative Reputation (RR), to select context providers with high RR values. The QoC evaluator generates the RR unit representing the match between QoC outcomes and QoC requirements. A mechanism of penalties also exists to indicate the applicable penalties with each QoC indicator's degradation in the context response compared to its guarantees.

3.2 Protocols for Multiple Interaction Patterns

As mentioned in Sect. 2.6, PIS middleware platforms leverage communication protocols upon different interaction patterns. We herein provide an overview of existing middleware-based IoT protocols. These protocols offer middleware primitives that aim to facilitate the development of IoT applications that include resource-constrained IoT devices. Karagiannis et al. (2015) compare the most promising IoT middleware protocols (more specifically, the ones mentioned here). Even though there are multiple IoT protocols, no single protocol has been adopted yet for IoT system development. This is mainly because the IoT is too diverse, including multiple data formats and (possibly highly) resource-constrained devices.

Protocols such as DPWS, OPC UA, CoAP, and XMPP have been introduced to support data exchange among peers based on the request-reply interaction pattern. OASIS introduced DPWS (Zeeb et al. 2007) in 2004 as an open standard, and it is suitable for supporting large-scale deployments and mobile devices. Nevertheless, the induced protocol overhead is noticeable and requires a large amount of RAM. The OPC Foundation designed OPC UA (Mahnke et al. 2009) in 2008 to target resource-constrained devices, but it implies a large payload unsuitable for IoT applications. IETF designed CoAP (Shelby et al. 2014), a lightweight protocol that supports highly resource-constrained devices and the delivery of small message payloads. Finally, XMPP (Saint-Andre 2011) is now a suitable protocol for IoT real-time communications, even though it uses XML data formats that create a significant computational overhead.

The publish-subscribe interaction pattern is an alternative to request-reply and offers time and space decoupled interactions. The Sun Microsystems' JMS standard has been one of the most successful asynchronous messaging technologies available by defining an API for building messaging systems. DDS (OMG 2015) is a messaging protocol designed for brokerless architectures and real-time applications. AMQP (OASIS 2012) is another messaging protocol designed to support applications with high message traffic rates. To support highly resource-constrained devices, MQTT (Banks and Gupta 2014) offers a publish-subscribe centralized architecture, but its performance decreases significantly when sending large message payloads. WebSockets (Fette 2011) were introduced to support real-time full-duplex interactions using only two bytes of overhead in message payloads.

3.3 Enabling Interoperability

Different data representations and APIs among IoT devices, platforms, and applications can be mapped with each other at the middleware layer. However, this alone does not make the interacting peers fully interoperable. There are indeed incompatibilities of IoT devices at the application layer, e.g., operation/resource names, data semantics, etc.

Ontologies (Gruber 1993) provide a common model for annotating content and thus help systems to interoperate. We review well-known ontologies for general sensor modeling. The W3C Semantic Sensor Network (SSN) ontology (Compton et al. 2012) presents a vocabulary to describe sensors and their observations, actuators, and their association to features of interest. Its central building block is the SOSA (Sensor, Observation, Sample, and Actuator) ontology (Janowicz et al. 2019), a standalone light-weight ontology that offers the core vocabulary for the descriptions. The Smart Appliances REFerence (SAREF) ontology (Daniele et al. 2015) follows a similar design to describe concepts required by smart applications. In SAREF, devices make measurements related to properties of interest (similar to sensors making observations in SSN). Depending on the application under development, developers must use the appropriate ontology. For example, the SAREF ontology is commonly used to model information of appliances in smart homes.

Several approaches to bridge middleware-based protocols have been proposed concerning APIS, protocols, and data representations, e.g., the QEST broker for CoAP and RESTful APIs (Collina et al. 2012), HTTP-CoAP proxy (Castellani et al. 2012), and Ponte for REST, CoAP, and MQTT (Banks and Gupta 2014). These approaches implement one-to-one mappings between existing protocols. Despite the simplicity, this is highly inefficient due to the vast development of IoT protocols. Negash et al. (2015, 2016) introduces the Lightweight Internet of Things Service Bus (LISA) for tackling IoT heterogeneity. Derhamy et al. (2017) introduced a protocol translator that utilizes an intermediate format to capture all protocol-specific information. XWARE (Roth et al. 2018) implements mediators to translate messages of IoT protocols by using an intermediate format. Finally, Georgantas et al. (2013) extended the Bouloukakis et al. (2019)'s work to deal with IoT heterogeneity using software abstractions and code generation.

While the above approaches considerably reduce the development effort, they do not consider semantic layer incompatibilities prevalent in the IoT. IoT platforms such as SemIoTic (Yus et al. 2019) provide end-to-end IoT interoperability in smart buildings by leveraging the SSN/SOSA ontologies and mediating adapters. In addition, it leverages the middleware-based interoperability approach that is further presented in Sect. 4.3.

3.4 Security and Privacy

In a comparison of 50 context-aware computing research projects, Perera et al. (2014) identified that only 11 projects (about 20%) provided security and privacy solutions. More recently, Alhirabi et al. (2020) reviewed the evolution of design notations, models, and languages that facilitate capturing the non-functional requirements of security and privacy. The majority of the requirement engineering efforts are focused on security. Among the 47 design notations analyzed in their study, security is supported by more than half (32 notations out of 47), while only three notations cover privacy. Even though a by-design approach has long been recommended for both security and privacy (Cavoukian and Dixon 2013), it is still not sufficiently put into practice by developers. Aljeraisy et al. (2021) highlight that there is still a relevant gap between legislation and design patterns that can help to translate and implement them.

Aljeraisy et al. (2021) analyzed data protection laws used across different countries, namely the European General Data Protection Regulations (GDPR), the Canadian Personal Information Protection and Electronic Documents Act (PIPEDA), the California Consumer Privacy Act (CCPA), the Australian Privacy Principles (APPs), and the New Zealand's Privacy Act 1993. The authors then retained the fundamental principles and individuals' rights to define the Combined Privacy Law Framework (CPLF) by eliminating duplication. Finally, they mapped CPLF with privacy-by-design (PbD) schemes (e.g., privacy principles, strategies, guidelines, and patterns) previously developed by different researchers to investigate the gaps in existing schemes. The results of this extensive study helped to identify where new privacy patterns should be defined. More than 70 privacy patterns have already been proposed in the literature (Colesky et al. 2022; Kargl et al. 2022) and they are a relevant, concrete mechanism to handle data usage and protection in a specific context. However, some principles and rights of CPLF are not achieved by any existing privacy pattern and call for further research.

While security and privacy research is very active, its integration into operational middleware is still limited. Fremantle and Scott (2017) analysed 54 IoT middleware frameworks and observed that they address security and privacy in very different ways. A majority of these middleware frameworks provide access control and authentication mechanisms, and others focus on providing protection for the content shared on the network. However, very few middleware frameworks support a sufficient coverage of the features required to support security and privacy for PIS.

3.5   Scalability

Without middleware, i.e., when applications directly obtain IoT data from sensors, existing coupling significantly hampers the system's scalability. Therefore, as formulated by Bellavista et al. (2012), PIS middleware architectures are classically first organized according to the following question: is the middleware centralized or decentralized? The centralized approach includes deploying middleware on a single host or cloud. The second approach has two subcategories depending on whether the distribution is hierarchical or not. Consequently, the basic solutions for scaling up follow these three classes of solutions.

The architectures of the first class of solutions have been referred to as Web of Things (Delicato et al. 2013) or, more recently, Cloud of Things (Dias et al. 2020). Scalability issues arising in these centralized architectures concern the complex processing of a huge quantity of data with many clients either producing or requesting data. Cugola and Margara (2012) surveyed solutions for complex event processing and stream processing.

The second class of solutions dealing with scalability targets this requirement at a local scale, a.k.a. localized scalability (Satyanarayanan 2001b). A collection of small clouds, i.e., cloudlets, typically are brought to lower latencies between so-called co-located clients: these smaller clouds are physically distributed to form smaller groups of clients. This architectural style corresponds to what we know as fog computing. Perera et al. (2017) surveyed such solutions for smart cities.

To target scalability at a global scale, an architecture based on publish-subscribe is preferred as it favors decoupling. Eugster et al. (2003) distinguish three forms of decoupling, namely space, time, and synchronization decoupling. In this approach, some clients publish IoT data while others consume these data. As surveyed by Bellavista et al. (2012), a first set of solutions organize an overlay of brokers responsible for routing IoT data from producers to subscribers. Producers push data to their access broker, and brokers forward them to the consumers that have subscribed to these data. A data model and a filtering model define the non-scaling variables of publish-subscribe solutions: roughly speaking, topic-based filtering with opaque data scales better than content-based filtering with structured data or semi-structured data. In addition, the diameter of the overlay network of brokers is the other non-scaling variable. Kermarrec and Triantafillou (2013) surveyed a second set of solutions targeting non-broker-based routing and using topic-based filtering. These solutions are constructed as peer-to-peer systems: peer nodes simultaneously play the three roles, namely publishers, subscribers, and routers.

Finally, note that broker-based PIS middleware protocols such as AMQP and MQTT are topic-based and cloud-based, but without complex event processing or streaming. This is precisely the role of recent works such the one of Luckner et al. (2014), and of industrial platforms such as AWS IoT Core,[3] Google IoT Core,[4] Microsoft Azure IoT Hub,[5] and FIWARE,[6] to add complex event processing and streaming to publish-subscribe middleware standards. These platforms are proof, if any were needed, of the interest of major operators in working to integrate scalability into PIS middleware.

3.6   Energy Efficiency and Energy-Awareness

Middleware has recently explored some strategies for the IoT for energy efficiency and energy-awareness purposes. The most used strategy for energy efficiency is network adaptation. Network adaptation refers to introducing new protocols, mod-

---

[3] https://aws.amazon.com/iot-core/.

[4] https://cloud.google.com/iot-core.

[5] https://docs.microsoft.com/azure/architecture/reference-architectures/iot.

[6] https://www.fiware.org/.

ifying existing ones, and making network optimizations. Akkermans et al. (2016) proposed adapting a publish-subscribe middleware by adding a layer between the broker and the client applications to send notifications via IPv6 multicast rather than using several point-to-point messages. Kalbarczyk and Julien (2018) proposed Omni, a device-to-device middleware with periodic adaptive discovery of neighbor devices using lightweight discovery mechanisms in wireless local area networks. Discovered devices are only connected when data needs to be transferred, and the communication technology adapts both to the network energy efficiency and the volume of data.

Task offloading stands for using the network to transfer software components to other locations. For example, an application running on a mobile phone could send data to a server in a cloud or to another computer in its vicinity for data processing purposes. Several authors such as Aazam et al. (2020), Pasricha (2018), Song et al. (2017), Ivarez-Valera et al. (2019), and Shekhar et al. (2019) proposed middleware to offload software components to other nodes in the cloud or the fog as a means of saving energy on the source nodes. All these proposals show that task offloading has a benefit in terms of energy consumption for at least one of the nodes of the system.

The data filtering capability offered by some middleware proposes processing data to reduce the number or the size of messages according to specific criteria. Adaptive sampling and adaptive filtering (Giouroukis et al. 2020a) are two techniques that have emerged over the last decade. These techniques dynamically reconfigure rates and filter thresholds to trade-off data quality against resource utilization. de Oliveira et al. (2020) proposed a data stream processing workflow to be deployed at the network's edge to perform data cleaning tasks.

Another strategy used by middleware is to temporarily reduce the activity of some nodes to reduce the infrastructure energy consumption. This strategy is used for a time in data centers. For example, Binder and Suri (2009) presented a dispatch algorithm to concentrate services on a reduced number of servers so that they put inactive servers in a sleeping mode to save energy in the data center. In the context of the IoT, this strategy is used as well and is known as active node selection. For example, Cecchinel et al. (2019) proposed determining an optimal configuration of sensors towards extending their battery life. Sarkar et al. (2016) proposed to reduce interactions among the nodes of a wireless sensor network and hence the network's energy consumption. The data stream processing workflow proposed by de Oliveira et al. (2020) also includes active node selection. Active node selection can hence reduce energy consumption on some of the nodes of a PIS.

The second requirement concerning energy introduced in Sect. 2.10 is energy-awareness. The energy-awareness may be provided at the middleware or the application level (i.e., knowledge shared through middleware abstractions with the application components). At the former level, energy-awareness may be used to constrain the system's energy consumption through an energy budget configuration. For example, Padhy et al. (2017) proposed a middleware to minimize the total energy consumption of an IoT application while ensuring that the requested accuracy is met. The middleware intends to find the sensors that consume the minor energy while satisfying the sensing requirements and maximizing the overall accuracy under an energy budget. For the latter level, we found some examples where applications express energy requirements (e.g. Song et al. 2017) for deployment purposes. However, middleware does not usually expose energy consumption to upper layers.

Energy consumption is a recent concern for the community working on IoT middleware. Some middleware has mainly handled energy efficiency to reduce energy consumption only on some systems parts. We noticed a few middleware proposals providing energy-awareness to the upper layers.

4   PIS Middleware Proposals

We have been working on middleware for the IoT and PIS for some years. Different software is available in open source (Bouloukakis et al. 2022; Conan et al. 2022; Gomes et al. 2017b) and some of these proposals are presented below. Table 1 summarizes the requirements tackled by each of them.

4.1   QoC Management with QoCIM and Processing Functions

Based on the QoC criteria most frequently mentioned in the literature, it is possible to notice that no criteria can respond to all the needs of applications, each having its own method for computing the quality of context information. We have then focused our attention on realizing a model able to represent any type of QoC criteria. This resulted in QoCIM[7] (Quality of Context Information Model) (Marie et al. 2013), a meta-model dedicated to modeling QoC criteria and enforcing expressiveness, computability, and genericity of QoC management. QoCIM offers a flexible ideology, i.e., it defines a basis to design and represent any QoC criterion instead of providing a predefined list of supported QoC criteria. With QoCIM, a given QoC criterion can also be built upon other primitive or composed QoC criteria.

QoCIM is complemented with the specification and implementation of a set of functions for processing context information and its QoC metadata. The goal of these processing functions is to provide the developers of PIS with middleware programming facilities to process context information together with its associated QoC metadata efficiently. The functions manage three types of data: (1) context information sensed and collected from different sources; (2) QoC metadata modeled with QoCIM, each piece of QoC metadata corresponding to an instance of a QoC indicator, and (3) message encapsulating a piece of context information associated to a list of QoC metadata. There are functions for aggregation, filtering, inference, and fusion of context information with QoC metadata. These functions can be configured to determine what computing method to use and to indicate the number

---

[7] QoCIM is part of the M4IoT platform: https://www-inf.it-sudparis.eu/m4iot/.

of messages to be taken as input. The configurability of the functions is based on a declarative solution.

The *aggregation* function applies an aggregation operator onto a list of messages. The result is a message with the same abstraction level. The choice of the aggregation operator (arithmetical average, for instance) is specified in a configuration file. There is also a distinction between temporal aggregation and spatial aggregation. The former handles information coming from a single context source and produced during some time. The latter handles information coming from several context sources that periodically produce the same type of context information. The *filtering* function analyzes the message and decides to remove it or not, but the content of the message itself is never modified. The *inference* function applies an inference operator onto a list of messages. The result is only one message with a higher abstraction level. The *fusion* function executes a set of functions sequentially. The result is a list of messages with a higher abstraction level.

QoC management must take place throughout the whole chain of processing context information. A declarative programming approach allows qualifying context information and self-adapting QoC management due to potential physical limitations of the processing entities (Marie et al. 2016).

4.2 MUDEBS

Distributed-based event systems (DEBS) for broad IoT face unprecedented scales regarding the volume of exchanged data, number of participants, and communication distance. As many brokers may be involved, a high amount of messages may be exchanged when installing subscription filters and, most importantly, when routing numerous events from producers to consumers. MUDEBS[8] (Conan et al. 2017) take advantage of the inherently heterogeneous nature of broad IoT systems to control and limit the amount of exchanged data. Some sources of heterogeneity, such as geographical and group membership heterogeneity, may delimit visibility scopes for data distribution, with notifications being visible only in certain scopes. More precisely, Fiege et al. (2002) define scope as *an abstraction that bundles a set of clients (producers and consumers) in that the visibility of notifications published by a producer is confined to the consumers belonging to the same scope as the producer; a scope can recursively be a member of other scopes.* In MUDEBS, filtering is impacted by the visibility of notifications that are analyzed according to several dimensions of scopes. A client advertises or subscribes by providing a filter tagged with a set of scopes, with at most one scope per dimension, e.g., interest in geographical scopes or areas belonging to end-users scopes or groups. A notification is visible to a client if it is visible in all the dimensions. In summary,

---

[8] muDEBS is part of the M4IoT platform: https://www-inf.it-sudparis.eu/m4iot/.

MUDEBS targets scalability by scoping the distribution of data between producers and consumers.

IoT data can be exploited by pervasive applications to detect the users' current situation and provide them with the relevant services corresponding to their precise needs. The threats to the users' privacy appear more clearly and Chabridon et al. (2014) have shown that QoC and privacy are closely related and must be addressed together in order to find a workable solution. As a first step, Lim et al. (2015) identified models for a first set of attributes to be specified in privacy policies, namely purpose (intention of use), visibility (who has access), and retention (for how long data may be retained). Following these models, IoT producers specify privacy requirements and QoC guarantees in producer context contracts that are then registered in MUDEBS as XACML policies.[9] On their side, IoT consumers express their QoC requirements and the privacy guarantees that they are committed to fulfilling in consumer context contracts, mentioning at least for what purpose they are requesting access to some specific IoT data. Privacy guarantees take the form of ABAC information registered with the subscription filters. QoC guarantees and requirements are expressed by following the QoCIM model (see Sect. 4.1). As a second step, Denis et al. (2020) studied confidentiality under the semi-trusted broker assumption in which brokers are considered honest-but-curious, i.e., brokers route the publications to the interested consumers, but they can make use of the data for their own interest. More precisely, confidentiality concerns encompass (1) part or all of the constraints of the subscriptions, (2) part or all the information in the publication that is used for routing against subscriptions, and (3) the payload of the publications. The solution proposed in MUDEBS adapts an existing attribute-based encryption scheme and combines it with data splitting, a non-cryptographic method called for alleviating the cost of encrypted matching. Data splitting enables forming groups of attributes sent apart over several independent broker networks. It also prevents the identification of an end-user, and only attributes are encrypted to prevent data leakage.

4.3 DeX Mediators

IoT devices employ middleware-layer protocols such as MQTT, CoAP, ZeroMQ, and more to interact with each other. These protocols support different Quality of Service (QoS) semantics. They define multiple data-serialization formats (e.g., JSON, XML, protobuf, etc.) and different payloads suitable for constrained or healthy devices and follow different interaction patterns such as request-reply and publish-subscribe. IoT systems include heterogeneous IoT devices employing any of those protocols. In many cases, new heterogeneous IoT devices may be added to an IoT system in an on-demand fashion. For instance, in the logistic chain

---

[9] https://docs.oasis-open.org/xacml/3.0/xacml-3.0-core-spec-os-en.html.

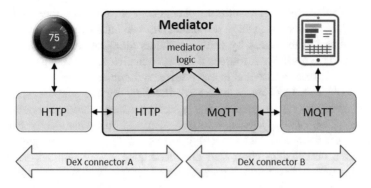

Fig. 1 Enabling data exchange via mediators

traceability scenario, IoT devices in the shipment must interact with the services of the IS that dynamically collect information for decision-making purposes. Therefore, generic, automated solutions must enable data exchange in such IoT systems.

The Data eXchange Mediator Synthesizer (DeXMS)[10] (Bouloukakis et al. 2019) addresses the heterogeneity of IoT devices and services by synthesizing software mediators. As depicted in Fig. 1, DeXMS relies on the Data eXchange (DeX) API, which implements POST and GET primitives for sending/receiving messages using existing IoT protocols such as CoAP, MQTT, XMPP, etc. In the illustration, the mediator converts temperature data from a package (in JSON format through the HTTP protocol) to be received from an IS dashboard (in XML format through the MQTT protocol). Considering a set of heterogeneous IoT devices that have to inter-connect with devices deployed in an IoT system, DeXMS accepts their input/output data representation models as input and synthesizes the required mediators. Based on the requirements defined in Sect. 2, DeXMS provides a semi-automated manner to tackle interoperability among devices employing middleware-layer protocols (classified to diverse interaction patterns). Regarding the application-layer, DeXMS enables developers to manually perform data mappings between applications semantics. More details on DeXMS can be found in the work of Bouloukakis et al. (2019).

4.4 QoDisco

A pervasive context encompasses a distributed plethora of heterogeneous resources (sensors, actuators, services) with different functionalities and communication

---

[10] https://gitlab.inria.fr/dexms.

protocols. In this scenario, a well-known challenge for both machines and users is finding, selecting, and using these resources. Discovering services play a significant role in addressing this issue by enabling clients (applications, middleware, end-users) to retrieve available resources based on complex search criteria considering contextual information essential in a pervasive environment.

QoDisco[11] is a QoC-aware federated discovery service supporting multiple-attribute searches, range queries, and synchronous/asynchronous operations. It encompasses an ontology-based information model for semantically describing resources, services, and QoC-related information. QoDisco is structured upon a distributed architecture composed of a federation of autonomous repositories cooperating with each other to perform data and service discovery tasks. It provides an API to perform discovery tasks in such repositories, and each repository provides operations for querying and updating records. Clients are responsible for semantically annotating resource data (such as the ones provided by sensors) by using the concepts of the QoDisco information model. When receiving a discovery request, QoDisco searches for resource descriptions or data stored in the available repositories, thereby hiding the heterogeneity.

The semantic description of resources defined by the QoDisco information model relies on: (1) the SAN ontology (Spalazzi et al. 2014), an extension of the W3C's SSN ontology (Barnaghi et al. 2011) that provides concepts, attributes, and properties to model both sensors and actuators; (2) part of the SOUPA ontology (Chen et al. 2005) aiming at including location-related concepts to describe spatial locations of entities in terms of latitude, longitude, altitude, distance, and surface, as well as symbolic representations of space and spatial relationships; (3) the OWL-S ontology for semantically modeling services exposed by the resources; and (4) part of the QoCIM meta-model (Marie et al. 2013) to describe QoC-related concerns (see Sect. 4.1). This information model supports the QoC management requirement and tackles data format heterogeneity using ontologies.

Due to the dynamic context in which the IoT resources operate, QoDisco handles both synchronous calls and asynchronous notifications. The former relies on request-reply interactions towards providing resource information at the moment of the search. The latter is based on publish-subscribe interactions to notify clients in case of resource removal, insertion, or update. More details on QoDisco can be found in the work of Gomes et al. (2019).

4.5   IoTVar

IoTVar[12] is a middleware that provides developers with abstractions for IoT variables. From a variable declaration, IoTVar automatically discovers matching

---

[11] https://github.com/porfiriogomes/qodisco.

[12] IoTVar is part of the M4IoT platform: https://www-inf.it-sudparis.eu/m4iot/.

data-producer objects and transparently deals with updates to these variables thanks to transparent interaction with IoT systems. IoTVar offers an abstraction level to interact with virtualized sensors. It drastically minimizes the number of lines of code to be written by the client application developer to obtain up-to-date sensor data from several hundreds of lines of code to a single dozen.

The IoTVar architecture has been designed to integrate new IoT platforms and IoT systems. For this purpose, it exposes an interface that can easily be implemented for integrating with new platforms. The architecture was focused not only on developing the IoT applications but also on expanding the middleware to support multiple IoT platforms. IoTVar is currently integrated with FIWARE, OneM2M (oneM2M Partners 2019), and MuDEBS (Conan et al. 2017) IoT platforms. More details on IoTVar can be found in the work of Borges et al. (2019).

IoTVar responds to some of the previously mentioned PIS requirements. The multiple IoT platforms supported by IoTVar have different data models and API access and use different protocols to retrieve sensor data. For the sake of interoperability, IoTVar includes data unmarshallers, IoT protocols handlers, and IoT API handlers, as well as it supports both publish-subscribe and request-reply interaction patterns to be chosen according to efficiency considerations. IoTVar also supports application development by providing an API accessible through code in the Java programming language and enabling IoT developers to access sensor data easily. The developer will declare environment variables by providing a simple IoT variable declaration. Those IoT variables will be automatically updated.

5 Open Challenges for Future PIS Middleware

Next-generation PIS are deployed at an unprecedented scale with components on connected mobile devices and remote servers in cloud and fog intermediaries. In this context, handling requirements from an end-to-end perspective is challenging. At the same time, mastering requirements such as privacy and sustainability becomes essential and even more complex. This section highlights some open challenges that can commission research on future PIS middleware.

5.1 Enabling End-to-End Interoperability

As mentioned in Sect. 3.3, existing middleware approaches enable interoperability at each layer (i.e., application, middleware, network) independently. However, enabling IoT interoperability requires introducing end-to-end approaches. This is challenging due to: (1) the difficulty to select a unique data model and IoT protocol to develop cross-domain IoT applications, which results in composing multiple IoT protocols and data models; (2) the existence of numerous IoT protocols to support diverse types of devices (healthy/constrained/tiny in terms of resources);

(3) the diversity of data models to cover multiple application domains (healthcare, autonomous driving, etc.); and (4) end-to-end approaches are usually developed for specific application domains (e.g., smart buildings) and it is difficult to adapt them to other domains. Therefore, advanced end-to-end interoperability approaches must be introduced while considering those challenges.

5.2 PIS Adaptive Middleware

Previous research on the so-called adaptive middleware can indeed contribute to support dynamic adaptation in PIS, including proposals on context-aware applications (Huebscher and McCann 2006), ubiquitous computing (Yau and Karim 2004), wireless sensor networks (Portocarrero et al. 2016), IoT (Cavalcanti et al. 2021), cyber-physical systems (García-Vallis and Baldoni 2015), and cloud computing (Rafique et al. 2017). *Adaptive middleware* can be defined as a kind of middleware that enables modifying the behavior of a distributed application in response to changes in requirements or operating conditions (Sadjadi and McKinley 2003). To the best of our knowledge, the literature has still not explored building adaptive middleware to support PIS and provide these systems with dynamic adaptation capabilities.

Designing adaptive middleware needs to consider some 5W1H (What? Who? Where? When? Why? How?) issues typically associated with self-adaptive software systems (Salehie and Tahvildari 2009). It is necessary to understand (1) the need for adapting the middleware to changes in application requirements and context, (2) the time at which the adaptation needs to be triggered, whether proactively or reactively, (3) the extent of the adaptation in terms of how many components should be subjected to the adaptation, and (4) how the adaptation actions can be executed and implemented (Rosa et al. 2020). Designing PIS middleware with adequate support for dynamic adaptation should hence cope with these issues.

5.3 Support to Develop PIS Relying on Middleware

Middleware platforms are well-acknowledged to leverage the development of distributed applications, but this does not seem to be the case for PIS yet. Indeed, there is still no available programming model for PIS relying on middleware while coping with the characteristics of this class of systems. Biegel and Cahill (2015) highlight that existing solutions and approaches in the literature are not currently able to address the requirements for PIS middleware comprehensively, but rather only a subset of them. The authors also point out the significant effort necessary from application developers to deal with these requirements, an issue that hampers a broader adoption of PIS middleware in industrial settings. Therefore, a programming model able to ease the development of PIS relying on middleware is desirable.

The development of PIS relying on middleware faces other challenges. On the one hand, the proliferation of physical devices and platforms to support PIS may lead these systems to become primarily vendor/platform- and hardware-specific (Taivalsaari and Mikkonen 2017). This may also pose difficulties in finding the most suitable solution (or set of solutions) for a specific application and deepen users' lack of experience and knowledge on understanding the implications for current and future needs. PIS middleware should hence enable applications to benefit from using different devices and platforms while relieving developers from dealing with their specificities through proper high-level abstractions.

5.4 Privacy and Security

Security for PIS is still a significant challenge as attacks are relatively easy in an open, connected world. Many devices were not designed for security, and their high number increases the attack surface, as well as their integration within the Internet that exposes them to numerous potential attackers. We underline some specific areas where research challenges need to be addressed by PIS middleware in the short term: (1) the need for low-cost cryptography primitives suitable for devices with limited resources; (2) security analysis of new low-power wireless wide area network technologies; and (3) the need for frameworks and protocols to facilitate the development of devices where security is considered from the design stage.

Considering privacy, our connected world has allowed unprecedented growth in personal data collection practices, with intrusion in our private life. The lack of transparency, the fact that many services and devices behave like black boxes, and the lack of user control raise major research challenges to enable PIS middleware to enforce data protection and privacy patterns. In addition, robust anonymization, which effectively resists deanonymization attacks while preserving data utility, remains an open research topic.

With resource-constrained devices and sustainability objectives, resource consumption of security and privacy solutions is gaining importance. We consider that this also opens some new research directions where concerns for security, privacy, and sustainability can be addressed jointly in PIS middleware.

5.5 Context Data Sampling and Filtering

As discussed in Sect. 3.5, many contributions exist that enable scaling PIS solutions deployed in Clouds. Among the next challenges, for scaling PIS deployed in highly distributed environments such as connected mobile devices and with fog intermediaries, the contextual data filtering module of a PIS middleware should strive to increase the system's scalability by controlling and reducing the amount of transmitted data. Giouroukis et al. (2020b) classify filtering techniques into (1) time-based, i.e., sending data is suppressed until certain time conditions become true, and (2) change-based, i.e., sending data is suppressed as long as the contextual data are equal or similar to that previously transmitted. Of course, any combination of time-based and change-based filtering techniques is possible. For example, in the illustrative logistic chain traceability system, some applications may request to receive location updates only if the new location is not identical to the previous one and if an interval of at least 10 min has elapsed.

Adaptive sampling is, of course, closely related to adaptive filtering. For instance, tuning sensor sampling frequency enforces network usage optimization and can be performed according to the frequency of requests from deployed software applications. As another significant outcome, PIS middleware obtains a self-adaptive platform with an extended sensor battery life while ensuring good data quality and freshness.

Put together, selection-based filtering of publish-subscribe systems enables the system to limit dissemination to some scopes, contrary to system-wide scoping. Context-based filtering uses context data of different context dimensions to route IoT data at the application layer. In contrast, adaptive filtering enables the system to decide whether some IoT data are worth passing on intermediaries, depending on whether a sensor value is similar to previous values or evolves predictably. These issues are still not solved and are certainly a very fruitful area for future research.

5.6 PIS Sustainability

In the last decade, the number of existing PIS has grown, coming with new facilities for the end-users and rising computer power demand. However, sustainability in IT is from now on a first-class concern for enterprises. This demand has to be taken into account by PIS middleware designers.

As seen in Sect. 3.6, many strategies have been proposed so far by middleware targeting energy efficiency. However, those strategies mainly target one of the components of the system. Considering energy efficiency at the scale of the whole system is still a challenge.

Even though middleware eases the task of application developers when dealing with energy efficiency, a developer may face difficulties in evaluating the energy consumption of the system. An important research direction to foster energy efficiency in PIS is providing energy-awareness at the middleware level. Some techniques such as static code analysis (Vekris et al. 2012) and profilers to detect software energy and performance bugs (Nistor and Ravindranath 2014) have been proposed in the last years aiming at statically easing the identification of energy-consuming components. Energy awareness may also be provided at runtime through abstractions expressing energy requirements and evaluating energy consumption. These abstractions based on measures and energy consumption models have yet to be integrated in middleware. We believe that energy-awareness may significantly increase the efficiency of the systems as the awareness brings a broader view of where and how the many resources (CPU, network, energy, etc.) used by an application are behaving in terms of energy consumption.

6 Conclusion

In this chapter, we have considered PIS middleware in the context of the IoT. This middleware provides applications with an easy integration of context data collected from connected objects spread over the Internet. This context comes with new challenges and requirements. In addition to context-awareness, middleware should tackle scalability, privacy and interoperability and provide applications with new abstractions representing the physical environment and ensure the quality of the data that may be used for decision-making.

We have shown through the state of the art that middleware has proposed semantic interoperability for handling heterogeneities and large-scale publish-subscribe architectures to tackle scalability. However, while middleware has already enabled new kinds of PIS in various domains such as transport traceability, healthcare, and smart cities, the middleware community still faces new challenges, such as providing high-level programming model for PIS, supporting PIS dynamic adaptation, disseminating and filtering large volumes of data, end-to-end privacy and interoperability handling, as well as enabling the deployment of sustainable applications.

Acknowledgments This work is a contribution to the Energy4Climate Interdisciplinary Center (E4C) of IP Paris and École des Ponts ParisTech, supported by 3rd Programme d'Investissements d'Avenir [ANR-18-EUR-0006-02]. It has been partially funded by the "Futur & Ruptures" program from Institut Mines-Télécom, Fondation Mines-Télécom, and Institut Carnot.

References

Aazam M, Islam SU, Lone ST, Abbas A (2020) Cloud of things (cot): Cloud-fog-IoT task offloading for sustainable internet of things. IEEE Transactions on Sustainable Computing pp 1–1, DOI https://doi.org/10.1109/TSUSC.2020.3028615

Ahmed M, Taconet C, Ould M, Chabridon S, Bouzeghoub A (2021) IoT Data Qualification for a Logistic Chain Traceability Smart Contract. Sensors 21(6):2239

Akkermans S, Bachiller R, Matthys N, Joosen W, Hughes D, Vučinić M (2016) Towards efficient publish-subscribe middleware in the IoT with IPv6 multicast. In: 2016 IEEE International Conference on Communications (ICC), pp 1–6

Alhirabi N, Rana O, Perera C (2020) Security and Privacy Requirements for the Internet of Things: A Survey. ACM Trans Internet Things 2(1):6:1–6:37

Aljeraisy A, Barati M, Rana O, Perera C (2021) Privacy Laws and Privacy by Design Schemes for the Internet of Things: A Developer's Perspective. ACM Comput Surv 54(5):102:1–102:38

Bacon J, Moody K, Bates J, Ma C, McNeil A, Seidel O, Spiteri M (2000) Generic support for distributed applications. Computer 33(3):68–76, DOI https://doi.org/10.1109/2.825698

Banks A, Gupta R (2014) Mqtt version 3.1. 1

Barnaghi P, et al. (2011) Semantic Sensor Network XG Final Report. Tech. rep., W3C, URL http://www.w3.org/2005/Incubator/ssn/XGR-ssn-20110628/

Bellavista P, Corradi A, Fanelli M, Foschini L (2012) A Survey of Context Data Distribution for Mobile Ubiquitous Systems. ACM Computing Survey 44(4):24:1–24:45

Biegel G, Cahill V (2007) Requirements for middleware for pervasive information systems. In: Pervasive Information Systems, M.E. Sharpe, Armonk, NY, pp 102–118

Biegel G, Cahill V (2015) Requirements for middleware for pervasive information systems. In: Kourouthanassis PE, Giaglis GM (eds) Pervasive information systems, Routledge, USA, pp 86–102

Binder W, Suri N (2009) Green computing: Energy consumption optimized service hosting. In: 35th Conference on Current Trends in Theory and Practice of Computer Science (SOFSEM), Spindleruv Mlýn, Czech Republic, Springer, Lecture Notes in Computer Science, vol 5404, pp 117–128

Blair GS, Schmidt DC, Taconet C (2016) Middleware for Internet distribution in the context of cloud computing and the Internet of Things - Editorial Introduction. Ann des Télécommunications 71(3–4):87–92

Borges PV, Taconet C, Chabridon S, Conan D, Batista T, Cavalcante E, Batista C (2019) Mastering Interactions with Internet of Things Platforms through the IoTVar Middleware. In: 13th Int. Conf. on Ubiquitous Computing and Ambient Intelligence (UCAmI), MDPI Proceedings, vol 31, p 78

Bouloukakis G, Georgantas N, Ntumba P, Issarny V (2019) Automated Synthesis of Mediators for Middleware-layer Protocol Interoperability in the IoT. Future Generation Computer Systems 101:1271–1294

Bouloukakis G, et al. (2022) DeXMS, The Data eXchange Mediator Synthesizer Framework. https://gitlab.inria.fr/dexms

Buchholz T, Kupper A, Schiffers M (2003) Quality of context information: What it is and why we need it. In: 10th Int. Workshop of the HP OpenView University Association (HPOVUA), Geneva, Switzerland

Castellani AP, Fossati T, Loreto S (2012) HTTP-CoAP cross protocol proxy: an implementation viewpoint. In: 9th IEEE Int. Conf. on Mobile Ad-Hoc and Sensor Systems, (MASS)

Cavalcanti D, Carvalho R, Rosa N (2021) Adaptive middleware of things. In: Proceedings of the 2021 IEEE Symposium on Computers and Communications, IEEE, USA

Cavoukian A, Dixon M (2013) Privacy and security by design: An enterprise architecture approach. Tech. rep., Information and Privacy Commissioner of Ontario, Canada, https://www.ipc.on.ca

Cecchinel C, Fouquet F, Mosser S, Collet P (2019) Leveraging live machine learning and deep sleep to support a self-adaptive efficient configuration of battery powered sensors. Future Generation Computer Systems 92:225–240

Chabridon S, Laborde R, Desprats T, Oglaza A, Marie P, Machara Marquez S (2014) A Survey on Addressing Privacy together with Quality of Context for Context Management in the Internet of Things. Annals of Telecommunications 69(1):47–62

Chaudhuri A, Cavoukian A (2018) The Proactive and Preventive Privacy (3P) Framework for IoT Privacy by Design. EDPACS 57(1):1–16

Chen H, Finin T, Joshi A (2005) The SOUPA ontology for Pervasive Computing. In: Ontologies for agents: Theory and experiences, Whitestein Series in Software Agent Technologies, Switzerland, pp 233–258

Colesky M, Hoepman JH, Boesch C, Kargl F, Kopp H, Mosby P, Métayer DL, Drozd O, del Álamo JM, Martín YS, Caiza JC, Gupta M, Doty N (2022) Privacy Patterns. https://privacypatterns.org

Collina M, Corazza GE, Vanelli-Coralli A (2012) Introducing the QEST broker: Scaling the iot by bridging MQTT and REST. In: 23rd IEEE Int. Symposium on Personal, Indoor and Mobile Radio Communications (PIMRC)

Compton M, Barnaghi P, Bermudez L, García-Castro R, Corcho O, Cox S, Graybeal J, Hauswirth M, Henson C, Herzog A, Huang V, Janowicz K, Kelsey WD, Le Phuoc D, Lefort L, Leggieri M, Neuhaus H, Nikolov A, Page K, Passant A, Sheth A, Taylor K (2012) The SSN ontology of the W3C semantic sensor network incubator group. Journal of Web Semantics 17

Conan D, Lim L, Taconet C, Chabridon S, Lecocq C (2017) A Multiscale Approach for a Distributed Event-Based Internet of Things. In: Proc. of 15th IEEE Int. Conf. on Pervasive Intelligence and Computing (PICOM), Orlando, USA, pp 844–852

Conan D, et al. (2022) M4IoT Frameworks, Middleware for the Internet of Things. https://www-inf.it-sudparis.eu/m4iot/

Cugola G, Margara A (2012) Processing Flows of Information: From Data Stream to Complex Event Processing. ACM Computing Survey 44(3):15:1–15:62

Daniele L, den Hartog F, Roes J (2015) The Smart Appliances REFerence (SAREF) Ontology. In: Proc. of International Workshop Formal Ontologies Meet Industries

Delicato F, Pires P, Batista T (2013) Middleware Solutions for the Internet of Things. Springer Briefs in Computer Science, Springer

Deng M, Wuyts K, Scandariato R, Preneel B, Joosen W (2011) A privacy threat analysis framework: Supporting the elicitation and fulfillment of privacy requirements. Requirements Engineering 16(1):3–32

Denis N, Chaffardon P, Conan D, Laurent M, Chabridon S, Leneutre J (2020) Privacy-preserving Content-based Publish/Subscribe with Encrypted Matching and Data Splitting. In: 17th Int. Joint Conf. on e-Business and Telecommunications (SECRYPT), INSTICC, SciTePress, Paris, France, pp 405–414

Derhamy H, Eliasson J, Delsing J (2017) IoT interoperability—on-demand and low latency transparent multiprotocol translator. IEEE Internet of Things Journal 4(5)

Dey A, Abowd G (2000) Towards a better understanding of context and context-awareness. In: Proceedings of the PrCHI 2000 Workshop on the What, Who, Where, When and How of Context-Awareness

Dias D, Delicato F, Pires P, Rocha A, Nakagawa E (2020) An Overview of Reference Architectures for Cloud of Things. In: Proc. of the 35th ACM Symposium on Applied Computing, New York, NY, USA, pp 1498–1505

Duboc L, Rosenblum D, Wicks T (2007) A Framework for Characterization and Analysis of Software System Scalability. In: Proceedings of the the 6th Joint Meeting of the European Software Engineering Conference and the ACM SIGSOFT Symposium on The Foundations of Software Engineering, Dubrovnik, Croatia, pp 375–384

Endler M, Silva F (2018) Past, Present and Future of the ContextNet IoMT Middleware. Open Journal of Internet Of Things (OJIOT) 4(1):7–23, Special Issue: Int. Workshop on Very Large Internet of Things (VLIoT), in conjunction with the VLDB Conference in Rio de Janeiro, Brazil

Eugster P, Felber P, Guerraoui R, Kermarrec AM (2003) The Many Faces of Publish/Subscribe. ACM Computing Survey 35(2)

Ferreboeuf H, Efoui-Hess M, Verne X (2021) Impact environnemental du numérique : Tendances à 5 ans et gouvernance de la 5G. Tech. rep., The Shift project

Fette I (2011) The websocket protocol

Fiege L, Mezini M, Mühl G, Buchmann A (2002) Engineering Event-Based Systems with Scopes. In: Magnusson B (ed) Proc. 16th European Conference on Object-Oriented Programming, Springer, Málaga, Spain, Lecture Notes in Computer Science, vol 2374, pp 309–333

Fremantle P, Scott PJ (2017) A survey of secure middleware for the internet of things. PeerJ Comput Sci 3:e114

García-Vallis M, Baldoni R (2015) Adaptive middleware design for CPS: Considerations on the OS, resource managers, and the network at run-time. In: 14th Int. Workshop on Adaptive and Reflective Middleware, ACM, USA, DOI 10.1145/2834965.2834968

Georgantas N, Bouloukakis G, Beauche S, Issarny V (2013) Service-oriented distributed applications in the future internet: The case for interaction paradigm interoperability. In: Lau K, Lamersdorf W, Pimentel E (eds) 2nd European Conf. on Service-Oriented and Cloud Computing, ESOCC, vol 8135

Giouroukis D, Dadiani A, Traub J, Zeuch S, Markl V (2020a) A Survey of Adaptive Sampling and Filtering Algorithms for the Internet of Things. In: Proceedings of the 14th ACM International Conference on Distributed and Event-Based Systems, Association for Computing Machinery, New York, NY, USA, DEBS '20, p 27–38, DOI https://doi.org/10.1145/3401025.3403777

Giouroukis D, Dadiani A, Traub J, Zeuch S, Markl V (2020b) A Survey of Adaptive Sampling and Filtering Algorithms for the Internet of Things. In: Proc. 14th ACM International Conference on Distributed Event-Based Systems, Montreal, Quebec, Canada, pp 27–38

Gomes B, Muniz LCM, da Silva e Silva FJ, dos Santos DV, Lopes RF, Coutinho LR, Carvalho FO, Endler M (2017a) A Middleware with Comprehensive Quality of Context Support for the Internet of Things Applications. Sensors 17(12):2853

Gomes P, Cavalcante E, Batista T, Taconet C, Conan D, Chabridon S, Delicato F, Pires P (2019) A semantic-based discovery service for the internet of things. Journal of Internet Services and Applications 10

Gomes P, et al. (2017b) QoDisco. https://github.com/porfiriogomes/qodisco

Gruber TR (1993) A translation approach to portable ontology specifications. Knowledge Acquisition 5(2)

Hassan MG, Hirst R, Siemieniuch C, Zobaa A (2009) The impact of energy awareness on energy efficiency. Int Journal of Sustainable Engineering 2(4):284–297

Henricksen K, Indulska J (2004) Modelling and using imperfect context information. In: Pervasive Computing and Communications Workshops, 2004. Proceedings of the Second IEEE Annual Conference on, pp 33–37

Howard M, Lipner S (2006) The Security Development Lifecycle. Microsoft Press, USA

Huebscher MC, McCann JA (2006) An adaptive middleware framework for context-aware applications. Pervasive and Ubiquitous Computing 10:12–20

ISO/IEC 25010 (2011) Systems and software engineering - Systems and software Quality Requirements and Evaluation (SQuaRE) - System and software quality models. Tech. rep., ISO

ISO/IEC 25012 (2008) Data Quality model. URL https://iso25000.com/index.php/en/iso-25000-standards/iso-25012

Ivarez-Valera HH, Dalmau M, Roose P, Herzog C (2019) The architecture of kaligreen V2: A middleware aware of hardware opportunities to save energy. In: Alsmirat MA, Jararweh Y (eds) Sixth International Conference on Internet of Things: Systems, Management and Security, IOTSMS 2019, Granada, Spain, October 22–25, 2019, IEEE, pp 79–86

Jagarlamudi KS, Zaslavsky A, Loke SW, Hassani A, Medvedev A (2021) Quality and Cost Aware Service Selection in IoT-Context Management Platforms. In: Int. Conferences on Internet of Things (iThings), Green Computing & Communications (GreenCom), Cyber, Physical & Social Computing (CPSCom), Smart Data (SmartData) and Congress on Cybermatics (Cybermatics), IEEE, pp 89–98

Janowicz K, Haller A, Cox SJ, Le Phuoc D, Lefrançois M (2019) SOSA: A lightweight ontology for sensors, observations, samples, and actuators. Journal of Web Semantics 56

Joint Committee for Guides in Metrology (2008) Evaluation of measurement data - guide to the expression of uncertainty in measurement. https://www.bipm.org/documents/20126/2071204/JCGM_100_2008_E.pdf

Kalbarczyk T, Julien C (2018) Omni: An Application Framework for Seamless Device-to-Device Interaction in the Wild. In: 19th Int. Middleware Conf., ACM, Rennes, France, p 161–173

Karagiannis V, et al. (2015) A Survey on Application Layer Protocols for the Internet of Things. Transaction on IoT and Cloud Computing 3:11–17

Kargl F, Métayer DL, Gupta M, Colesky M, Hoepman JH, del Álamo JM, Martín YS, Boesch C, Kopp H, Mosby P, Doty N, Drozd O (2022) Privacy Patterns, Collecting Patterns for Better Privacy. https://privacypatterns.eu

Kermarrec AM, Triantafillou P (2013) XL Peer-to-Peer Pub/Sub Systems. ACM Computing Survey 46(2):16:1–16:45

Kourouthanassis PE, Giaglis GM (2007) Pervasive Information Systems. Advances in Management Information Systems (AMIS) Vol. 10:. M.E. Sharpe, Armonk, NY

Kourouthanassis PE, Giaglis GM (2015) Toward pervasiveness: Four eras of information systems development. In: Kourouthanassis PE, Giaglis GM (eds) Pervasive information systems, Routledge, USA, pp 3–25

Krakowiak S (2009) Middleware Architecture with Patterns and Frameworks. https://lig-membres. imag.fr/krakowia/Files/MW-Book/Chapters/Preface/preface.html

Lim L, Marie P, Conan D, Chabridon S, Desprats T, Manzoor A (2015) Enhancing context data distribution for the internet of things using qoc-awareness and attribute-based access control. Annals of Telecommunications pp 1–12

López J, Rios R, Bao F, Wang G (2017) Evolving privacy: From sensors to the internet of things. Future Gener Comput Syst 75:46–57

Luckner M, Grzenda M, Kunicki R, Legierski J (2014) IoT Architecture for Urban Data-Centric Services and Applications. ACM Transactions on Internet Technology 20(3):29:1–29:30

Mahnke W, Leitner SH, Damm M (2009) OPC unified architecture. Springer Science & Business Media

Marie P, Desprats T, Chabridon S, Sibilla M (2013) QoCIM: A meta-model for Quality of Context. In: Modeling and Using Context, LNCS, vol 8175

Marie P, Desprats T, Chabridon S, Sibilla M (2016) Enabling Self-Configuration of QoC-Centric Fog Computing Entities. In: Intl IEEE Conf. on Advanced and Trusted Computing, Smart World Congress (UIC/ATC/ScalCom/CBDCom/IoP/SmartWorld), Toulouse, France

Negash B, Rahmani AM, Westerlund T, Liljeberg P, Tenhunen H (2015) Lisa: Lightweight internet of things service bus architecture. Procedia Computer Science 52

Negash B, Rahmani AM, Westerlund T, Liljeberg P, Tenhunen H (2016) Lisa 2.0: lightweight internet of things service bus architecture using node centric networking. Journal of Ambient Intelligence and Humanized Computing 7(3)

Nistor A, Ravindranath L (2014) SunCat: Helping developers understand and predict performance problems in smartphone applications. In: Int. Symp. on Software Testing and Analysis, ACM, USA, p 282–292

Noureddine A, Rouvoy R, Seinturier L (2013) A review of middleware approaches for energy management in distributed environments. Softw Pract Exp 43(9):1071–1100

OASIS (2012) Advanced Message Queuing Protocol (AMQP) version 1.0. http://docs.oasis-open. org/amqp/core/v1.0/os/amqp-core-complete-v1.0-os.pdf

de Oliveira EA, Delicato F, Mattoso M (2020) An energy-aware data cleaning workflow for real-time stream processing in the internet of things. In: Anais do IV Workshop de Computação Urbana, SBC, Porto Alegre, RS, Brasil, pp 71–83

OMG (2015) Data Distribution Service, v. 1.4. https://www.omg.org/spec/DDS/

Padhy S, Chang HY, Hou TF, Chou J, King CT, Hsu CH (2017) A Middleware Solution for Optimal Sensor Management of IoT Applications on LTE Devices. In: Quality, Reliability, Security and Robustness in Heterogeneous Networks (QSHINE), vol 199, Springer, pp 283–292

Pang C, Hindle A, Adams B, Hassan AE (2016) What do programmers know about software energy consumption? IEEE Software 33(03):83–89

Paradis CV, Kazman R, Tamburri DA (2021) Architectural tactics for energy efficiency: Review of the literature and research roadmap. In: 54th Hawaii International Conference on System Sciences (HICSS), pp 1–10

oneM2M Partners (2019) oneM2M Services Platform. Release 3

Pasricha S (2018) Overcoming Energy and Reliability Challenges for IoT and Mobile Devices with Data Analytics. In: 31st Int. Conf. on VLSI Design (VLSID)

Penzenstadler B (2015) From requirements engineering to green requirements engineering. In: Calero C, Piattini M (eds) Green in Software Engineering, Springer

Perera C, Zaslavsky AB, Christen P, Georgakopoulos D (2014) Context aware computing for the internet of things: A survey. IEEE Commun Surv Tutorials 16(1):414–454

Perera C, Qin Y, Estrella J, Reiff-Marganiec S, Vasilakos A (2017) Fog Computing for Sustainable Smart Cities: A Survey. ACM Computing Survey 50(3):32:1–32:43

Portocarrero JMT, Delicato FC, Pires PF, Rodrigues TC, Batista TV (2016) SAMSON: Self-adaptive middleware for wireless sensor networks. In: 31st Annual ACM Symposium on Applied Computing, ACM, USA

Rafique A, Van Landuyt D, Reniers V, Jossen W (2017) Towards an adaptive middleware for efficient multi-cloud data storage. In: 4th Workshop on CrossCloud Infrastructures & Platforms, ACM, USA

Raychoudhury V, Cao J, Kumar M, Zhang D (2013) Middleware for pervasive computing: A survey. Pervasive Mob Comput 9(2):177–200

Rosa N, Cavalcanti D, Campos G, Silva A (2020) Adaptive middleware in Go - a software architecture approach. Journal of Internet Services and Applications 11(3), DOI https://doi.org/10.1186/s13174-020-00124-5

Roth FM, Becker C, Vega G, Lalanda P (2018) XWARE - A customizable interoperability framework for pervasive computing systems. Pervasive Mob Comput 47

Sadjadi SM, McKinley PK (2003) A survey of adaptive middleware. Tech. rep., Michigan State University, USA

Saint-Andre P (2011) Extensible messaging and presence protocol (xmpp): Core

Salehie M, Tahvildari L (2009) Self-adaptive Software: Landscape and Research Challenges. ACM Transactions on Autonomous and Adaptive Systems 4(2)

Sarkar C, Rao VS, Venkatesha Prasad R, Das SN, Misra S, Vasilakos A (2016) Vsf: An energy-efficient sensing framework using virtual sensors. IEEE Sensors Journal 16(12):5046–5059, DOI https://doi.org/10.1109/JSEN.2016.2546839

Satyanarayanan M (2001a) Pervasive computing: vision and challenges. Personal Communications, IEEE 8(4):10–17, DOI https://doi.org/10.1109/98.943998

Satyanarayanan M (2001b) Pervasive Computing: Vision and Challenges. IEEE Personal Communications 8(4):10–17

Sedlmeir J, Buhl HU, Fridgen G, Keller R (2020) The energy consumption of blockchain technology: beyond myth. Business & Information Systems Engineering 62(6):599–608

Shekhar S, Chhokra A, Sun H, Gokhale A, Dubey A, Koutsoukos X (2019) URMILA: A Performance and Mobility-Aware Fog/Edge Resource Management Middleware. In: 22nd IEEE Int. Symposium on Real-Time Distributed Computing (ISORC), pp 118–125

Shelby Z, et al. (2014) The constrained application protocol (coap)

Song Z, Le M, Kwon YW, Tilevich E (2017) Extemporaneous micro-mobile service execution without code sharing. In: 2017 IEEE 37th International Conference on Distributed Computing Systems Workshops (ICDCSW), pp 181–186, DOI https://doi.org/10.1109/ICDCSW.2017.70

Spalazzi L, Taccari G, Bernardini A (2014) An internet of things ontology for earthquake emergency evaluation and response. In: Proceedings of the 2014 International Conference on Collaboration Technologies and Systems (CTS 2014), pp 528–534

Taivalsaari A, Mikkonen T (2017) A roadmap to the Programmable World: Software challenges in the IoT era. IEEE Software 34(1):72–80, DOI https://doi.org/10.1109/MS.2017.26

Teixeira S, Agrizzi BA, Filho JGP, Rossetto S, Pereira ISA, Costa PD, Branco AF, Martinelli RR (2020) LAURA architecture: Towards a simpler way of building situation-aware and business-aware IoT applications. Journal of Systems and Software 161:110494

Truong HL, Dustdar S (2015) Principles for engineering IoT cloud systems. IEEE Cloud Computing 2(2):68–76, DOI https://doi.org/10.1109/MCC.2015.23

Vekris P, Jhala R, Lerner S, Agarwal Y (2012) Towards verifying Android apps for the absence of no-sleep energy bugs. In: Proceedings of the 2012 Workshop on Power-Aware Computing and Systems, USENIX Association, USA

Verdecchia R, Lago P, Ebert C, de Vries C (2021) Green it and green software. IEEE Software 38(6):7–15, DOI https://doi.org/10.1109/MS.2021.3102254

Weiser M (1991) The Computer for the 21st Century. Scientific American, Special Issue on Communications, Computers, and Networks 265(3):66–75

Yau SS, Karim F (2004) An adaptive middleware for context-sensitive communications for real-time applications in ubiquitous computing environments. Real-Time Systems 26:29–61

Yus R, Bouloukakis G, Mehrotra S, Venkatasubramanian N (2019) Abstracting interactions with IoT devices towards a semantic vision of smart spaces. In: 6th ACM Int. Conf. on Systems for Energy-Efficient Buildings, Cities, and Transportation, BuildSys

Zeeb E, Bobek A, Bohn H, Golatowski F (2007) Service-oriented architectures for embedded systems using devices profile for web services. In: 21st International Conference on Advanced Information Networking and Applications Workshops (AINAW'07), IEEE, vol 1, pp 956–963

Edge Computing and Learning

Philippe Lalanda

1 Introduction

The massive deployment of intelligent and communicating objects in our living environments generates immense quantities of data, unmatched in the past (Becker et al. 2019). This data, collected on the field, provides past, present and future information on physical phenomena and running infrastructures, but also on activities and behaviour of people. This information, which can be sensitive and private, must be secured so that it cannot be acquired by parties not entitled to it. This is for example the case for data related to individuals, such as medical data or location data, but also for confidential data concerning organizations, whether private or governmental.

Many of these smart objects are now connected to information systems through successive gateways and networks. This makes it possible to set up new high value-added services allowing, for example, to bring more flexibility to production activities, to better monitor the health of patients, or to set up more intelligent living spaces like smart cities, smart homes, or smart stations. It is safe to assume that most leading-edge companies could no longer do without this information.

Today, information systems are often located in cloud data centers. This implies constant and costly communications between connected objects and data centers that are usually located at a great distance. This architectural solution does not scale well and is challenged by the massive increase in data to be transported and stored in the cloud. Also, it appears that, in many cases, data is badly identified and looses its relevance rather quickly. Essentially, the data is kept for fear of losing important information. This only further clutters the communication channels and storage devices.

P. Lalanda (✉)
Grenoble University, Grenoble, France
e-mail: philippe.lalanda@univ-grenoble-alpes.fr

In fact, with the installation of tens of billions of connected objects, it is simply not appropriate to upload all the data that can be collected on the field to cloud data centers. There are several reasons for this. First, this architecture leads to a central collection of data, which is problematic for privacy-sensitive users. Also, this approach is very expensive. For instance, running a single Amazon EC2 instance of type "a1.2xlarge" with 8 cores and 16 GiB RAM costs 0.23 dollar per hour. Finally, in addition to that, recent trends in pervasive computing, like augmented reality and machine learning for instance, increase the number of applications that require fast processing of large amounts of data captured by devices. Analysing this data in the cloud does not meet the response time requirements of these applications due to the high communication latency between the devices and the cloud infrastructure (Sarkar et al. 2018). The same applies for highly interactive applications or games that require fast responses (Choy et al. 2012).

This major evolution, in both the amount of data and the application needs, has marked the end of all-cloud solutions and the inevitable emergence of more decentralized architectures where computations are done near the data sources. This new architectural approach is based on edge computing (Shi and Dustdar 2016; Garcia Lopez et al. 2015; Vaquero and Rodero-Merino 2015; Varghese et al. 2016), which refers to all the enabling technologies allowing computation to be performed at the edge of the network. It can be defined as any computing and network resources along the path between data sources and cloud infrastructures (Shi and Dustdar 2016; Shi et al. 2016). Typical resource providers in edge computing environments are electronic boxes of various types, personal computers, HMIs, smartphones, and even more powerfull "regional" servers, attached to cellular base stations for instance, that are in the close vicinity of the data sources. As we will see in more details, edge computing improves latency and security. It also leads to a better utilization of existing hardware (e.g., unused office PCs) (Hasan et al. 2015; Miluzzo et al. 2012) and economic benefits for both consumers and providers (Miluzzo et al. 2012; Fernando et al. 2012).

The aim of this chapter is to study this trend towards more distributed architectures and to study the associated software challenges. It is also to present a second major trend, namely the use of AI techniques on the edge. We will see that the effects of this second major evolution are profound. They call into question the software techniques currently used for the development and deployment of pervasive applications. This chapter is organized as follows. First, the notion of edge is defined and illustrated with examples from different pervasive spaces. Then, the main challenges related to the implementation of pervasive applications on the edge are presented. The solutions provided by the current pervasive platforms will then be detailed. Finally, we will turn to the notion of machine learning on the edge. We will show the main challenges at the different stages of the application lifecycle and outline some solutions currently being explored.

2   Edge Computing in Pervasive Computing

2.1   *Principles and Examples*

As introduced, edge computing is not a technique per se, but rather an architectural pattern that aims to decentralize calculations and data management as close as possible to the field devices. This decentralization is done opportunistically according to the available machines in the vicinity of the data sources and to the available networks. This results in very varied and often heterogeneous software architectures. The availability of appropriate resources is highly dependent on the domains, but also on technological opportunities. For example, in the Telco domain, the massive deployment of cellular based stations has made possible the development of MEC (multi-access edge computing) where new services for specific customers or classes of customers are now installed.

The use of edge computing is now a reality in many areas such as smart homes, smart buildings, smart cities, smart cars, or smart manufacturing. Let us take two examples to illustrate this point. Let us start with the smart home domain which is informative and illustrative. A smart home is a house or an apartment equipped with electronic devices providing sensing and actuating capabilities. Although most existing homes were not designed to be smart, the emergence of low consumption wireless devices has allowed the easy instrumentation of homes and the development of increasingly intelligent services. These services, however, are characterized by stringent requirements regarding security, response times or interaction facilities. For example, the detection of a fall must be done as soon as possible and should not be revealed to unauthorized persons. Also, in general, it is often necessary to have smooth interactions with the inhabitants to allow a good acceptance of the technology, which implies very short response times.

There is actually no shortage of computer resources in smart homes. Precisely, depending on the configuration, the edge infrastructure can include the following elements (see Fig. 1):

- smart communication-enable devices capable of hosting significant pieces of code like some connected cameras for example,

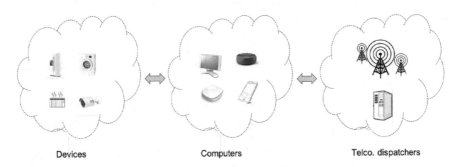

Devices   Computers   Telco. dispatchers

Fig. 1 Smart Home Computing resources

- electronic appliances like Internet or TV boxes. Such boxes host more and more applications related, for instance, to home automation or to the safety or well-being of people.
- vocal assistants are getting more and more popular and can also host applications just like boxes.
- laptop or desktop computers. Such computers can also run various comfort, security or automation applications. WiFi signals between Internet boxes and personal computers can even be used to detect movements or identify people.
- smartphones and tablets. Such devices, more and more powerful, are able to run the above mentioned applications but also resource intensive games or augmented reality functions.
- telecom dispatchers located in the close neighborhood. Such equipment is regularly upgraded by the operators to accommodate more and more network functions but also applications. They can, for example, perform added-value analytic on the electrical, gas or water consumption in a house.

It should be noted that edge computers are not just about CPU performances. They must integrate various communication protocols, wired or wireless, and advanced middleware to support the deployment, execution and adaptation of applications. We will come back to this fundamental point later in this chapter.

Let us now turn to a second example, Industry 4.0. The purpose of this initiative is to bring together new technologies and production processes to enable the emergence of smart, connected manufacturing. The term, coined in 2011 by a government-funded German project, refers to what could be the fourth industrial revolution (Forschungsunion 2013). Industry 4.0 envisions new production techniques, new materials, and the generalized adoption of digital technologies. We focus here on the latter point, and in particular on the adoption of dense and pervasive networks of sensors and actuators in industrial environments in order to complement existing devices and systems. The generalized use of sensors/actuators allows the integration of field devices controlling operations on a plant floor and supervision systems, usually located in IT facilities. Among many benefits, such integration allows the systematic oversight and improvement of production activities and resource management and an overall increase in safety and sustainability of production systems. It also leads to more flexibility in production processes, which can be reconfigured to meet changing demands and enable novel products.

Given this new context, the notion of edge is now prevalent in manufacturing production environments. These environments are characterized by a great heterogeneity, but we can nevertheless identify some common computing nodes that can host edge-type functions (see Fig. 2). This is the case for example of the following elements:

- desktop computers. Such computers are usually quite numerous in the plant floor and not used at full power. They can house various analytic allowing to follow and possibly adjust the processes in progress.
- smartphone and tablets. These devices are now heavily used in the plant floor, in particular to run augmented reality applications in order to get information without opening any industrial box for instance.

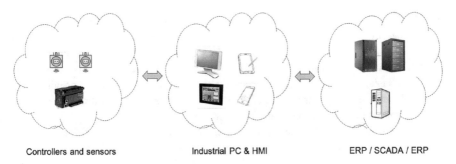

Controllers and sensors   Industrial PC & HMI   ERP / SCADA / ERP

Fig. 2 Smart Manufacturing resources

- HMI devices. These appliances are very present in production environments and constitute prime computing and storage resources. They are often quite powerful and, above all, are usually connected to a number of production equipment via integrated fieldbus connectors.
- IT servers. Several major software packages, such as MES (Manufacturing Execution System), ERP (Enterprise resource Planing) or SCADA (Supervisory Control and Data Acquisition), run on servers located near the automation islands, usually in the same building. These servers are increasingly used to deploy new software functions.

It is very interesting to note that the new sensors integrated on the plant floor must not interfere with the control functions. They provide different information that allows, for example, to set up analytics or to better configure manufacturing devices (Lalanda et al. 2017), but they are not intended to replace the current controllers like PLCs (Programmable Logic Controllers) for instance.

There are many other areas today where edge infrastructures are put in place successfully. For instance, autonomous vehicles rely more and more on edge resources in order to process big amount of data in real time. Data collected from in-vehicle sensors are processed locally in order to reduce latency and to deal with intermittent network connection. Also, autonomous vehicles are able to opportunistically use edge servers located in the vicinity to offload some computing or receive software updates. In another very popular domain, content delivery networks have deployed servers situated close to the users in order to allow rapid loading of websites and to support smooth video streaming.

2.2 Terminology

The great diversity of the domains and their use of the edge have led to the introduction of particular terminologies. In particular, the terms device edge, far edge and near edge are often used today:

- The Device edge, also called the IoT (Internet of Things) edge, includes low to medium power computers, directly connected to sensors/actuators by non-Internet protocols like field buses or WiFi. They correspond for instance to Internet boxes and smartphones in a smart home, or HMI and tablets in a smart plant. These are the elements closest to data sources and are usually provide ultra low latency and high throughput. Due to their geographical location, they provide optimal conditions for managing data security.
- The Far Edge, also called user edge, corresponds to powerful computing infrastructures that are deployed purposefully in the vicinity of the data sources, typically within a distance of some kilometers. They usually provide low latency, good throughput and also high scalability. For example, telecom companies may deploy far edge facilities in the cell phone towers they own, near the mobile base stations. Such infrastructures can also be found in large factories, big shopping centers or smart buildings. Far edge computers are designed to run resource-intensive applications that are specific to the location in which they are deployed.
- The Near Edge, also called enterprise edge, corresponds very powerful computing infrastructures that are deployed in a central location, usually connected to one of several Far Edge facilities. In fact, they look like small data centers designed to run generic services needed by the applications deployed on Device or Far edges. They generally provide very large computing and storage capacities.

It clearly appears here that the notion of edge covers a great diversity of locations and technologies. Edge infrastructures are actually installed in order to meet the needs but also to the financial resources of the owner companies. Typically, Near Edge infrastructures are only set up and managed by large companies that can afford to own them. Gaming, Live video streaming applications are good examples of applications that require the installation of advanced infrastructures both in the Near and Far edges.

3 Edge Pervasive Applications

Executing services at the edge and managing their life cycle is however challenging due to the dynamic, heterogeneous, and stochastic nature of the pervasive computing environments. This is further complicated by the fact that some edge computers have limited resources that must be managed explicitly. In addition, developers and administrators can no longer benefit from advanced services provided by cloud infrastructures and must use *edge-specific* tools that are often less sophisticated. As we will see here, there is nevertheless a rapid and significant improvement in these tools, often inspired by those previously developed for the cloud.

3.1 Challenges

3.1.1 Application Design

A first challenge, of course, is the definition of distributed architectures where computation and data management are appropriately distributed between devices, edge resources and cloud data centers. Such architectures are dependent on the targeted applications and are difficult to generalize from one domain to another. Also, the optimal distribution of computational and data oriented components may evolve over time. Today, there are a number of research works around the dynamic and autonomic distribution of these architectural elements along a device/edge/cloud continuum (Shi and Dustdar 2016).

Another issue is the design and implementation of applications, or parts of applications, that are intended to be placed on edge machines. They are usually executed on heterogeneous computers, often limited in terms of resources. This imposes strong constraints on the development teams regarding the programming language, the COTS (Components Off The Shelves) and the architectural patterns that can be used. For instance, a language as popular as Java is not well suited to constrained environments because of its heavy software stack. Similarly, some communication middleware can be too costly in terms of memory footprint or CPU required. These constraints concerning the tools and patterns that can be used also extend to deployment, updates and monitoring activities.

3.1.2 Application Security

Security is a major concern for any pervasive system. It is true that, by nature, edge computing considerably limits the transfer of data to remote servers, and thus significantly reduces the risks of interception or tampering. But, in a way, the security problems are partly transferred from the network to the edge computers, which can result in centralized hotspots for data security. These machines must be perfectly secure to counter any malicious attack. Remember that pervasive data, in a house or a factory, betrays the activities and habits of the occupants and, as a consequence, are highly prized.

Securing an edge computer, like a gateway for instance, is particularly costly and has a profound impact on all enclosing developments. It is indeed a matter of securing both the services provided by the computer (communication, middleware for execution, deployment, etc.) and all the applications. Concerning the latter, all the internal software components and their interaction must be secured. This requires specific architectural patterns and techniques, high-level skills and often leads to long development times. Nevertheless, despite all these difficulties, advanced security is a requirement that often comes first in many industries when it comes to deploying applications on the edge (Lalanda et al. 2021).

3.1.3 Application Data

Another major constraint is directly related to the quality, dynamism and hetero-geneity of the data. Regarding quality, cleaning data is a critical first step since it can be incomplete, uncertain or noisy. Pre-processing data is thus necessary to obtain reliable and well presented data. In addition, some data is simply not available on all environments or it may come and go depending on the availability of certain sensors. Recovery mechanisms, sometimes complex, must be put in place at the edge or a the applications levels to avoid crashes when data is not or no longer available. This is generally more difficult than in the cloud where applications are not directly connected to data sources but rather to databases.

The notion of data model, that is the way data is structured and named, is also of major importance. In most domains, such as manufacturing, there are several standards for data models, pushed by competing vendors. The correspondence between data collected on a field bus, often identified by simple register numbers, and a structured, symbolic data model has then to be done for each application or for each edge machine. It is important to have tools that facilitate this rather technical operation which consists in aligning data from communication frames, in Modbus (see modbus.org) for instance, with higher level models, like OPC/UA for example (see opcfoundation.org).

3.1.4 Application Context

Abstracting is a fundamental technique in software engineering and is particularly important in edge computing. This allows applications to rely on high-level data that matches their computational needs, and thus facilitates their programming and management in general. Data models, introduced here before, provide a certain level of abstraction which nevertheless remains limited since they usually focus on a single device or on a single function. The notion of pervasive context, introduced in the 1990s by Schilit et al. (1994), allows to aggregate and extend information provided by different devices. Dey and Abowd define context as "any information that can be used to characterize the situation of an entity. An entity is a person, place, or object that is considered relevant to the interaction between a user and an application, including the user and applications themselves" (Dey and Abowd 1999). Contextual information thus covers various aspects related to users (like localization, interaction, physiological parameters, or general expectations and preferences), environments (like temperature, pressure, or CO_2 levels), and characteristics of the supporting computing infrastructure.

Collecting information to build a relevant, useful context and keeping it up to date has proved to be particularly complex. In most cases, it is necessary to integrate disparate devices, applications and network protocols in order to get the needed information. Also, as previously said, pervasive environments are highly dynamic and volatile. Devices can connect and disconnect without warning, quality of the network connectivity can dramatically vary, and failures can happen anytime on various system levels. A number of context management platforms with specific properties have been introduced (see Becker et al. 2013 for instance) but research on that topic is still going on. An open question regarding context, and by extension data models, is to know whether its construction should be application-specific or not.

3.1.5 Application Placement

Edge environments can be complex and composed of several computers, including mobile ones. The question of placing applications on the right machine(s) is therefore paramount. Note that the placement of tasks has always been crucial in pervasive systems to meet requirements related to ed or energy consumption. For instance, the completion time of a remote execution depends heavily on the speed of the selected provider device. The choice of the offloading target happens either statically or dynamically. An example for static placement is for instance Clone2Clone (Kosta et al. 2013). In this approach, each provider serves a fixed set of devices. Most offloading approaches, however, perform dynamic placement, i.e., a separate choice of the executing provider for each offloadable part.

Dynamic offloading has been applied in a variety of distributed computing paradigms including cluster and grid computing. Effective placement in grid computing systems often requires some knowledge about context, which also makes sense in edge environments. Context-aware placement gathers context information about the surrounding computing environment and is therefore able to react to changes. A context-aware placement approach can consider a number of context dimensions such as provider performance (Jonathan et al. 2017) and reliability (Edinger et al. 2017), system load (Ousterhout et al. 2013), task complexity (Flinn et al. 2002), data size (Cicconetti et al. 2019) or bandwidth (Kosta et al. 2012). Motivated by these observations, several novel placement approaches like Voltaire (Breitbach et al. 2021) apply ML to benefit from past experience. The core advantage is that the placement approach adjusts itself to the current environment and learns from past performance to improve continuously. Based on several input features of an upcoming task, e.g., the corresponding application, the input data size, the parameters, and the current system load, the ML-based approaches estimate whether offloading is expected to be beneficial.

3.2 Pervasive Platforms

The most common solution today to face the challenges previously mentioned is to use a specific platform, also called middleware, to host the applications. Such middleware provides a development language adapted to the targeted domain (pervasive in this case) as well as a set of technical services that are used, in more or less transparent ways, by the applications. These services can concern any of the

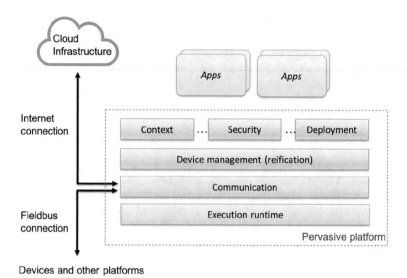

Fig. 3 Pervasive middleware

above issues like communication, data management, security, self-awareness or data contextualization. Decoupling applications and technical services is a well-known approach in software engineering, referred to as separation of concerns, which has proven successful in many areas. It relieves programmers of complicated code by moving it to the platform. This approach is illustrated by Fig. 3 where platform-dependent services are built on top of the execution runtime. Various techniques can be used to implement those services.

In the pervasive domain, numerous platforms have been developed and evaluated. In the smart home domain for instance, let us mention iCasa (Lalanda and Hamon 2020), PCOM (Becker et al. 2004), AutoHome (Bourcier et al. 2011), DigiHome (Romero et al. 2013) or Microsoft's HomeOS (Dixon et al. 2012). Most of these platforms first dealt with the definition of a programming language for the applications adapted to the dynamicity of pervasive environments. Also, many of them strongly focused on the reification of devices, i.e. their transformation into objects that can be manipulated by the defined programming language. For this, the service approach has often been favored. The service-oriented computing paradigm promotes the development of applications through the late composition of independent and modular software elements, called services (Papazoglou 2003). Services are dynamically published on a registry and, thus, made available to potential consumers that can invoke them, possibly with a quality of service contract. In our case, devices are presented as services that come and go, and that can be used by the pervasive applications.

Another element brought by most platforms is some notion of execution context. This serves as an abstraction layer between the physical world and the applications run on the platform. Context provides information about the surrounding physical environment but also the current state of execution of the running applications if needed. Some information is static, most of it is very dynamic though. The context module usually constitutes the only means for applications to interact with physical devices. Research on context-aware computing dates back to the 1990s. Schilit et al. (1994) introduced a still current definition of context and details of a comprehensive context management platform. Since then, a number of context management platforms with specific properties have been introduced. Various technologies have been developed, including tuples, object-orientation, databases with SQL-like approaches, or ontologies. Context can also be used implicitly, where the spatial distribution of data is implicitly used as context. More recently, contextual information has been represented as services (Lalanda and Hamon 2020). Here, context appears as a dynamic set of services. Depending on the availability of context sources and the applications needs, different services can be published and withdrawn.

Let us focus on the iCasa platform for illustration. A particularity of this platform is to use the service paradigm for many of its constituent elements. It is based on the iPOJO service-oriented component model (Escoffier et al. 2007), which in turn is based on the OSGi framework. Applications are all programmed in iPOJO and seamlessly interact with physical devices and remote platforms through services provided by the context module. Applications can be dynamically updated, completely or partially, by relying on the deployment mechanisms specific to OSGi and iPOJO. All the contextual information is presented as services. Precisely, the context appears as a dynamic set of iPOJO components. Context is dynamic in order to reflect the changing nature of the execution environment but also to deal with applications evolving needs. Context adaptations are carried out by an autonomic manager that follows the applications requirements and the available resources. Contextual services are then opportunistically and seamlessly used by the pervasive applications. The context module also tracks any change about a used contextual service and triggers a callback to alert consumer applications.

Finally, a communication manager (Bardin et al. 2010) reifies devices as iPOJO components. This manager supports an open set of protocols, including Zwave, Zigbee, X10, UPnP, DPWS and Bluetooth. Whenever a device disappears or a remote service becomes unreachable, the manager detects the disruption and removes the corresponding component. If the services provided by that component were needed by an application, the communication manager tries to find a new device or a remote service satisfying the needs (Roth et al. 2018).

3.3   Conclusion

Moving applications to the edge has many advantages, but also raises significant technical and architectural issues. Many pervasive platforms have been proposed and are often distinguished according to their areas of focus. For example, the platforms used for industry are often more robust and less dynamic than those used on smartphones or in smart homes.

Nevertheless, all these platforms offer interesting solutions for application, device, context and security management for instance. The service-oriented approach plays a major role in many cases and has proved successful. As we have seen, the service paradigm allows both to reify objects as services in pervasive platforms and to build modular and dynamic applications. It also facilitates interoperability between platforms by publishing their various functional capabilities as services (Roth et al. 2018).

Nevertheless, this service-based approach finds its limits when the amount of data to be processed increases. The service approach sees computing elements, including devices or contextual elements, essentially as service providers. The fact is that most of them are also data providers. In some domains, like smart manufacturing, they are even intense data providers. Work is then needed to allow interactions of almost continuous data flows between pervasive elements in service-based environments.

4   Machine Learning on the Edge

4.1   Principles

In the last few years, Machine Learning (ML) based approaches have received a very strong interest for the development of pervasive applications. This can be explained by the difficulty to build models of dynamic phenomena in complex physical environments. The goal of an ML system is to train an algorithm to automatically make decisions by identifying patterns that may be hidden within massive data sets whose exact nature is unknown and therefore cannot be programmed explicitly. The growing attention towards machine learning stems from different sources: efficient algorithms, availability of massive amounts of data in pervasive environments, advances in high-performance computing, broad accessibility of these technologies, and impressive successes reported by industry, academia, and research communities, in fields such as vision, natural language processing or decision making.

The development of software systems based on learning techniques is however very different than the development of "traditional" software systems since the behavior of the system is not specified in the code by programmers but it is learned by a machine from data. To do so, two main workflows are set up. The first workflow, called model development, is primarily performed by data scientists. This workflow assumes that a business problem has been properly identified along with sources of historical data. During the first steps, raw historical data is analyzed, cleaned and transformed into appropriate numeric representations called features. Feature engineering is a complex task which purpose is to find out the most relevant data representations given the available data, the task at hand and the targeted model.

Features are then used to train a model with a carefully chosen machine learning algorithm.

Once a model has been developed, it is deployed on a target execution machine. This is the essence of the second workflow that is often implemented by software engineers. Its purpose is first to collect appropriate data and build features. The data is then used to make predictions. As the name suggests, predictions are only ... predictions. They are founded on data which has not been seen during the training phase and can therefore be incorrect. Finally, collected data might be set aside in order to be used for further training.

The use of Machine Learning techniques opens the way for many new, more advanced applications on the edge. The expected added value motivates many manufacturers and service providers, in both the industrial and consumer sectors. But the development of these new applications raises formidable challenges that are not addressed by traditional software engineering techniques. ML-based applications are not developed in the same way as more traditional applications. They bring together different teams with new skills. Also they are built, tested, installed, configured, run, monitored and updated differently. In a word, they implement totally different life cycles.

4.2   A Variety of Actors

First of all, it should be understood that ML-based components are usually only a small part of a system. They are often developed independently and integrated into a larger software architecture. Thus, implementing ML applications on the edge involves several different actors, with different cultures and skills. These actors develop complementary software components, learning-based and more traditional, that have to be assembled within an architecture. This architecture is usually deployed on a single edge machine, resulting in complex engineering work to allow interaction between programs of a differing nature. This generates important constraints on the edge platform in terms of execution mechanisms and technical services to be offered.

To illustrate this problem, let us take the example of analytic development in a smart plant (Lalanda et al. 2017). To do this, three complementary profiles, and usually three distinct teams, are needed:

- A team of software engineers who are in charge of managing the platform and programming specific code related for instance to data collection or data mediation (Morand et al. 2011; Garcia et al. 2010)
- A team of domain experts who are in charge of defining and developing the business-oriented analytics,
- A team of data scientists who are in charge of developing learning-based models and keeping them relevant and up to date. This includes selecting the needed data, creating the appropriate features, choosing the learning algorithm to be used, etc.

This diversity, if it is a source of value, is also a source of difficulties, misunderstandings and cultural gaps. These different actors use different environments, tools, processes and programming languages. On this last point, for instance, domain experts generally use Matlab for analytics, data scientists make use of Python to build models, and computer engineers user languages such as Java, Go, or C to develop business code or technical services.

4.3   A Specific Life-Cycle

The development of "traditional" software systems is carried out according to activities that are now well defined: requirement management, design specification, implementation, and validation. Deployment then starts when a software system has been duly approved for delivery. It handles the transfer, installation, configuration, and integration of concrete artefacts therein. It also initiates the different executable components and deals with subsequent updates. Maintenance begins after the software initial installation. Its purpose is to modify the software being used in order to fix bugs, to improve quality of service, or to address new conditions for execution. Maintenance comprises a number of activities, ranging from the "simple" reconfiguration of certain parameters to more complex operations, like the development of new pieces of code or the migration to new running platforms. Simply put, system administrators, or autonomic managers, observe the systems at run time, change local configurations when needed, and otherwise send a request to developers if something serious happens.

The development of a prediction model takes a completely different turn because of the focus on data. Here, no requirements, design or coding, just data. The initial development uses historical data; its relevance depends on the quality of the available data and adequacy of the selected learning algorithm. In the case of pervasive applications, this data must come from the field, or from very high quality simulations, to be usable. Tests are done against a subset of the available data, set aside for this purpose. As illustrated by Fig. 4 (left part), it is an iterative process where the steps of data collection, feature selection and model training are repeated until a satisfactory result is obtained.

Model deployment activities look like traditional deployment tasks but are nevertheless significantly different (see Fig. 4, right part). First of all, the model is transferred to the execution (edge) machine and installed like any other software artifact. It is also configured to fit properly into its execution environment. Configuration can be complex and actually depends on lot on the services provided by the host middleware. In some cases, the model has to be further trained with local data in order to adjust to the specificity of the execution environment. Then appropriate data has to be collected in order to run the model, which can thus provide the expected predictions. The model is constantly monitored by system administrators, through appropriate tools. Finally, an update step completes the loop. The purpose of this

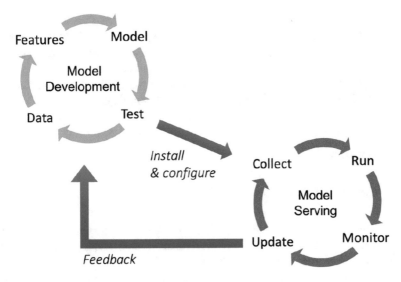

Fig. 4 Life-cycle of ML-based components

step is either to update the model directly on site or to send data back to the data scientist teams to allow them to implement off-line updates.

A model is updated when a new one has been devised by data scientists, which happens fairly often. This can be done to enhance its performance, to improve its compactness, or even to extend its functional scope. Sometimes, this also comes with a change in the input data, which may require updates on data gathering activities. Finally, let us note that the models are extremely sensitive to data evolution, even very slight one. The smallest modification can invalidate a prediction model. Therefore, they must be continuously adapted to the execution environment and the corresponding data to stay relevant.

4.4 Conclusion

The use of learning techniques on the edge is today more than a trend, it is a must. However, it raises major issues. It requires the creation of development teams with different and complementary skills, using different languages, processes and tools. Such heterogeneity is difficult to manage from a human point of view but also from a technical point of view. It requires to build architectures, and middleware, capable of integrating very different modules in order to form a single system.

Strong heterogeneity is also introduced in the management of the software components life cycle. Learning-based components have their own cycle, entirely data-driven, that is very different from the one of more traditional software components. While the major activities remain the same, they are treated in a very different way and require, here again, specific skills and tools. All these differences call into question the current Software Engineering techniques and processes but also the support that has to be provided by the edge platforms.

Throughout the following section, we examine the challenges associated with each of the life cycle activities and outline possible solutions.

5   Challenges

5.1   Model Development

To start with, a consistent and sufficiently large dataset is needed to create a relevant initial model. The data must be complete, well distributed, and clean. A low quality of data inevitably leads to models of little value.

It is therefore necessary to set up a structured and systematic data collection campaign. To provide real value, this data must be collected in the field, for example with some of the edge machines that will be used to run the models later. Such campaigns take time and effort and must be integrated into the development cycle. The most difficult part is to obtain data corresponding to extreme, problematic or even dangerous cases. Often, it is necessary to use simulation to do so, with all the risks that this entails for the actual quality of the data.

The choice of an adapted learning algorithm is also of major importance. It must take into account the specificity of the domain but also those of the targeted execution machines. As explained earlier, machines on the edge are often characterized by limited computing and storage capabilities. The learning models must therefore have a size in accordance with these limitations, which is often challenging since data scientists tend to build large models to get better performances.

5.2   Installation

A learning model is usually only a (small) part of a larger software system. It is encapsulated in a software component and inserted into an encompassing software architecture. Within this architecture, it interacts with other components to implement higher-level functionality.

The installation of a learning-based component in a target environment can be done individually or with the architecture (and all other components). In the latter case, all components are compiled and linked together to create an executable. It is this executable that is installed on the clients site. This approach is easier to manage because most of the work is done off-line but, in general, it makes individual component updates more technically complicated, if not impossible. This is a problem because learning-based components are updated often and usually at a different rate than other more traditional components.

The alternative is therefore to deploy the learning-based components independently and integrate them with the encompassing architecture afterwards. However, this requires a middleware capable of managing components with autonomous life cycles, and, as previously said, written with different programming languages.

5.3 Configuration

The learning models are built off-line with data usually coming from purpose-built facilities, or from selected customers' sites. But, in any case, data remains relatively specific to these training environments, as do the models obtained. Thus, when models are deployed to clients' sites, it is necessary to adapt them to their new conditions of execution. This problem is particularly acute in pervasive computing where there is no two environments alike.

By nature, model configuration is done on site, at the edge level, using data collected from the environment. Two approaches are possible. The first is to use a large amount of data that has been previously collected and stored for this purpose. With this data, the general model received can be efficiently fine-tuned. This approach is very effective but requires significant storage capacity on the edge. The second approach, which does not rely on such capacity, is to use data collected after the general model is received. Here, fine tuning is not usable because the well-known catastrophic forgetting problem occurs very quickly. It is necessary to use Continual Learning techniques, like regularization for instance, to adapt the learning model. Continual Learning, also called lifelong learning or online machine learning, is the ability of a model to learn continually from an infinite stream of data, gradually integrating new acquired knowledge into old knowledge (Chen and Liu 2018). This however results in complex algorithms.

5.4 Data Collection

The use of prediction models adds constraints when running pervasive applications. Indeed, it is not only necessary to collect data to make punctual predictions when the model is invoked, but also to allow the continuous improvement of the models. An update can only be meaningful if it is based on a sufficient amount of data, and it is therefore needed to collect data very regularly in order to reach a critical mass. Simply put, data must be continuously retrieved in order to keep models relevant and in sync with their execution environment.

This is a significant difference from current practices where data is fetched only to meet occasional application needs. Often, as explained in Sect. 4, context modules, general or application-specific, are built by pervasive platforms. But these contexts usually contain little data and keep only significant data. At best, caching techniques are implemented to save recent data and then provide more responsiveness (Lalanda et al. 2018).

Moreover, when supervised learning is used by the learning algorithms, collected data must be labeled, which means that ground truth is associated with it. Data labeling is well known to be a complex activity. It can be done manually by users or experts via dedicated tools. But this approach is seen as boring and massively rejected by the involved people. It is also very error-prone. In some cases, labels can be calculated automatically, often with a delay, using other data. This approach is safer but requires to collect even more data and to create specific code to effectively compute the labels and associate them with the corresponding data.

5.5 Model Execution

Resorting to predictions for the execution of an application is a powerful but risky approach. In some cases, it is always beneficial because it provides information that would not otherwise be available. Even if the prediction is not perfect, its mere existence is better than the absence of information. Especially if, on average, it is accurate. But, in other cases, an inaccurate prediction can lead to important malfunctions, or even endanger the existence of people or infrastructures.

Guaranteeing the relevance of a prediction seems difficult without human intervention, because it depends on the correlation between training data and runtime data, but also on runtime environments that cannot be completely characterized (some information cannot be captured by sensors). A commonly used approach is to multiply the models on a runtime platform. Several models, based on different algorithms and sometimes on different features, are deployed and used together. Then, as in redundancy approaches, voting techniques can determine the "good" predictions. Using several models is likely to be more robust since final results are based on the output of several models. As in redundancy approaches, voting techniques can be used to select a prediction. However, here again, support from the pervasive platform is highly effective to realize those functions.

5.6 Model Monitoring

Monitoring is a systematic collection of relevant information with the purpose of understanding, evaluating and controlling the system. For the models, it is a matter of presenting the data used, the predictions made and, if appropriate, all other data allowing to understand or verify the results provided. Let us note that the monitoring function can be adaptive by either adapting the focus of what is being monitored— deciding on which components are monitored and when, or adapting the amount of times or numbers of samples that are required.

It is of major importance to include human, essentially experts, in the monitoring activity. A simple solution is to monitor the applications behavior and switch to a human mode when some tasks (data collection, model predictions, and so on) are uncertain. Here, visualization tools are definitively needed to assist the domain experts in reviewing the current tasks and in providing help. It is also needed to define a global process making explicit the situations and moments where human can be included.

5.7 Model Update

Trained models are data dependent, making it necessary to retrain them when data changes. Data drifts happen very frequently. This is the case for instance in the manufacturing domain due to the natural wear of certain parts. The decision to initiate re-training is however delicate because it is costly, both in money and in carbon footprint. At its simplest, it can be done on a periodic basis. A more complex solution, and also more effective, would be to rely on observations from monitoring. For example, changes in the value or distribution of data can be observed, or an expert can identify suspicious results.

A major decision is to then know where the new training has to be done. Doing it at the data center level is a natural solution since the most significant computing resources are there. However, this poses a major problem: the (labeled) data collected on the edge must be uploaded to the cloud. This raises obvious security problems and also significant financial costs. This approach is sometimes simply rejected by users who do not want their data stored in a cloud.

The second solution is to build the new model directly on the edge. This brings the opposite advantages to the previous approach but also the opposite problems. In particular, it requires considerable computing and storage capacities on the edge to train a model, quite different from the capacities needed to simply run a model. Such capacities are not always available. Another problem is that, if they each build their own model, the clients using the initial learning model will quickly diverge and not be able to share their data. Nevertheless, there are significant developments in edge machines that tend towards this solution. For example, smartphones are more and more equipped with electronic cards adapted to models training.

6 Recent Trends

As demonstrated in the previous section, challenges to develop ML-based pervasive applications on the edge are not only about developing the best models and algorithms but also to provide support for the entire applications lifecycle. The current techniques are unfortunately not adapted to support activities related to data collection, model installation and configuration, model monitoring and model frequent updates. There is a clear need to provide new Software Engineering support for these different steps.

In this last part, we explore two promising trends to deal with these new challenges: the use of microservices in pervasive platforms and the notion of Federated Learning.

6.1 Microservice-Based Platform

Microservices can be seen as an extension of the service-oriented architectural style as described previously. It structures a software application as a set of loosely coupled components, called microservices, interacting with each others. Microservices implement specific services that are integrated in a global architecture in order to deliver the expected functionality of an application. Each microservice can implement its own life cycle: it is developed, deployed and maintained individually. It can be thus modified independently without impacting the overall architecture. Microservices are actually a combination of service-based and component-based architectures.

Microservices use lightweight APIs to communicate with each other. While REST APIs have often been used to enable interactions between microservices, there is no requirement to do so. A clear benefit of using REST is that updates of a resource can be limited to the microservice containing that resource. However, not all domains are suitable for a REST expression of the possible results of a component and, moreover, this approach requires relatively rare technical skills. We believe that techniques such as gRPC are preferable today, even if they induce a stronger coupling between the microservices.

Communication between microservices can also be implemented with events. Such events can be used to send business data but also control or synchronization data between the different microservices. In this case, it is interesting to use a communication middleware implementing a publish/subscribe pattern allowing high dynamicity in the interactions between microservices.

Today, a common way to implement microservice-based architectures is to use container-based solutions like Dockers or Kubernetes. These solutions automate the management, deployment, and scaling of services across multiple servers by abstracting the underlying infrastructure.

Today, edge platforms based on microservice architectures are emerging. This indeed solves some of the problems mentioned in this chapter, including the need to decouple the life cycles of traditional and machine learning components. Figure 5 presents the new architecture of the iCasa platform (Lalanda et al. 2021). The different technical services (data collection, data storage, context, ML manager) are implemented on dockers. Thus, each of these elements can be:

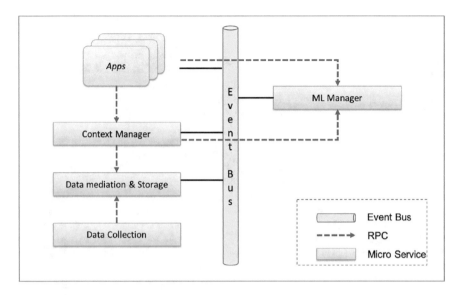

Fig. 5 Microservice-based platform

- built and deployed independently,
- considered as an independent process that can be implemented in any language, using any framework,
- easily managed with container-based solutions.

6.2 Federated Learning

Federated Learning promotes the computation of local models on devices and the aggregation of these models on a server to produce a new model that is sent back to clients for use and further training. When the client model has been significantly updated or when a certain time has elapsed, the client model is sent to the server for a new aggregation (see Fig. 6). A core incentive of FL in pervasive computing is to utilize mutual learning goals between clients to indirectly share knowledge with one another. However, effective collaboration between unmoderated clients, is still a challenge. This is due to statistical heterogeneity (differences in individuals' usage) and system heterogeneity (difference between client data caused by different system traits).

A key point in Federated Learning is the way specialized models are aggregated. In the case of deep learning, two families of algorithms can be considered. The first strategy is to emphasize generalization. The aggregation algorithm considers local models in their entirety and builds a new model that potentially calls into question all layers and all weights associated with neurons. This approach is shown

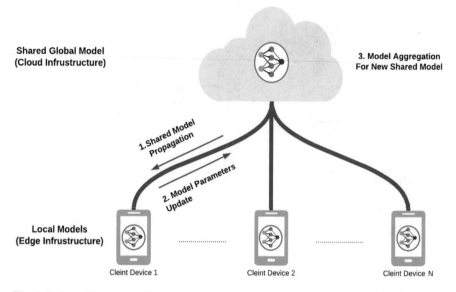

Fig. 6 Federated learning architecture

in FedAvg (McMahan et al. 2017) and FedMA (Wang et al. 2020) algorithms. The second strategy focuses more on client specialization. Here, the algorithm does not question certain parts of the local models. Precisely, only the base layers are sent to the server for generalization, while the last layers are kept unchanged. This approach is used in FedPer algorithm (Arivazhagan et al. 2019).

Federated Learning has been only recently used to implement pervasive services and, ultimately, does not address all the specifics of this domain well. However, this clearly solves the heterogeneity problems of pervasive environments and also improves the security issues. With this approach, data is not sent to a cloud for retraining. It is only the models that are transferred, which is much better for privacy preservation.

7 Conclusion

The integration of machine learning-based models in pervasive information systems is more than a trend, it is a necessity. It allows to face evolving, uncertain, and incompletely characterized environments.

However, this raises unprecedented technological and scientific challenges, notably by calling into question current software engineering practices. It requires bringing together communities that are not familiar with each other and developing new tools, in particular middleware for deployment, execution and integration of models. These models have their own life cycle that must be managed explicitly.

In this chapter, we have mentioned two avenues that seem promising, although of course insufficient. The use of microservices within a single execution unit allows the decoupling of the execution of models and traditional software components. Also, distributed learning approaches such as Federated Learning allow to improve models while keeping their specificity at the client level.

References

Becker, C., Julien, C., Lalanda, P., Zambonelli, F.: Pervasive computing middleware: current trends and emerging challenges. CCF Transactions on Pervasive Computing and Interaction **1**(1) (2019)

Sarkar, S., Chatterjee, S., Misra, S.: Assessment of the suitability of fog computing in the context of internet of things. IEEE Trans. Cloud Comput. **6**(1) (2018)

Choy, S., Wong, B., Simon, G., Rosenberg, C.: The Brewing Storm in Cloud Gaming: A Measurement Study on Cloud to End-User Latency. In proc. IEEE NetGames, 2012 (2012)

Shi, W., Dustdar, S.: The promise of edge computing. Comp. **49**(5) (2016)

Garcia Lopez, P., Montresor, A., Epema, D., Datta, A., Higashino, T., Iamnitchi, A., Barcellos, M., Felber, P., Riviere, E.: Edge-centric computing: Vision and challenges. ACM SIGCOMM Comput. Commun. Rev. **45**(5) (2015)

Vaquero, L.M., Rodero-Merino, L.: Finding your way in the fog: Towards a comprehensive definition of fog computing. ACM SIGCOMM Comput. Commun. **44**(5) (2015)

Varghese, B., Wang, N., Barbhuiya, S., Kilpatrick, P., Nikolopoulos, D.S.: Challenges and Opportunities in Edge Computing. in Proc. IEEE SmartCloud. IEEE, 2016 (2016)

Shi, W., Cao, J., Zhang, Q., Li, Y., Xu, L.: Edge computing: Vision and challenges. IEEE Internet Things J. **3**(5) (2016)

Hasan, R., Hossain, M.M., Khan, R.: Aura: An IoT Based Cloud Infrastructure for Localized Mobile Computation Outsourcing. in Proc. MobileCloud, 2015 (2015)

Miluzzo, E., Cáceres, R., Chen, Y.F.: Vision: mClouds - Computing on Clouds of Mobile Devices. in Proc. ACM MCS., 2012 (2012)

Morand, D., Garcia, I., Lalanda, P.: Autonomic enterprise service bus, ETFA2011, (2011), pp. 1–8. https://doi.org/10.1109/ETFA.2011.6059231

Garcia, G., Pedraza, B., Debbabi, P.L., Hamon, C.: Towards a Service Mediation Framework for Dynamic Applications, 2010 IEEE Asia-Pacific Services Computing Conference, (2010), pp. 3–10. https://doi.org/10.1109/APSCC.2010.90

Fernando, N., Loke, S.W., Rahayu, W.: Dynamic Mobile Cloud Computing: Ad hoc and Opportunistic Job Sharing. in Proc. IEEE UCC., 2011 (2012)

Forschungsunion, Acatech: Recommendations for implementing the strategic initiative industrie 4.0. Technical report, Final report of the Industrie 4.0 Working Group (2013)

Lalanda, P., Morand, D., Chollet, S.: Autonomic mediation middleware for smart manufacturing. IEEE Internet Computing **21**(1) (2017)

Lalanda, P., Vega, G., Cervantes, H., Morand, D.: Architecture and pervasive platform for machine learning services in Industry 4.0. in Proceedings of the International Conference on Pervasive Computing and Communications (PerCom) and other Affiliated Events (PerCom Workshops). (2021)

Schilit, B., Adams, N., Want, R.: Context-aware computing applications. In First IEEE Workshop on Mobile Computing Systems and Applications (WMCSA) (1994)

Dey, A.K., Abowd, G.D.: Context-aware computing applications. In Proc. HUC. Springer (1999)

Becker, C., VanSyckel, S., Schiele, G.: Ubiquitous information technologies and applications. Lecture Notes in Electrical Engineering, **214**(1). (2013)

Kosta, S., Perta, V.C., Stefa, J., Hui, P., Mei, A.: Clone2Clone (C2C): Peer-to-Peer Networking of Smartphones on the Cloud. in Proc. HotCloud. USENIX. (2013)

Jonathan, A., Ryden, M., Oh, K., Chandra, A., Weissman, J.: Nebula: Distributed edge cloud for data intensive computing. IEEE Trans. Parallel Distrib. Syst. **28**(11) (2017)

Edinger, J., Schäfer, D., Krupitzer, C., Raychoudhury, V., Becker, C.: Fault-Avoidance Strategies for Context-Aware Schedulers in Pervasive Computing Systems. in Proceedings of the International Conference on Pervasive Computing and Communications (PerCom). (2017)

Ousterhout, K., Wendell, P., Zaharia, M., Stoica, I.: Sparrow: Distributed, Low Latency Scheduling. in Proceedings of ACM SOSP. (2013)

Flinn, J., Park, S., Satyanarayanan, M.: Balancing Performance, Energy, and Quality in Pervasive Computing. in Proceedings of IEEE ICDCS. (2002)

Cicconetti, C., Conti, M., Passarella, A.: Low-Latency Distributed Computation Offloading for Pervasive Environments. in Proceedings of the International Conference on Pervasive Computing and Communications (PerCom). (2019)

Kosta, S., Aucinas, A., Hui, P., Mortier, R., Zhang, X.: ThinkAir: Dynamic Resource Allocation and Parallel Execution in the Cloud for Mobile Code Offloading. in Proceedings of IEEE INFOCOM. (2012)

Breitbach, M., Edinger, J., Kaupmees, S., Trötsch, H., Krupitzer, C., Becker, C.: Voltaire: Precise EnergyAware Code Offloading Decisions with Machine Learning. in Proceedings of the International Conference on Pervasive Computing and Communications (PerCom). (2021)

Lalanda, P., Hamon, C.: A service-oriented edge platform for cyber-physical systems. CCF Transactions on Pervasive Computing and Interaction **2**(3) (2020)

Becker, C., Handte, M., Schiele, G., Rothermel, K.: PCOM - A Component System for Pervasive Computing. in Proceedings of the International Conference on Pervasive Computing and Communications (PerCom). (2004)

Bourcier, J., Diaconescu, A., Lalanda, P., McCann, J.A.: An autonomic management framework for pervasive home applications. TAAS **6**(1) (2011)

Romero, D., Hermosillo, G., Taherkordi, A., Nzekwa, R., Rouvoy, R., Eliassen, F.: The digihome service-oriented platform. Softw., Pract. Exper. **43**(10) (2013)

Dixon, C., Mahajan, R., Agarwal, S., Brush, A.J.B., Lee, B., Saroiu, S., Bahl, P.: An operating system for the home. Proceedings of the 9th USENIX Symposium on Networked Systems Design and Implementation (NSDI), San Jose, CA, USA. (2012)

Papazoglou, M.: Service-oriented computing: Concepts, characteristics and directions. In 4th International Conference on Web Information Systems Engineering (WISE), Rome, Italy. (2003)

Escoffier, C., Hall, R.S., Lalanda, P.: iPOJO: An extensible service oriented component framework. in Proceedings of the IEEE International Conference on Service Computing (SCC) (2007)

Bardin, J., Lalanda, P., Escoffier, C.: Towards an Automatic Integration of Heterogeneous Services and Devices. in Proceedings of the IEEE International Conference on Asian-Pacific Service Computing (APSCC) (2010)

Roth, F.M., Becker, C., Vega, G., Lalanda, P.: Xware—a customizable interoperability framework for pervasive computing systems. Pervasive and mobile computing **47** (2018)

Chen, Z., Liu, B.: Lifelong machine learning. Synthesis Lectures on Artificial Intelligence and Machine Learning, vol. 12, number 3 (2018)

Lalanda, P., Mertz, J., Nunes, I.: Autonomic caching management in industrial smart gateways. in Proceedings of IEEE Industrial Cyber-Physical Systems (ICPS) (2018)

McMahan, B., Moore, E., Ramage, D., Hampson, S., y Arcas, B.A.: Communication-Efficient Learning of Deep Networks from Decentralized Data. In: Proceedings of the 20th International Conference on Artificial Intelligence and Statistics, vol. 54. Fort Lauderdale, USA, pp. 1273–1282 (2017)

Wang, H., Yurochkin, M., Sun, Y., Papailiopoulos, D.S., Khazaeni, Y.: Federated learning with matched averaging. CoRR **abs/2002.06440** (2020) arXiv:2002.06440

Arivazhagan, M.G., Aggarwal, V., Singh, A.K., Choudhary, S.: Federated learning with personalization layers. arXiv:1912.00818v1 (2019)

PIS: IoT & Industry 4.0 Challenges

Frédéric Le Mouël and Oscar Carrillo

1 Introduction

Industry 4.0—a term coined by H. Kagermann et al.—was introduced as the Fourth Industrial Revolution in the context of the development of the German economy (Kagermann et al. 2011). Following the First Industrial Revolution with water and steam engine as a source of power, the Second Industrial Revolution with mass production and globalization, the Third Industrial Revolution with automation and digitization, the Fourth Industrial Revolution concept was popularized by K. Schwab from The World Economic Forum (Schwab 2016, 2017). Industry 4.0 stands out as the evolution from digital manufacturing to smart factories (cf Fig. 1).

Despite significant efforts from the research community, no unanimous definition of Industry 4.0 is currently adopted (Boyes et al. 2018; Kiangala and Wang 2019; Lasi et al. 2014; Piccarozzi et al. 2018; Qin et al. 2016). Its characterization (Buer et al. 2018) or roadmap (Beier et al. 2020; Paravizo et al. 2018) are not clearly defined. Its complexity makes it difficult to focus on scope, objectives, and holistic development (Buer et al. 2018; Derigent et al. 2021; Meissner et al. 2017).

Rupp et al. have compiled keywords, concepts, and citations in an exhaustive bibliometric analysis within the scope of research literature and have formed a concise definition of the Industry 4.0 paradigm:

F. Le Mouël (✉)
Univ Lyon, INSA Lyon, Inria, CITI, Villeurbanne, France
e-mail: frederic.le-mouel@insa-lyon.fr

O. Carrillo
Univ Lyon, CPE, INSA Lyon, Inria, CITI, Villeurbanne, France
e-mail: oscar.carrillo@cpe.fr

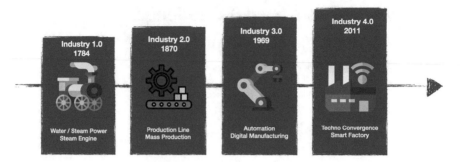

Fig. 1 Industry 4.0—The Fourth Revolution

"Industry 4.0 is the implementation of Cyber-Physical Systems for creating Smart Factories by using the Internet of Things, Big Data, Cloud Computing, Artificial Intelligence and Communication Technologies for Information and Communication in Real-Time over the Value Chain." Rupp et al. (2021)

From this clearly technology-oriented definition, Industry 4.0 emerges as the convergence of four major technological trends (cf Fig. 2):

Physical World Digitalization The first requirement to optimize any kind of value chain is to have information about ongoing processes. The *Internet of Things (IoT)* refers to physical objects or groups of objects with sensing and communication abilities that connect and exchange data over public or private networks. Machines or humans are embedded with electronic sensors or actuators to generate data. *Cyber Physical Systems (CPS)* are systems including mechanisms where physical objects, humans, and software are closely intertwined to create new levels of sociotechnical interactions. CPS involves transdisciplinary approaches—merging the theory of cybernetics, mechatronics, design and process science. The principal aim is to produce constant interactions between the real physical world and a virtual world representation to indicate the best decisions (Boyes et al. 2018).

On-Demand Computing On-demand computing is an enterprise-level delivery model in which computing resources are made available to the user when needed. *Cloud Computing* is a key technology of on-demand computing. Cloud Computing is the on-demand availability of different remote services over the Internet, especially data storage, networking, and computing power. *Edge and Fog Computing* are also key technologies complementary to Cloud Computing. Edge and Fog Computing are distributed computing paradigms bringing computation and data storage closer to the data sources. Edge Computing architectures perform computation and storage on the embedded devices or the gateway at the network's edge, in close proximity to the physical location of sensors creating the data. Fog Computing

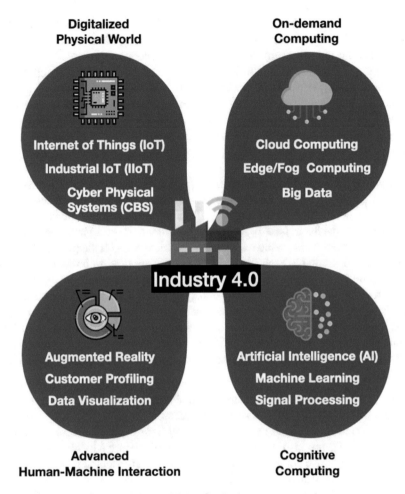

Fig. 2 Industry 4.0—the four major enabling technologies

architectures act as mediators between the edge, the core network, and the cloud for various purposes, such as data processing or data geo-distribution (Hong and Varghese 2019). Finally, *Big Data* refers to structured, semi-structured, and unstructured datasets that are too large or complex to be dealt with by traditional data-processing application software. Big Data requires the previous computing architectures to be stored and analyzed to reveal patterns, trends, and associations, especially those relating to human behavior and interactions (Chen et al. 2014; Khan et al. 2017).

Cognitive Computing Cognitive Computing refers to technology platforms that mimic the way the human brain works by incorporating advanced aspects of artificial intelligence and signal processing. *Signal Processing* focuses on analyzing, modifying, and synthesizing signals such as scientific measurements, sound, natural language, and images or videos. After any data capture, filtering noise from data and structuring the signal impacts any future knowledge representation. *Artificial intelligence (AI)* refers to intelligence demonstrated by machines, as opposed to the natural intelligence displayed by animals and humans. Traditional goals of AI include knowledge representation, reasoning, perception, planning, learning, processing, and decision-making. *Machine Learning* is a subset of AI that has recently regained popularity with advances in artificial neural networks, deep learning, and reinforcement learning (Lee et al. 2018; Verbraeken et al. 2020).

Advanced Human-Machine Interaction Advanced human-machine interaction is the field studying the design and the use of computer technology interfacing between people and computers. Following the effort to provide multi-modal interfaces (audio, visual, feedback-based), *Augmented Reality (AR)* and *Virtual Reality (VR)* are key technologies where the reality of the physical world is supported and mixed with the use of digital 3D models. AR/VR are mainly used to build and assemble complex components and architectures, and to read and document technical systems in real-time (Xiong et al. 2021). *3D-printing* is, at the same time, a physical world augmentation and an advanced human-machine interacting system. 3D-printing plays an essential role in Industry 4.0 by enabling the direct production of high-complexity digital 3D models, making it suitable for individual production of experimental small-sized batches to large production with high added-value (Rong et al. 2018).

This chapter focuses on Industry 4.0-enabling technologies to digitalize the physical world and how to apply them to industrial and manufacturing contexts - hereby referred to as *The Industrial Internet of Things (IIoT)*. Interactions of the IIoT sensing part are also detailed in regards of adaptation capabilities of the on-demand and cognitive computing, and advanced human-machine interaction parts.

The chapter is structured as follows: Sect. 2 details the current state-of-the-art. Section 3 presents existing protocols, architectures and standards. Section 4 identifies gaps and challenges that need to be addressed in future research directions, before to conclude in Sect. 5.

2 State of the Art

In IIoT environments, a machine/device can communicate and share information seamlessly inside or outside the industrial ecosystem. The interoperability is a key point to guaranteeing these exchanges in the industrial ecosystem. IIoT interoperability is most of the time referred to as Machine-to-Machine/Device-to-Device communication interoperability (M2M/D2D), where multiple devices can exchange knowledge and their understanding of the context (e.g., mockups, constraints, processes, states, operations, etc.) within a single hop or multiple hop distance. The main goal is to establish a robust and ubiquitous communication among the heterogeneous embedded devices in the network. Machine connectivity, proximity, identification, and messaging are the cornerstones for conceptual M2M/D2D communications in IIoT environments.

There are several challenges to designing an interoperable IIoT environment, and here are the two main ones:

1. a massive amount of heterogeneous IIoT devices are sharing resources, and the majority of the IIoT devices are constrained in terms of storage and processing,
2. the industrial IIoT applications mainly rely on a composition model with an advanced single and centralized orchestrator (Praveen Kumar et al. 2019).

On one hand, several organizations and collaborative institutes such as IEEE[1], IETF[2], and 3GPP[3] explicitly develop and standardize industrial M2M communications. OM2M is one of the universal M2M platforms for industrial applications, where computing devices, gateways, and networks are the building blocks of the ETSI-M2M standard (Ali et al. 2017). Table 1 categorizes IIoT research activities according to the main criteria involved to reach an adaptive and extensible system:

- **Heterogeneity:** IIoT devices are heterogeneous in terms of hardware capabilities, network interfaces and data format supported to interact.
- **Transparency:** We classify transparency capabilities of IIoT systems in two levels: technical integration or platform integration. Technical integration is the possibility to deal with the interoperability issue—either at the network level with compatible protocols, or at the data level with supported data format, or at the semantic level with substitution rules. Platform integration allows to deal with higher levels of interoperability issues—either to integrate new devices, to communicate cross-domain, or to rule all the actors of a domain or sector-specific architecture.
- **Adaptation:** Adaptation criteria in our classification refer to protocol and platform capabilities to adapt and optimize their energy, latency and throughput.
- **Opportunistic:** Opportunistic criteria show the ability of the IIoT system to discover and benefit from its context. In IIoT systems, we particularly classify the system scaling ability in this criteria.
- **Determinism:** Determinism criteria describes the ability of the IIoT system to reproduce the same result from a given context.
- **Automatic:** Automatic criteria validate the IIoT system's ability to automatically make a decision and adapt to an unknown context.
- **Interaction capabilities:** In Industry 4.0, IIoT systems grab context information, to be processed by the cognitive computing part, and to be displayed by the Human-Machine Interaction part. The interaction criteria do not expose the

---

[1] https://standards.ieee.org.

[2] https://www.ietf.org/standards.

[3] https://www.3gpp.org/specifications.

Table 1 Summary of existing IIoT approaches according to PIS criteria

Authors	Context	Heterogeneity			Transparency	Adaptation				Determinism	Automatic	Interactive
		Network	Machine	Data		Energy	Latency	Throughput	Opportunistic			
Pradhan et al. (2018)	Smart City	LTE, IEEE 802.11b/g/n, LoRaWAN, NATO IST 147, MQTT	RFID, spo2, heart, muscle sensors	XML, JSON	Technical (Network)				✗	✗		
Guan et al. (2017)	Smart City	ZigBee, MQTT, WLAN	Smartphone, gateway	VICINITY API	Technical (Network)				✗	✗	✓	
Pramukantoro et al. (2018)	Smart City	6LoWPAN, Bluetooth, CoAP, MQTT, Websocket	ESP 32, ESP 8266, RPI		Technical (network)	✗	✓		✗	✗		
Žarko et al. (2019)	Smart City	HTTPs, AMQP		JSON, RDF	Technical (data)					✗		✓
Pramukantoro et al. (2017)	Smart City	IEEE 802.11b/g/n, CoAP, MQTT, Websocket	MCU, DHT 22, gateway	JSON	Technical (data)	✗	✗	✓	✓	✗		
Doumbouya et al. (2014)	Healthcare, mobility		Smartphone	XML, XTML	Technical (data)					✗		
Alaya et al. (2015)	Smart City	HTTP, CoAP		IoT-O semantic	Technical (semantic)					✗		
Yang and Wei (2019)	Smart City			Rules, SIA, Tabdoc	Technical (semantic)	✗	✓	✓	✗	✗	✓	✓
Epple et al. (2017)	Smart factory			IEC61360	Technical (semantic)					✗		

Reference	Domain	Communication	Devices	Data format	Type							
Ray et al. (2019)	Smart City, healthcare	Bluetooth, IEEE 802.11b/g/n, MQTT	Motor, GRS sensor, gateway		Platform (device)	✗	✓	✓	✗	✗		
Xiao et al. (2014)	Smart *	HTTP		XMPCDC, XMP	Platform (device)	✗	✓	✓	✗	✗		✓
Negash et al. (2019)	Smart factory	HTTP, Zigbee, BLE			Platform (device)	✗	✓	✓	✗	✗	✓	
Golchay et al. (2011)	Smart City, mobility	IEEE 802.11b/g/n, LTE	Gateway, smartphone	JSON	Platform (device)	✓	✓	✓	✗	✗		
Fraile et al. (2018)	Smart factory	IP			Platform (cross-domain)		✓			✗	✓	
Valtolina et al. (2019)	Smart City			JSON, ontology	Platform (cross-domain)	✗	✓	✗	✗	✗		✓
Bröring et al. (2017)	Smart City	BIG IoT API: HTTP, MQTT, CoAP		JSON-LD, XML	Platform (cross-domain)				✗			
Pereira et al. (2016a)	Healthcare	HTTP, CoAP	Gateway, smartphone	JSON	Platform (architecture)	✓	✓	✗	✗	✗		
Gyrard et al. (2014)	Smart City, healthcare	SenML	RFID	OWL	Platform (architecture)		✓		✗			
Pereira et al. (2016b)	Smart City, Healthcare, Mobility	HSUPA, HSDPA, IPv4, HTTP	Gateway, smartphone, GPS	JSON	Platform (architecture)	✓	✓	✗	✗	✗		

HMI's ability to visualize data, but the HMI's ability to maintain and administrate the IIoT system itself.

The first nine rows of the table show that standardizing communications leads to technical transparency—either at the protocol level, for data format, or semantic integration. These approaches optimize device point-to-point communications, such as latency or throughput criteria. They even sometimes take opportunistic advantages of network characteristics, but can not globally optimize the energy of the whole network and system (Mao et al. 2021).

On the other hand, a possible solution to these challenges is categorizing devices into tiers and orchestrating edge-fog-cloud technology into the IIoT environment. Mature cloud technology provides unlimited data collection and sharing resources across distributed IIoT environments, and fog networking supports the industrial processing chain by delivering a faster response to delay-critical industrial applications. In 2011, Cisco introduced the Fog Computing paradigm to process low-latency industrial applications near the sensing devices (Bonomi et al. 2012), or even on edge devices/gateways (Bajic et al. 2019; Cao et al. 2020). Later OpenFog Consortium[4]—now merged with the Industrial Internet Consortium[5]—was founded to develop and standardize Fog Computing (OpenFog Consortium 2018). Fog Computing supports QoS-aware data processing, productivity, mobility, and agility, making interoperable IIoT ecosystems geographically distributed over the network. Cloud computing and its supporting technologies—such as container-based cloud, serverless computing, and cloudlet—support interoperable data processing enabling big data analysis, data migration, and data virtualization by providing a pay-as-you service model. Some standards associated with cloud interoperability are ISO/IEC 19941 (ISO/IEC 2017), IEEE P2301 (IEEE 2020), and OCCI (Ahmed-Nacer et al. 2017). Furthermore, some modeling languages like TOSCA (Binz et al. 2014), CAML (Bergmayr et al. 2014a), HOT (Markelov 2016) support cross-cloud data transfer, where data can be moved from one service provider to another service provider without modifying the structure and format of the data (Bergmayr et al. 2014b).

By incorporating edge-fog-cloud infrastructures into healthcare (Javaid and Haleem 2019), agriculture (Liu et al. 2021), smart city/building/home (Aheleroff et al. 2020; Karaköse and Yetiş 2017), logistics (Barreto et al. 2017; Lin and Yang 2018), automotive sector (Cronin et al. 2019), and manufacturing (Frank et al. 2019; Ghobakhloo 2020; Pilloni 2018; Wu et al. 2017), many—domestic or international (Bettiol et al. 2020)—companies have developed their IIoT environments with the creation of added value (Akdil et al. 2018; Elango 2022; Josefsson 2020) and contribution to circular economies (Dantas et al. 2021). Despite these efforts, as shown in Table 1, very few approaches are automatic, take advantage of the

---

[4] https://web.archive.org/web/20181222131011/http://www.openfogconsortium.org.

[5] https://www.iiconsortium.org.

context in an interactive way, and—because of the unpredictable nature of IIoT communications—none are deterministic.

3   Existing Solutions

Existing solutions are presented in the following sections, first, with a bottom-up approach in Sect. 3.1, describing IIoT protocols allowing to built IIoT environment connections. Then, Sect. 3.2 details the top-down approaches with Industry 4.0 architectures, allowing to build the global IIoT view. Finally, Sect. 3.3 presents existing adopted standards.

3.1   IIoT Protocols

Connectivity in today's world includes a set of heterogeneous devices (e.g., sensors, smartphones), network architectures (e.g., Ad hoc, Bluetooth), and large distributed environments (e.g., Ethernet, HomePlug). This complexity is a big challenging issue for industries (Spachos and Plataniotis 2020). On top of that, devices have their own distinct issues and goals such as energy, latency, scalability, safety that further extend these challenges to the next level. The IIoT main goal is how to build a device-friendly protocol stack so that the devices can communicate with each other, inter-operate, exchange their knowledge and meet their desired objectives (Palattella et al. 2013). However, the existing OSI and IP models are unsuitable to adopt the distributive nature of IIoT and the diverse interoperability issues (Sharma and Gondhi 2018). It, therefore, requires a separate protocol stack, which is scalable, flexible, cost-efficient, and business-oriented.

Several academic efforts and standardized institutes (e.g., IETF (Moran 2021) and ITU-T[6] (ITU-T Study Group 20 2020)) defined 4-levels of IoT protocol stack for ultra-reliable and low-latency communication with the objective of incorporating large numbers of low-powered IoT devices.

IIoT applications can become more efficient, intelligent, flexible, and diverse by considering the benefits of new networking technologies. Therefore, in order to meet the specific IIoT requirements, several design objectives need to be considered. Table 2 summarises popular IoT/IIoT interoperable protocols, giving their characteristics and detailing their abilities according to PIS criteria:

- **Adaptation to power consumption:** Power supply is one of the prerequisites for establishing an industrial technology center for any country. Moreover, this metric is directly related to the economy. Industries such as smart grids,

---

[6] https://www.itu.int/en/itutelecom.

Table 2 Summary of existing IIoT protocols according to PIS criteria

OSI layer	Protocol	Standard	Context	Characteristics					Adaptation			Transp.	Opportunistic
				Transport	Frequency	Range	Data rate	Messaging	Power	Security	QoS	Interop.	Reliability
Physical	Zigbee	IEEE802.15.4	Industry	–	2.4 GHz	10–100 m	250 kbps	–	Low	✓	✓	✓	✓
Physical	RFID	ISO/IEC	Industry	–	960 MHz	200 mm	640 kbps	–	Low	✓	–	✓	✓
Physical	NFC	ISO/IEC	Smartphones	–	13.56 MHz	4m	424 kbps	–	Low	✓	–	✓	✓
Full stack	SigFox	SigFox	Industry	Both	862–928 MHz	50 km	1 kbps	–	Low	✓	✓	✓	✓
Full Stack	NB-IoT	3GPP	Smart City	Both	200 KHz	10 km	1 Mbps	–	Low	✓	✓	✓	✓
Datalink	Z-Wave	IEEE 802.15.4	Smart Home	UDP	915 MHz	30–100 m	100 kbps	–	Low	✓	–	✓	✓
Datalink	HomePlug GP	IEEE 1901-2010	Industry	–	28 MHz	2 km	1 Mbps	–	Low	✓	✓	✓	✓
Datalink	Dash7	ISO/IEC 18000-7	Industry	–	433 MHz	5 km	200 kbps	–	Low	✓	✓	✓	✓
Datalink	LoRaWAN	LoRaWANR 1.0	Smart City	–	868,915 MHz	15 km	50 kbps	–	Low	✓	✓	✓	✓
Datalink	Bluetooth	IEEE 802.15.1	Smart Home	TCP	2.4 GHz	10–150 m	1 Mbps	–	Low	✓	✗	✗	✓
Datalink	BLE	IEEE 802.15.1	Industry	–	2.5 GHz	100 m	2 Mbps	–	Low	✓	✗	✓	✗
Network	6LoWPAN	IEEE 802.15.4	Infrastructure	–	–	–	–	–	Low	✗	–	✓	✗
Network	WiFi	IEEE802.11	Transport	UDP	2.4–5 GHz	50 m	200 Mbps	–	Medium	✓	✗	✓	✗
Network	RPL	IETF	Routing	–	–	–	–	–	Low	✓	✓	✓	✓
Network	IPv4	RFC 3927	Identification	TCP	–	–	–	–	Low	✓	✓	✓	✗
Network	IPv6	IETF	Identification	Both	–	–	–	–	Low	✓	✓	✗	✓
Application	HTTP	HTTP 1.1	Healthcare	Both	–	–	–	Req\Res	High	✓	✓	✗	✓
Application	CoAP	RFC 7252	Industry	UDP	–	–	–	Req\Res	Low	✓	✓	✗	✓

Layer	Protocol	Standard	Type	Transport			Pattern	ReqRes			
Application	XMPP	IETF	Industry	TCP	–	–	ReqRes	High	✗	✗	✓
Application	WebSocket	IETF	Industry	TCP	–	–	Pub\Sub	Low	✗	✗	✓
Application	MQTT	ISO/IEC 20922	Industry	TCP	–	–	PubSub	Low	✗	✓	✓
Application	Mosquitto	MQTT v3.1	Messaging	TCP	–	–	PubSub	Medium	✗	✓	✓
Application	HiveMQ	HiveMQ 4	Messaging	TCP	–	–	PubSub	Low	✗	✓	✓
Application	VerneMQ	VerneMQ	Messaging	TCP	–	–	PubSub	Low	✓	✓	✓
Application	ZeroMQ	ZeroMQ	Industry	TCP	–	–	Both	Low	✓	✓	✓
Application	paho MQTT	paho MQTT	Messaging	TCP	–	–	PubSub	Low	✗	✓	✓
Application	AMQP	OASIS	Messaging	TCP	–	–	PubSub	Low	✓	✓	✓
Application	Rabbit MQ	Rabbit MQ	Messaging	TCP	–	–	Both	High	✓	✓	✓
Application	WS-N	WS-N	Industry	–	–	–	PubSub	High	✓	✗	✗
Application	STOMP	STOMP 1.2	Industry	TCP	–	–	PubSub	Medium	✗	✗	✓
Application	DDS	DDS 1.4	Industry	Both	–	–	PubSub	High	✗	✓	✓

smart cities, mining and manufacturing are the most affected areas of the power supply. Therefore, an interoperable IIoT ecosystem also demands energy-efficient communication protocols between lightweight IIoT devices.

- **Security adaptation:** Industrial digital technology encourages the connection of new devices, thereby increasing new thread factors and unknown risks to the industrial installations. These threads can be internal or external. Network segmentation, user access, and policy management are the three critical factors of industrial security (Benias and Markopoulos 2017).
- **Adaptive QoS:** QoS network resource management and system capabilities for IoT communications are supported with a secure backbone. QoS can include delays, latency and bandwidth variations, and packet loss to provide stable and reliable services through traffic monitoring, resource usage, and channel subscription/allocation constraints. From the user's point of view, QoS parameters can be user satisfaction, cost, processing time, and other network- or system-level parameters.
- **Transparency through interoperability:** Protocol transparency is the ability of a device or application to work independent of the type of protocol used, and a device or application that can work as such is deemed protocol transparent. For protocols, we considered the transparency through the interoperability if the user/application is—or not—concerned with the intermediate operations needed to convert when disconnecting, discovering, or recovering.
- **Opportunistic reliability:** This criterion is the ability of an object to reach a target under specified conditions for a given time, and to adapt to new context conditions. Reliability is a key performance metric for calculating the correlation between actual and optimal production volumes in industrial environments where the main goal is to increase revenue generation.

Such protocol stack includes the sensing layer protocols (e.g., WSN, BLE, and RFID), network-layer protocols (e.g., cellular networks, IPv6, Internet), discovery protocols (e.g., DNS-SD, mDNS, Physical Web), semantic protocols (e.g., Web Thing Model, JSON-LD), device management protocols (e.g., OMA-DM, TR-069), service layer protocol (e.g., COAP, HTTP), and application layer protocols (e.g., DNS, DNP, SNMP, LwM2M, mobile application, and device management) (Lerche et al. 2012). Several updates have been made to incorporate this model into more communication technologies. Ray et al. (2019) have designed a new protocol stack by incorporating gateway level into the existing model. Other works (Agiwal et al. 2016; Vasudev et al. 2020; Wang et al. 2021) also added a separate security layer to secure the industrial network.. Over time, several new protocols have been designed (e.g., NFC, IEEE802.11, Bluetooth Mesh, and 5G) (Zezulka et al. 2018), and existing protocols modified (e.g., MQTT, CoAP, CoAP+, and CoAP++) to achieve interoperability (Iglesias-Urkia et al. 2017). In addition, several industrial proprietary and open-source application protocols such as 6LowPAN (Bonavolontà et al. 2017) and WirelessHART were proposed for industrial application (Devan et al. 2021). ISA100.11a has been designed for automation (Adriano et al. 2018). SigFox has been introduced for M2M communication (Goursaud and Gorce 2015).

BLE has been redesigned for low-powered communication, NB-IoT for smart metering. And LTE-MTC has been introduced for machine-level communication to make interoperable connectivity among heterogeneous devices (Dangana et al. 2021; Mogensen et al. 2019).

3.2 Industry 4.0 Architectures

An architecture represents a robust and ground-level understanding related to the scenarios that help to recognize problems and difficulties. A Reference Architecture (RA) provides a template solution for an architecture for a particular domain— in our precise case for Industry 4.0 (Clements et al. 2010). The key idea of designing a reference architecture (such as, for example, service-oriented architecture (SOA)) is to highlight modularity, scalability, adaptiveness, and interoperability among the connected heterogeneous devices in a real-time environment. Over the past decades, several reference architectures have been designed to establish IoT/IIoT ecosystems. Sarkar et al. (2022) have introduced a four-layer fog framework to handle latency-sensitive IoT applications. Mukherjee et al. (2019) have demonstrated three-level IIoT architecture for interoperable data processing. Viriyasitavat et al. (2019) have introduced a secure IoT architecture. Several other efforts (Al-Masri 2018; Bedhief et al. 2019; Hou et al. 2019; Pallewatta et al. 2022) also proposed more profitable multi-tier IIoT architectures to meet industrial application requirements. Some standardized RAs (e.g., IEC30166 (ISO/IEC 2020), RAMI (Hankel and Rexroth 2015), BIG IoT (Bröring et al. 2017), IBM Industry 4.0 (Kiradjiev 2017), FIWARE (Barriga et al. 2022; Cirillo et al. 2019), Arrowhead[7] (Delsing 2017), Open Connectivity Foundation[8] (Park 2017), ThingWorx[9]) have been proposed to address issues in the manufacturing industry (Wang 2020). Some popular commercial reference architectures are AWS IoT[10], Azure IoT[11], Google Cloud IoT[12], and Predix IIoT[13]. Two standardizing organizations, namely Industrial Internet Consortium (IIC) and Platform Industrie 4.0[14], proposed RAMI 4.0 and IIRA architectures. These organizations are mainly focus on Industry 4.0 and interoperable IIoT-related research issues (Hankel and Rexroth 2015). In the same vein, the architecture

---

[7] https://arrowhead.eu/why-how/what-is-it/architecture.

[8] https://openconnectivity.org.

[9] https://www.ptc.com/en/products/thingworx.

[10] https://aws.amazon.com/iot.

[11] https://azure.microsoft.com/overview/iot.

[12] https://cloud.google.com/solutions/iot.

[13] https://www.ge.com/digital/iiot-platform.

[14] https://www.plattform-i40.de.

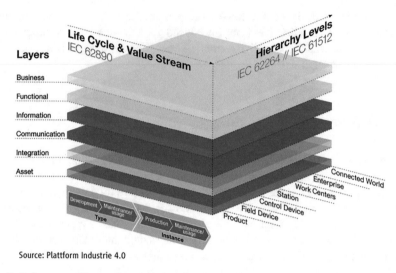

Source: Plattform Industrie 4.0

Fig. 3 Reference architectural model industrie 4.0 (RAMI 4.0)

of IBM Industry 4.0[15] and the NIST[16] services-based architecture[17] are other popular design architectures. We focus on these four popular industrial reference architectures, which are discussed below:

1. **RAMI 4.0:** In a smart industry, the production objects must communicate automatically and autonomously with other devices (Hankel and Rexroth 2015). To create a unified platform, industries and research institutions collaborated to design RAMI 4.0 in 2015, supporting a service-oriented architecture. RAMI 4.0 provides an interoperable framework by introducing a set of conceptual interoperability layers that combine all hierarchical IT components in a layer and life cycle model for the manufacturing industry (cf Fig. 3). These are the integration layer, the business layer, the information layer, the functional layer, the asset layer, and the communication layer. With RAMI 4.0, complex processes are separated into easily accessible packages to provide data protection and IT security. The key objectives of RAMI 4.0 are to extend business and organization models, connect physical things to the real world, and transform the underlying world into a digital world.

2. **IIRA:** The term IIRA stands for Investment, Innovation & Research Alliance. This standardized architecture was first released in 2015 to encourage system architects from the industrial domain to build their own structures based on

[15] https://www.ibm.com/topics/industry-4-0.

[16] https://www.nist.gov.

[17] https://www.nist.gov/programs-projects/service-oriented-architectures-smart-manufacturing-project.

shared knowledge and principles (IIConsortium Architecture Task Group 2019). The IIRA Reference Architecture provides a set of core principles and a common foundation for creating, reporting, communicating, and executing among IoT participants. It also permits building the system on top of IIoT - with no restrictions on the use of particular specifications or requirements of protocols. Similar to RAMI 4.0, the key features of this model are safety, security, resiliency, privacy, scalability, and reliability.

3. **IBM Industry 4.0 Architecture:** In 2017, IBM designed Industry 4.0 Reference Architecture to manage devices and provide cognitive services to users (Kiradjiev 2017). This standardized architecture consists of two layers, namely the device layer and the platform layer. In the device layer (also called the edge layer), smart devices share the generated data with gateway devices and hybrid cloud servers. Furthermore, the platform layer is divided into the plant and enterprise layers, which are commonly used for data visualization and cloud data management. The platform layer also provides infrastructure services, application development, security, and data analytics through the API platform. IBM Industry 4.0 architecture also allows OPC-UA communication standards.

4. **NIST Service-Oriented Reference Architecture:** NIST has also proposed one of the most popular service-oriented reference architectures for the manufacturing industry (Ivezic et al. 2018; Lu et al. 2016). This architecture combines information technology and operational technology via a manufacturing service bus. It offers a business intelligence service that ensures communication between all the stakeholders. The design objectives of NIST RA are to provide real-time industrial services, operational services, virtual services, IT services, data analysis, and application management.

Even though the architectures vary by application domains, sensing devices, gateway, fog/edge server, and cloud infrastructures are the most common components in all architectures. Figure 4, for instance, presents an architecture, where heterogeneous devices and technologies are combined to achieve interoperability in a real-time environment. Here, the gateway devices are mainly designed for handling cross-domain interoperability (Patel et al. 2018), edge/fog servers are in charge of handling delay-critical industrial applications, and the cloud servers are deployed for storage and data analysis (Valtolina et al. 2019).

3.3 Standards

To achieve a good business assistance and a high productivity in the industrial environment, IIoT-related technologies must be engineered and standardized to analyze the specification of data exchange, manufacturing, and communication technologies requirements among the heterogeneous objects. The future of IIoT mainly relies on technology standardizations (e.g., IEEE 802.15.4a (Molisch et al. 2004), IETF) that include interoperability, usability, trustworthiness, and zero downtime business

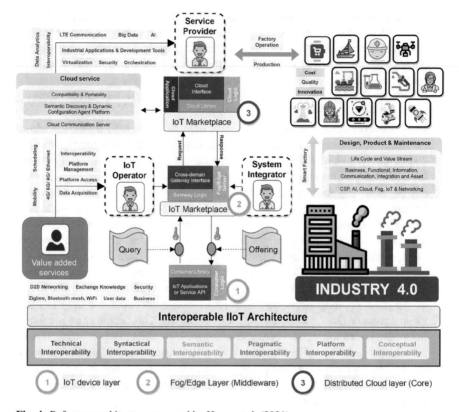

Fig. 4 Reference architecture proposed by Hazra et al. (2021)

operations. Currently, several industrial consortiums, organizations (IEEE, W3C[18], OASIS[19]) and IoT management frameworks such as ITU-T, OCF, and oneM2M[20] are controlling the standardization of numerous IIoT technology (Kim et al. 2016). Further, standardization helps to shorten the chance of business monopoly and encourages new startups and services to grow.

Over time, many domain-specific standardizing organizations and institutes have worked (both collaboratively or individually) on a number of industry issues related to IIoT connectivity and communication, architecture, infrastructure and interoperability to provide services in various fields (e.g., mobility, smart city, manufacturing, agriculture, etc.) (Robert et al. 2017). Among them, some prominent workgroups emerged, such as standardized organizations for connectivity (3GPP[21],

---

[18] https://www.w3.org.

[19] https://www.oasis-open.org.

[20] https://www.onem2m.org.

[21] https://www.3gpp.org.

IETF6Lo[22], IEC[23], OSGi[24] (Manzaroli et al. 2010), ETSI DASH7[25]), standardized organizations for interoperability (IEEE PLC[26], IPv6 Forum[27], OMA[28],[29] (Delgado et al. 2005), oneM2M, DMTF[30], SNIA[31] (Zhang et al. 2013)), standardized organizations for application (OSGi), standardized organizations for infrastructure (ETSI TETRA[32], ITU-T, IEEE, IEC, OSGi), standardized organizations for IoT architecture (IEEE, ITU-T, ISO/IEC JTC1[33]), standardized organizations for devices and sensor technology (3GPP, ETSI ERM[34], ISO/IEC, M2.COM[35]), standardized organizations for security and privacy (IEEE, ETSI DECT[36], ISO/IEC). We present a brief comparative analysis of standardized organizations and standards in Table 3. We divide our classification according to three main aspects:

1. **Challenge:** IIoT issues can be tackled at different levels to allow different manufacturers to have chip/hardware compatibility - inside the device, through the interactions - network connectivity or interoperability, inside the infrastructure, in the applications, or even though the global organization of the architecture.
2. **Context:** Standards can be used in different vertical application domains. Addressing specific domains completely guide the standard definitions.
3. **Goals/Responsibilities:** According to the level challenged, each standard can provide different abilities. Knowing the core responsibilities of each standard is essential to orient the standard choices to integrate into a Reference Architecture.

Moreover, some academic researchers have also been brought in to solve some standardization problems for industrial applications. For example, Weyrich and Ebert (2016) have talked about IIoT architectures and standards for an industrial environment. Deng et al. (2019) have highlighted the importance of IEEE 802.11ba for green IIoT in fast-paced industrial applications. Similarly, other works (Chi et al. 2014; Leonardi et al. 2019; Wang et al. 2019) also significantly impacted the IIoT domain, especially for long-range communications. However, there is still much

---

[22] https://tools.ietf.org/wg/6lo.

[23] https://iec.ch.

[24] https://www.osgi.org.

[25] https://www.dash7-alliance.org.

[26] https://standards.ieee.org/industry-connections/interoperability-and-compliance-testing.

[27] https://www.ipv6forum.com.

[28] https://omaspecworks.org.

[29] https://technical.openmobilealliance.org.

[30] https://www.dmtf.org.

[31] https://www.snia.org.

[32] https://www.etsi.org/technologies/tetra.

[33] https://jtc1info.org.

[34] https://www.etsi.org/committee/1398-erm.

[35] https://www.bosch-sensortec.com/news/sensor-platform-m2-com.html.

[36] https://www.etsi.org/committee/dect.

Table 3 Summary of existing IIoT standards

Challenge	Organization	Standards	Context	Goals/Responsibilities
Device	3GPP	GPRS, LTE-Advanced Pro, HSPA	Smart device, industry, agriculture, smart city	Radio transmission, M2M communication, low latency network, high data rate
Device	ETSI	ETSI EN 301 406, ETSI TS 102 939 1	Smart device, industry, agriculture, smart city	Home automation, low energy radio transmission, security and authentication, cellular network
Device	IEEE - ISO/IEC	ISO/IEC/IEEE 21451-1:2010, ISO/IEC/IEEE 21450:2010	Agriculture, industry, smart city	Device interoperability, TIM and TEDS, smart interface, sensing and actuating
Device	IETF CoRE	CoAP	Smart city, agriculture, mobility, industry	Protocol design, request-response model, time-dependent access, transmission consistency
Device	oneM2M	BBF	Smart city, agriculture, mobility, industry	Message flow, protocol management, standard communication, M2M connectivity
Interoperability	AllSeen	AllJoyn	Smart device	Among D2D and software applications, secure communication, client/server model, interoperability testing
Interoperability	IEEE PLC	IEEE 1905.1a	Smart environment	Mac and physical layer design, smart home technology, wired and wireless
Interoperability	oneM2M	ETSI TS 118 112/118 123	Agriculture, smart device, mobility	Interoperability testing, ontology, smart home applications, data management
Connectivity	3GPP	ETSI TS 123 002, NB-IoT, LTE-ADVANCED	Smart city, agriculture, smart device, mobility	Core networking, delay-sensitive applications, network optimization, data transmission over a cellular network, radio telecommunication
Connectivity	ETSI DECT	ETSI TS 102 939-2, ETSI EN 300 175	Smart city, industry	M2M communication, industrial automation, low power communication, bi-directional data transmission
Connectivity	IEEE 802	IEEE 802.11 / 802.15.4	Smart device, mobility	Wireless transmission, MAC and physical layer design, unlicensed spectrum, WPAN and LR-WPANs
Connectivity	OASIS	MQTT	Smart device, mobility	M2M communication, publish/subscribe messaging, resource discovery, QoS guarantees

Infrastructure	ETSI TETRA	ETSI EN 300 392	Agriculture, smart environment	Digital radio system, bi-directional communication, large scale communication, transportation
Infrastructure	IEEE	802.11s	Agriculture, smart environment, smart device, mobility	Public WiFi, follow mesh topology, high data rate, mesh gateway
Infrastructure	ITU-T	ITU G.992.x, ITU G.651, ITU G.652	Smart device, mobility, agriculture, industry	Delay sensitive IoT data, audio, and video, QoS guaranteed, fiber technology
Infrastructure	oneM2M	ETSI TS 118 102, ETSI TS 118 101	Agriculture, smart device, smart environment, industry	IoT deployment, platform service, middleware interoperability
Infrastructure	IEC	IEC 61508	Agriculture, smart device, mobility, smart environment, industry	Safety system, control system, Industry application
Application	BBF	TR-069/CPE	Smart environment	Remote device management, application service management, auto configuration service, gateway and router
Application	OMA	OMA-DM/LWM2M	Smart device, smart environment	Data synchronization, mobility and fault detection, lightweight data model, device management
Architecture	IEEE	P2413	Agriculture, smart device	Industrial technology, agricultural framework, D2D communication, SOA architecture
Architecture	ICC	IIRA	Agriculture, smart device, smart environment	Framework for RA, device interoperability, high level abstraction, industrial viewpoint
Architecture	ITU-T	ITU-T Y.2060	Agriculture, smart device, smart environment	Four layer reference architecture, security management, cross-domain communication, business architecture
Architecture	oneM2M	ETSI TS 118 101	Smart city, smart device, mobility, agriculture, industry	M2M communication, service layer, end-to-end transmission, functional architecture

room for improvement, especially concerning the interoperability challenge in the Industry 4.0 landscape.

4 Discussions

To face the great evolution of technologies, industries need to be flexible to adapt to new requirements and anticipate new needs. Future research still needs to address many challenges to guarantee a good fit between IIoT technologies and companies' businesses. We conclude this chapter by identifying some fundamental research challenges and future trends:

- **IIoT security issues:** Security is one of the essential criteria of Industry 4.0, which has always received the greatest attention from industry and the great public. For example, banking systems, telecommunication and retail sectors are always in need of securing their transactions from third parties (Khanboubi et al. 2019; Liu et al. 2019). This security challenge is even more significant as IIoT pushes the classically-closed IT security limits to be semipermeable to attacks (Figueroa-Lorenzo et al. 2020; Tournier et al. 2021). Digital society demands a more secure and reliable technology, where data can be distributed over the network and transactions validated and stored in chronological order. Blockchain is a decentralized and distributed technology that allows user data to be stored securely in a distributed way in the network, reducing the ability of data tampering. Even if costly (Sedlmeir et al. 2020), by incorporating blockchain into the industrial environment, both users and industry can securely connect without the help of a third party and create trust by having no central authority (Huo et al. 2022). Cybersecurity evolves toward the convergence of AI, IoT, blockchain and Edge Computing (Muhati et al. 2022) to detect cross-domain attacks (Tournier et al. 2020), to mitigate risks (Silva and Lepikson 2022) by using advanced machine learning techniques, such as deep learning/reinforcement learning, to discover network patterns, identify and prevent intrusions (Latif et al. 2021; Vaiyapuri et al. 2021).
- **IIoT ecosystem with energy harvesting:** IoT is an undeniable precursor to making useful measurements and controls for the Industry 4.0. Sensor deployment implies a massive demand for low-power battery-free/rechargeable wireless devices deployment. Additionally, recharging and replacing the batteries of hundreds or even thousands of IIoT devices can be laborious or even impractical (de Wolff 2021). To address this challenge, several energy harvesting approaches such as low-powered communication protocols, light energy harvesting, kinetic energy harvesting, and thermal energy harvesting have been designed for IIoT applications (Sanislav et al. 2021). However, such strategies are not entirely suitable for dense IIoT deployment. As the IIoT devices are often deployed in unstable weather-dependent (Murphy et al. 2021) or faulty environments (Ahmed et al. 2020, 2021), relying on a single energy

harvesting technique can lead to a number of other problems, such as power shortages, hardware failures, and intermittent uptime. To overcome this energy bottleneck, two or more energy harvesting techniques need to be integrated into IIoT devices for efficient power management (Sah and Amgoth 2020), hybrid energy storage technologies for harvesting systems can be used (Altinel and Karabulut Kurt 2019), and low-tech & green IIoT could be consider to reduce energy and temperature and CO_2 emission rate in the environment (Hu et al. 2021; Patsavellas and Salonitis 2019). These later points remain big challenges for the industry.

- **IIoT network and infrastructure virtualization:** 5G and its preceding 4G—known as LTE-Advanced—are known to build IoT-enabled intelligent services and application-oriented ecosystem. The increasing 5G demand for high-quality multimedia data and low-latency applications triggered several issues in industrial networks, especially the efficient, safe and secure allocation of resources (Brettel et al. 2014; Hazra et al. 2021). To implement this vision realistically in IIoT environments, the physical network must be divided into several separate logical networks of various sizes and configurations to allocate these resources to different types of services with different properties to guarantee. Virtualization through SDN and NFV bridges this gap between network configuration and network resources management (Barakabitze et al. 2020). Several efforts have been made on combining SDN/NFV solutions with edge/fog/cloud architectures to develop new services and control over the network (Chalapathi et al. 2021). Container-based SDN controller with edge/fog federations has been proposed to make an interoperable industrial network (Hou et al. 2019; Rufino et al. 2017). Manufacturing companies can virtually control production with efficient delay-tolerant service provisioning and on-demand specific resource optimization, such as through WSN (Nkomo et al. 2018) or 3D-reconstruction (Badat et al. 2020). However, researchers still need to consider several other issues such as computing on IoT nodes (Blanco and Le Mouël 2020), distributed scheduling, load balancing, easy network and cluster programmability (Fortier et al. 2021), multi-tenant services, hybrid SDN controllers, and 6G low-latency mobile service requirements (Du et al. 2020; Qadir et al. 2022) to take total control over the industrial networks.

- **IIoT standardization:** IoT protocols and their standardization are pillars of establishing IIoT ecosystems. Internet standards have shown a convergence adoption time of 10 to 20 years. IIoT domain is even more complex, having vertical-silo application domains. Several network protocols for IoT have been designed and standardized to address various challenges like naming, addressing, routing, flow control, congestion avoidance, and large-scale industrial deployment. These protocols, however, need to be adapted to the industrial requirements. Industrial applications are characterized by extreme conditions environments (high humidity, extreme temperatures, electromagnetic interference) that complicate the integration of low latency, real-time, determinism, frequent packet loss, and reliability properties in the definition of generic standards (Qiu et al. 2022; Sari et al. 2020; Vitturi et al. 2019). Standardization of the semantic representation and interoperability of the knowledge and the D2D interactions is also a great issue (Burns et al. 2019), and an agreed methodology among manufacturers would have to be established to meet the roadmap for standardization of Industry 4.0 proposed by Platform Industrie 4.0 (Platform Industrie 4.0 2019).

- **From Industry 4.0 to Society 5.0:** Some studies analyze the complex, mutually generative range of economic, social and political transformations of the First, Second and Third Industrial Revolutions, and argument that the same criteria cannot be found about the alleged Fourth Industrial Revolution (Moll 2021). Technologies undoubtedly continue to alter work, and lead to new varieties of work, but this evolution must also meet the broader social, cultural and geopolitical transformations to constitute a revolution. Society 5.0 concept has been introduced in Japan (Deguchi et al. 2020) and reframes two kinds of relationships: the relationship between technology and society and the technology-mediated relationship between individuals and society. Industry 4.0 advocates smart factories, while Society 5.0 calls for a supersmart society. The two visions differ in terms of measuring outcomes. Industry 4.0 aspires to create new added value and minimize manufacturing costs. Such down-to-earth outcomes allow for relatively simple and clear-cut performance metrics, such as productivity. By contrast, Society 5.0 aspires to create a supersmart society. The metrics, in this case, are much more complex. Metrics, such as sustainability, are of great importance (Beier et al. 2020; Ghobakhloo 2020). Having different social and industrial goals can greatly affect the interpretive structural modelling techniques structuring contextual relationships among the Industry 4.0 architectural functions. And can so, as a consequence, totally affect the way to deploy IIoT devices, infrastructures and services. Corporate social responsibilities, environmental dimensions (Potocan et al. 2021) or happiness (Ravina Ripoll et al. 2022) are metrics to be considered and technological deployment consequences are to be studied. Society 5.0 focuses heavily on the public impact of technologies and on the need to create a better society.

5 Conclusions

Industry 4.0 is a revolution transforming the industry with the emergence of IoT and related technologies. This revolution drives global industrial architectures into an advanced level of digitization and productivity—where customers can experiment with customized on-demand requirements. Customer satisfaction and company productivity can thus go hand in hand. This chapter mainly focused on Industry 4.0 connectivity capabilities—towards the Industrial Internet of Things—needed to capture the context. Specifically, we have stretched on this digitalization of the physical world from an industrial perspective. We have shortened the way protocols, architectures, and standards help companies adopt the emerging Industry 4.0 technologies. Finally, we have summarized our discussion by briefly reviewing several research challenges and future scopes.

References

Adriano JD, Rosario ECd, Rodrigues JJ (2018) Wireless sensor networks in industry 4.0: WirelessHART and ISA100.11a. In: 13th IEEE International Conference on Industry Applications (INDUSCON), pp 924–929, DOI https://doi.org/10.1109/INDUSCON.2018.8627177, URL https://ieeexplore.ieee.org/document/8627177

Agiwal M, Roy A, Saxena N (2016) Next generation 5G wireless networks: A comprehensive survey. IEEE Communications Surveys & Tutorials 18(3):1617–1655, DOI https://doi.org/10.1109/COMST.2016.2532458, URL https://ieeexplore.ieee.org/document/7414384

Aheleroff S, Xu X, Lu Y, Aristizabal M, Pablo Velásquez J, Joa B, Valencia Y (2020) IoT-enabled smart appliances under industry 4.0: A case study. Advanced Engineering Informatics 43:101043, DOI https://doi.org/10.1016/j.aei.2020.101043, URL https://www.sciencedirect.com/science/article/pii/S1474034620300124

Ahmed S, Le Mouël F, Stouls N (2020) Resilient IoT-based monitoring system for crude oil pipelines. In: 7th International Conference on Internet of Things: Systems, Management and Security (IOTSMS), pp 1–7, DOI https://doi.org/10.1109/IOTSMS52051.2020.9340197, URL https://ieeexplore.ieee.org/document/9340197

Ahmed S, Le Mouël F, Stouls N, Lipeme Kouyi G (2021) HyDiLLEch: A WSN-based distributed leak detection and localisation in crude oil pipelines. In: Barolli L, Woungang I, Enokido T (eds) Advanced Information Networking and Applications, Springer International Publishing, Cham, pp 626–637, URL https://link.springer.com/chapter/10.1007/978-3-030-75100-5_54

Ahmed-Nacer M, Gaaloul W, Tata S (2017) OCCI-compliant cloud configuration simulation. In: IEEE International Conference on Edge Computing (EDGE), pp 73–81, DOI https://doi.org/10.1109/IEEE.EDGE.2017.18, URL https://ieeexplore.ieee.org/document/8029259

Akdil KY, Ustundag A, Cevikcan E (2018) Maturity and Readiness Model for Industry 4.0 Strategy, Springer International Publishing, Cham, pp 61–94. URL https://doi.org/10.1007/978-3-319-57870-5_4

Al-Masri E (2018) QoS-aware IIoT microservices architecture. In: IEEE International Conference on Industrial Internet, ICII 2018, Seattle, WA, USA, October 21–23, 2018, IEEE, pp 171–172, DOI https://doi.org/10.1109/ICII.2018.00030

Alaya MB, Medjiah S, Monteil T, Drira K (2015) Toward semantic interoperability in oneM2M architecture. IEEE Communications Magazine 53(12):35–41, DOI https://doi.org/10.1109/MCOM.2015.7355582, URL https://ieeexplore.ieee.org/document/7355582

Ali A, Shah GA, Farooq MO, Ghani U (2017) Technologies and challenges in developing machine-to-machine applications: A survey. Journal of Network and Computer Applications 83:124–139, DOI https://doi.org/10.1016/j.jnca.2017.02.002, URL https://www.sciencedirect.com/science/article/pii/S1084804517300620

Altinel D, Karabulut Kurt G (2019) Modeling of multiple energy sources for hybrid energy harvesting iot systems. IEEE Internet of Things Journal 6(6):10846–10854, DOI https://doi.org/10.1109/JIOT.2019.2942071, URL https://ieeexplore.ieee.org/document/8843930

Žarko IP, Mueller S, Płociennik M, Rajtar T, Jacoby M, Pardi M, Insolvibile G, Glykantzis V, Antonić A, Kušek M, Soursos S (2019) The symbIoTe solution for semantic and syntactic interoperability of cloud-based IoT platforms. In: Global IoT Summit (GIoTS), pp 1–6, DOI https://doi.org/10.1109/GIOTS.2019.8766420, URL https://ieeexplore.ieee.org/document/8766420

Badat L, Vidal V, Pioli L, Mehaut JF, Honorio L, Dantas MA (2020) An IIoT edge environment as a main support to a 3D reconstruction virtualization application. In: Anais do XVIII Workshop em Clouds e Aplicações, SBC, Porto Alegre, RS, Brasil, pp 1–12, DOI https://doi.org/10.5753/wcga.2020.12440, URL https://sol.sbc.org.br/index.php/wcga/article/view/12440

Bajic B, Cosic I, Katalinic B, Moraca S, Lazarevic M, Rikalovic A (2019) Edge computing vs. cloud computing: Challenges and opportunities in industry 4.0. In: 30th DAAAM International Symposium, DAAAM International, Vienna, Austria, DOI https://doi.org/10.2507/30th.daaam.proceedings.120, URL https://www.daaam.info/Downloads/Pdfs/proceedings/proceedings_2019/120.pdf

Barakabitze AA, Ahmad A, Mijumbi R, Hines A (2020) 5G network slicing using SDN and NFV: A survey of taxonomy, architectures and future challenges. Computer Networks 167:106984, DOI https://doi.org/10.1016/j.comnet.2019.106984, URL https://www.sciencedirect.com/science/article/pii/S1389128619304773

Barreto L, Amaral A, Pereira T (2017) Industry 4.0 implications in logistics: an overview. Procedia Manufacturing 13:1245–1252, DOI https://doi.org/10.1016/j.promfg.2017.09.045, URL https://www.sciencedirect.com/science/article/pii/S2351978917306807, manufacturing Engineering Society International Conference 2017, MESIC 2017, 28–30 June 2017, Vigo (Pontevedra), Spain

Barriga JA, Clemente PJ, Hernández J, Pérez-Toledano MA (2022) SimulateIoT-FIWARE: Domain specific language to design, code generation and execute IoT simulation environments on FIWARE. IEEE Access 10:7800–7822, DOI https://doi.org/10.1109/ACCESS.2022.3142894, URL https://ieeexplore.ieee.org/document/9680737

Bedhief I, Foschini L, Bellavista P, Kassar M, Aguili T (2019) Toward self-adaptive software defined fog networking architecture for IIoT and industry 4.0. In: IEEE 24th International Workshop on Computer Aided Modeling and Design of Communication Links and Networks (CAMAD), pp 1–5, DOI https://doi.org/10.1109/CAMAD.2019.8858499, URL https://ieeexplore.ieee.org/document/8858499

Beier G, Ullrich A, Niehoff S, Reißig M, Habich M (2020) Industry 4.0: How it is defined from a sociotechnical perspective and how much sustainability it includes – a literature review. Journal of Cleaner Production 259:120856, DOI https://doi.org/10.1016/j.jclepro.2020.120856, URL https://www.sciencedirect.com/science/article/pii/S0959652620309033

Benias N, Markopoulos AP (2017) A review on the readiness level and cyber-security challenges in industry 4.0. In: South Eastern European Design Automation, Computer Engineering, Computer Networks and Social Media Conference (SEEDA-CECNSM), pp 1–5, DOI https://doi.org/10.23919/SEEDA-CECNSM.2017.8088234, URL https://ieeexplore.ieee.org/document/8088234

Bergmayr A, Troya J, Neubauer P, Wimmer M, Kappel G (2014a) UML-based cloud application modeling with libraries, profiles, and templates. In: Paige RF, Cabot J, Brambilla M, Rose LM, Hill JH (eds) 2nd International Workshop on Model-Driven Engineering on and for the Cloud co-located with the 17th International Conference on Model Driven Engineering Languages and Systems, CloudMDE@MoDELS 2014, Valencia, Spain, September 30, 2014, CEUR-WS.org, CEUR Workshop Proceedings, vol 1242, pp 56–65, URL http://ceur-ws.org/Vol-1242/paper7.pdf

Bergmayr A, Wimmer M, Kappel G, Grossniklaus M (2014b) Cloud modeling languages by example. In: IEEE 7th International Conference on Service-Oriented Computing and Applications, pp 137–146, DOI https://doi.org/10.1109/SOCA.2014.56, URL https://ieeexplore.ieee.org/document/6978602

Bettiol M, Capestro M, Marchi VD, Maria ED (2020) Industry 4.0 investments in manufacturing firms and internationalization. "Marco Fanno" Working Papers 0245, Dipartimento di Scienze Economiche "Marco Fanno", URL https://ideas.repec.org/p/pad/wpaper/0245.html

Binz T, Breitenbücher U, Kopp O, Leymann F (2014) TOSCA: Portable Automated Deployment and Management of Cloud Applications, Springer New York, New York, NY, pp 527–549. DOI https://doi.org/10.1007/978-1-4614-7535-4_22, URL https://doi.org/10.1007/978-1-4614-7535-4_22

Blanco DF, Le Mouël F (2020) Infrastructure de services cloud FaaS sur noeuds IoT. In: Conférence d'informatique en Parallélisme, Architecture et Systèmes (ComPAS'2020), Lyon, France, URL http://www.le-mouel.net/Research/Publications/Conferences/2020/COMPAS2020.pdf

Bonavolontà F, Tedesco A, Moriello RSL, Tufano A (2017) Enabling wireless technologies for industry 4.0: State of the art. In: IEEE International Workshop on Measurement and Networking (M&N), pp 1–5, DOI https://doi.org/10.1109/IWMN.2017.8078381, URL https://ieeexplore.ieee.org/document/8078381

Bonomi F, Milito R, Zhu J, Addepalli S (2012) Fog computing and its role in the internet of things. In: First Edition of the MCC Workshop on Mobile Cloud Computing, Association for Computing Machinery, New York, NY, USA, MCC '12, p 13–16, https://doi.org/10.1145/2342509.2342513

Boyes H, Hallaq B, Cunningham J, Watson T (2018) The industrial internet of things (IIoT): An analysis framework. Computers in Industry 101:1–12, DOI https://doi.org/10.1016/j.compind.2018.04.015, URL https://www.sciencedirect.com/science/article/pii/S0166361517307285

Brettel M, Friederichsen N, Keller M, Rosenberg M (2014) How virtualization, decentralization and network building change the manufacturing landscape: An industry 4.0 perspective. International Journal of Information and Communication Engineering 8(1):37 – 44, URL https://publications.waset.org/vol/85

Bröring A, Schmid S, Schindhelm CK, Khelil A, Käbisch S, Kramer D, Le Phuoc D, Mitic J, Anicic D, Teniente E (2017) Enabling IoT ecosystems through platform interoperability. IEEE Software 34(1):54–61, DOI https://doi.org/10.1109/MS.2017.2, URL https://ieeexplore.ieee.org/document/7819420

Buer SV, Fragapane GI, Strandhagen JO (2018) The data-driven process improvement cycle: Using digitalization for continuous improvement. IFAC-PapersOnLine 51(11):1035–1040, DOI https://doi.org/10.1016/j.ifacol.2018.08.471, URL https://www.sciencedirect.com/science/article/pii/S2405896318315994, 16th IFAC Symposium on Information Control Problems in Manufacturing INCOM 2018

Burns T, Cosgrove J, Doyle F (2019) A review of interoperability standards for industry 4.0. Procedia Manufacturing 38:646–653, DOI https://doi.org/10.1016/j.promfg.2020.01.083, URL https://www.sciencedirect.com/science/article/pii/S2351978920300846, 29th International Conference on Flexible Automation and Intelligent Manufacturing (FAIM 2019), June 24–28, 2019, Limerick, Ireland, Beyond Industry 4.0: Industrial Advances, Engineering Education and Intelligent Manufacturing

Cao K, Liu Y, Meng G, Sun Q (2020) An overview on edge computing research. IEEE Access 8:85714–85728, DOI https://doi.org/10.1109/ACCESS.2020.2991734, URL https://ieeexplore.ieee.org/document/9083958

Chalapathi GSS, Chamola V, Vaish A, Buyya R (2021) Industrial Internet of Things (IIoT) Applications of Edge and Fog Computing: A Review and Future Directions, Springer International Publishing, pp 293–325. URL https://doi.org/10.1007/978-3-030-57328-7_12

Chen M, Mao S, Liu Y (2014) Big data: A survey. Mobile Networks and Applications 19(2):171–209, DOI https://doi.org/10.1007/s11036-013-0489-0, URL https://doi.org/10.1007/s11036-013-0489-0

Chi Q, Yan H, Zhang C, Pang Z, Xu LD (2014) A reconfigurable smart sensor interface for industrial WSN in IoT environment. IEEE Transactions on Industrial Informatics 10(2):1417–1425, DOI https://doi.org/10.1109/TII.2014.2306798, URL https://ieeexplore.ieee.org/document/6742595

Cirillo F, Solmaz G, Berz EL, Bauer M, Cheng B, Kovacs E (2019) A standard-based open source IoT platform: FIWARE. IEEE Internet of Things Magazine 2(3):12–18, DOI https://doi.org/10.1109/IOTM.0001.1800022, URL https://ieeexplore.ieee.org/document/8950963

Clements P, Bachmann F, Bass L, Garlan D, Ivers J, Little R, Merson P, Nord R, Stafford J (2010) Documenting Software Architectures: Views and Beyond. SEI Series in Software Engineering, Addison-Wesley, Upper Saddle River, NJ, URL https://www.safaribooksonline.com/library/view/documenting-software-architectures/9780132488617/

Cronin C, Conway A, Walsh J (2019) Flexible manufacturing systems using IIoT in the automotive sector. Procedia Manufacturing 38:1652–1659, DOI https://doi.org/10.1016/j.promfg.2020.01.119, URL https://www.sciencedirect.com/science/article/pii/S2351978920301207, 29th International Conference on Flexible Automation and Intelligent Manufacturing (FAIM 2019), June 24–28, 2019, Limerick, Ireland, Beyond Industry 4.0: Industrial Advances, Engineering Education and Intelligent Manufacturing

Dangana M, Ansari S, Abbasi QH, Hussain S, Imran MA (2021) Suitability of NB-IoT for indoor industrial environment: A survey and insights. Sensors 21(16), DOI https://doi.org/10.3390/s21165284, URL https://www.mdpi.com/1424-8220/21/16/5284

Dantas T, de Souza E, Destro I, Hammes G, Rodriguez C, Soares S (2021) How the combination of circular economy and industry 4.0 can contribute towards achieving the sustainable development goals. Sustainable Production and Consumption 26:213–227, DOI https://doi.org/10.1016/j.spc.2020.10.005, URL https://www.sciencedirect.com/science/article/pii/S2352550920307983

Deguchi A, Hirai C, Matsuoka H, Nakano T, Oshima K, Tai M, Tani S (2020) What Is Society 5.0?, Springer Singapore, Singapore, pp 1–23. URL https://doi.org/10.1007/978-981-15-2989-4_1

Delgado J, Prados J, Rodriguez E (2005) Profiles for interoperability between MPEG-21 REL and OMA DRM. In: Seventh IEEE International Conference on E-Commerce Technology (CEC'05), pp 518–521, DOI https://doi.org/10.1109/ICECT.2005.69, URL https://ieeexplore.ieee.org/document/1524100

Delsing J (2017) IoT automation: Arrowhead framework. CRC Press, URL https://www.routledge.com/IoT-Automation-Arrowhead-Framework/Delsing/p/book/9780367658144

Deng DJ, Gan M, Guo YC, Yu J, Lin YP, Lien SY, Chen KC (2019) IEEE 802.11ba: Low-power wake-up radio for green IoT. IEEE Communications Magazine 57(7):106–112, DOI https://doi.org/10.1109/MCOM.2019.1800389, URL https://ieeexplore.ieee.org/document/8767087

Derigent W, Cardin O, Trentesaux D (2021) Industry 4.0: contributions of holonic manufacturing control architectures and future challenges. Journal of Intelligent Manufacturing 32(7):1797–1818, DOI https://doi.org/10.1007/s10845-020-01532-x, URL https://link.springer.com/article/10.1007/s10845-020-01532-x

Devan PAM, Hussin FA, Ibrahim R, Bingi K, Khanday FA (2021) A survey on the application of WirelessHART for industrial process monitoring and control. Sensors 21(15), DOI https://doi.org/10.3390/s21154951, URL https://www.mdpi.com/1424-8220/21/15/4951

Doumbouya MB, Kamsu-Foguem B, Kenfack H, Foguem C (2014) Telemedicine using mobile telecommunication: Towards syntactic interoperability in teleexpertise. Telematics and Informatics 31(4):648–659, DOI https://doi.org/10.1016/j.tele.2014.01.003, URL https://www.sciencedirect.com/science/article/pii/S0736585314000148

Du J, Jiang C, Wang J, Ren Y, Debbah M (2020) Machine learning for 6G wireless networks: Carrying forward enhanced bandwidth, massive access, and ultrareliable/low-latency service. IEEE Vehicular Technology Magazine 15(4):122–134, DOI https://doi.org/10.1109/MVT.2020.3019650, URL https://ieeexplore.ieee.org/document/9206115

Elango J (2022) Industry 4.0 – a deep analysis of use cases and technologies. URL https://blog.contus.com/industry-4-0-use-cases-technologies/

Epple U, Mertens M, Palm F, Azarmipour M (2017) Using properties as a semantic base for interoperability. IEEE Transactions on Industrial Informatics 13(6):3411–3419, DOI https://doi.org/10.1109/TII.2017.2741339, URL https://ieeexplore.ieee.org/document/8012453

Figueroa-Lorenzo S, Añorga J, Arrizabalaga S (2020) A survey of IIoT protocols: A measure of vulnerability risk analysis based on CVSS. ACM Computing Surveys 53(2), URL https://doi.org/10.1145/3381038

Fortier P, Le Mouël F, Ponge J (2021) Dyninka: a FaaS framework for distributed dataflow applications. In: 8th ACM SIGPLAN International Workshop on Reactive and Event-Based Languages and Systems, Association for Computing Machinery, New York, NY, USA, REBLS 2021, p 2–13, URL https://doi.org/10.1145/3486605.3486789

Fraile F, Tagawa T, Poler R, Ortiz A (2018) Trustworthy industrial IoT gateways for interoperability platforms and ecosystems. IEEE Internet of Things Journal 5(6):4506–4514, DOI https://doi.org/10.1109/JIOT.2018.2832041, URL https://ieeexplore.ieee.org/document/8353121

Frank AG, Dalenogare LS, Ayala NF (2019) Industry 4.0 technologies: Implementation patterns in manufacturing companies. International Journal of Production Economics 210:15–26, DOI https://doi.org/10.1016/j.ijpe.2019.01.004, URL https://www.sciencedirect.com/science/article/pii/S0925527319300040

Ghobakhloo M (2020) Industry 4.0, digitization, and opportunities for sustainability. Journal of Cleaner Production 252:119869, DOI https://doi.org/10.1016/j.jclepro.2019.119869, URL https://www.sciencedirect.com/science/article/pii/S0959652619347390

Golchay R, Le Mouël F, Frénot S, Ponge J (2011) Towards bridging IoT and cloud services: Proposing smartphones as mobile and autonomic service gateways. In: 7ème Journées Francophones de la Mobilité et Ubiquité (UbiMob'2011), Toulouse, France, pp 45–48, URL http://www.le-mouel.net/Research/Publications/Conferences/2011/UbiMob2011.pdf

Goursaud C, Gorce JM (2015) Dedicated networks for IoT: PHY / MAC state of the art and challenges. EAI Endorsed Transactions on Internet of Things 1(1), DOI https://doi.org/10.4108/eai.26-10-2015.150597, URL https://eudl.eu/doi/10.4108/eai.26-10-2015.150597

Guan Y, Vasquez JC, Guerrero JM, Samovich N, Vanya S, Oravec V, García-Castro R, Serena F, Poveda-Villalón M, Radojicic C, Heinz C, Grimm C, Tryferidis A, Tzovaras D, Dickerson K, Paralic M, Skokan M, Sabol T (2017) An open virtual neighbourhood network to connect IoT infrastructures and smart objects – Vicinity: IoT enables interoperability as a service. In: Global Internet of Things Summit (GIoTS), pp 1–6, DOI https://doi.org/10.1109/GIOTS.2017.8016233, URL https://ieeexplore.ieee.org/document/8016233

Gyrard A, Bonnet C, Boudaoud K (2014) Enrich machine-to-machine data with semantic web technologies for cross-domain applications. In: IEEE World Forum on Internet of Things (WF-IoT), pp 559–564, DOI https://doi.org/10.1109/WF-IoT.2014.6803229, URL https://ieeexplore.ieee.org/document/6803229

Hankel M, Rexroth B (2015) The reference architectural model industrie 4.0 (RAMI 4.0). ZVEI 2(2):4–9, URL https://przemysl-40.pl/wp-content/uploads/2010-The-Reference-Architectural-Model-Industrie-40.pdf

Hazra A, Adhikari M, Amgoth T, Srirama SN (2021) A comprehensive survey on interoperability for IIoT: Taxonomy, standards, and future directions. ACM Computing Surveys 55(1), URL https://doi.org/10.1145/3485130

Hong CH, Varghese B (2019) Resource management in fog/edge computing: A survey on architectures, infrastructure, and algorithms. ACM Computing Surveys 52(5), URL https://doi.org/10.1145/3326066

Hou X, Ren Z, Yang K, Chen C, Zhang H, Xiao Y (2019) IIoT-MEC: A novel mobile edge computing framework for 5G-enabled IIoT. In: IEEE Wireless Communications and Networking Conference (WCNC), pp 1–7, DOI https://doi.org/10.1109/WCNC.2019.8885703, URL https://ieeexplore.ieee.org/document/8885703

Hu N, Tian Z, Du X, Guizani N, Zhu Z (2021) Deep-Green: A dispersed energy-efficiency computing paradigm for green industrial IoT. IEEE Transactions on Green Communications and Networking 5(2):750–764, DOI https://doi.org/10.1109/TGCN.2021.3064683, URL https://ieeexplore.ieee.org/document/9372936

Huo R, Zeng S, Wang Z, Shang J, Chen W, Huang T, Wang S, Yu FR, Liu Y (2022) A comprehensive survey on blockchain in industrial internet of things: Motivations, research progresses, and future challenges. IEEE Communications Surveys & Tutorials 24(1):88–122, DOI https://doi.org/10.1109/COMST.2022.3141490, URL https://ieeexplore.ieee.org/document/9676337

IEEE (2020) IEEE 2301-2020: IEEE Guide for Cloud Portability and Interoperability Profiles (CPIP). IEEE, URL https://standards.ieee.org/ieee/2301/5077/

Iglesias-Urkia M, Orive A, Urbieta A (2017) Analysis of CoAP implementations for industrial internet of things: A survey. Procedia Computer Science 109:188–195, DOI https://doi.org/10.1016/j.procs.2017.05.323, URL https://www.sciencedirect.com/science/article/pii/S1877050917309870, 8th International Conference on Ambient Systems, Networks and Technologies, ANT-2017 and the 7th International Conference on Sustainable Energy Information Technology, SEIT 2017, 16–19 May 2017, Madeira, Portugal

IIConsortium Architecture Task Group (2019) The industrial internet of things volume G1: Reference architecture (IIRA). Tech. Rep. 1.9, Industrial Internet Consortium, URL https://www.iiconsortium.org/pdf/IIRA-v1.9.pdf

ISO/IEC (2017) 19941:2017(E): Information technology – Cloud computing – Interoperability and portability. ISO/IEC, URL https://www.standict.eu/standards-repository/standard/information-technology-cloud-computing-interoperability-and

ISO/IEC (2020) TR 30166: Internet of things (IoT) – Industrial IoT. ISO/IEC, URL https://www.iso.org/standard/53286.html?browse=tc

ITU-T Study Group 20 (2020) ITU-T Y.4475: Lightweight intelligent software framework for Internet of things devices. IUT-T, URL https://handle.itu.int/11.1002/1000/14377

Ivezic N, Ivezic N, Kulvatunyou B, Brandl D, Macchi M, Lu Y, Noller D, Davis J, Wuest T, Kiritsis D, et al. (2018) 2017 NIST/OAGi Workshop: Enabling Composable Service-Oriented Manufacturing Systems. US Department of Commerce, National Institute of Standards and Technology (NIST), URL https://view.ckcest.cn/AllFiles/ZKBG/Pages/511/NIST.AMS.100-15.pdf

Javaid M, Haleem A (2019) Industry 4.0 applications in medical field: A brief review. Current Medicine Research and Practice 9(3):102–109, DOI https://doi.org/10.1016/j.cmrp.2019.04.001, URL https://www.sciencedirect.com/science/article/pii/S2352081719300418

Josefsson E (2020) How to improve ROI for industry 4.0 use cases. URL https://www.ericsson.com/en/blog/2020/7/how-to-improve-roi-for-industry-4-0-use-cases

Kagermann H, Lukas WD, Wahlster W (2011) Industrie 4.0: Mit dem internet der dinge auf dem weg zur 4. industriellen revolution. VDI Nachrichten URL http://www.wolfgang-wahlster.de/wordpress/wp-content/uploads/Industrie_4_0_Mit_dem_Internet_der_Dinge_auf_dem_Weg_zur_vierten_industriellen_Revolution_pdf

Karaköse M, Yetiş H (2017) A cyberphysical system based mass-customization approach with integration of industry 4.0 and smart city. Wireless Communications and Mobile Computing 2017:1058081, DOI https://doi.org/10.1155/2017/1058081

Khan M, Wu X, Xu X, Dou W (2017) Big data challenges and opportunities in the hype of industry 4.0. In: IEEE International Conference on Communications (ICC), pp 1–6, DOI https://doi.org/10.1109/ICC.2017.7996801, URL https://ieeexplore.ieee.org/document/7996801

Khanboubi F, Boulmakoul A, Tabaa M (2019) Impact of digital trends using IoT on banking processes. Procedia Computer Science 151:77–84, DOI https://doi.org/10.1016/j.procs.2019.04.014, URL https://www.sciencedirect.com/science/article/pii/S1877050919304752, the 10th International Conference on Ambient Systems, Networks and Technologies (ANT 2019) / The 2nd International Conference on Emerging Data and Industry 4.0 (EDI40 2019) / Affiliated Workshops

Kiangala KS, Wang Z (2019) An industry 4.0 approach to develop auto parameter configuration of a bottling process in a small to medium scale industry using PLC and SCADA. Procedia Manufacturing 35:725–730, DOI https://doi.org/10.1016/j.promfg.2019.06.015, URL https://www.sciencedirect.com/science/article/pii/S2351978919307401, the 2nd International Conference on Sustainable Materials Processing and Manufacturing, SMPM 2019, 8–10 March 2019, Sun City, South Africa

Kim J, Yun J, Choi SC, Seed DN, Lu G, Bauer M, Al-Hezmi A, Campowsky K, Song J (2016) Standard-based IoT platforms interworking: implementation, experiences, and lessons learned. IEEE Communications Magazine 54(7):48–54, DOI https://doi.org/10.1109/MCOM.2016.7514163, URL https://ieeexplore.ieee.org/document/7514163

Kiradjiev P (2017) Announcing the IoT industrie 4.0 reference architecture. URL https://www.ibm.com/cloud/blog/announcements/iot-industrie-40-reference-architecture

Lasi H, Fettke P, Kemper HG, Feld T, Hoffmann M (2014) Industry 4.0. Business & information systems engineering 6(4):239–242, DOI https://doi.org/10.1007/s12599-014-0334-4

Latif S, Driss M, Boulila W, Huma Ze, Jamal SS, Idrees Z, Ahmad J (2021) Deep learning for the industrial internet of things (IIoT): A comprehensive survey of techniques, implementation frameworks, potential applications, and future directions. Sensors 21(22), DOI https://doi.org/10.3390/s21227518, URL https://www.mdpi.com/1424-8220/21/22/7518

Lee J, Davari H, Singh J, Pandhare V (2018) Industrial artificial intelligence for industry 4.0-based manufacturing systems. Manufacturing Letters 18:20–23, DOI https://doi.org/10.1016/j.mfglet. 2018.09.002, URL https://www.sciencedirect.com/science/article/pii/S2213846318301081

Leonardi L, Battaglia F, Lo Bello L (2019) RT-LoRa: A medium access strategy to support real-time flows over LoRa-based networks for industrial IoT applications. IEEE Internet of Things Journal 6(6):10812–10823, DOI https://doi.org/10.1109/JIOT.2019.2942776, URL https://ieeexplore.ieee.org/document/8845658

Lerche C, Hartke K, Kovatsch M (2012) Industry adoption of the internet of things: A constrained application protocol survey. In: IEEE 17th International Conference on Emerging Technologies & Factory Automation (ETFA 2012), pp 1–6, DOI https://doi.org/10.1109/ETFA.2012. 6489787, URL https://ieeexplore.ieee.org/document/6489787

Lin CC, Yang JW (2018) Cost-efficient deployment of fog computing systems at logistics centers in industry 4.0. IEEE Transactions on Industrial Informatics 14(10):4603–4611, DOI https:// doi.org/10.1109/TII.2018.2827920, URL https://ieeexplore.ieee.org/document/8339513

Liu D, Alahmadi A, Ni J, Lin X, Shen X (2019) Anonymous reputation system for IIoT-enabled retail marketing atop pos blockchain. IEEE Transactions on Industrial Informatics 15(6):3527–3537, DOI https://doi.org/10.1109/TII.2019.2898900, URL https://ieeexplore.ieee. org/document/8640264

Liu Y, Ma X, Shu L, Hancke GP, Abu-Mahfouz AM (2021) From industry 4.0 to agriculture 4.0: Current status, enabling technologies, and research challenges. IEEE Transactions on Industrial Informatics 17(6):4322–4334, DOI https://doi.org/10.1109/TII.2020.3003910, URL https://ieeexplore.ieee.org/document/9122412

Lu Y, Morris KC, Frechette S, et al. (2016) Current standards landscape for smart manufacturing systems. Tech. Rep. 8107, National Institute of Standards and Technology (NIST), URL https:// nvlpubs.nist.gov/nistpubs/ir/2016/NIST.IR.8107.pdf

Manzaroli D, Roffia L, Salmon Cinotti T, Ovaska E, Azzoni P, Nannini V, Mattarozzi S (2010) Smart-M3 and OSGi: The interoperability platform. In: The IEEE symposium on Computers and Communications, pp 1053–1058, DOI https://doi.org/10.1109/ISCC.2010.5546622, URL https://ieeexplore.ieee.org/document/5546622

Mao W, Zhao Z, Chang Z, Min G, Gao W (2021) Energy-efficient industrial internet of things: Overview and open issues. IEEE Transactions on Industrial Informatics 17(11):7225–7237, DOI https://doi.org/10.1109/TII.2021.3067026, URL https://ieeexplore.ieee.org/document/ 9381665

Markelov A (2016) Orchestration of OpenStack, Apress, Berkeley, CA, pp 119–130. DOI https://doi.org/10.1007/978-1-4842-2125-9_10, URL https://doi.org/10.1007/978-1-4842-2125-9_10

Meissner H, Ilsen R, Aurich JC (2017) Analysis of control architectures in the context of industry 4.0. Procedia CIRP 62:165–169, DOI https://doi.org/10.1016/j.procir.2016.06.113, URL https://www.sciencedirect.com/science/article/pii/S2212827117300641, 10th CIRP Conference on Intelligent Computation in Manufacturing Engineering - CIRP ICME '16. [Edited by: Roberto Teti, Manager Editor: Doriana M. D'Addona]

Mogensen RS, Rodriguez I, Berardinelli G, Fink A, Marcker R, Markussen S, Raunholt T, Kolding T, Pocovi G, Barbera S (2019) Implementation and trial evaluation of a wireless manufacturing execution system for industry 4.0. In: IEEE 90th Vehicular Technology Conference (VTC2019-Fall), pp 1–7, DOI https://doi.org/10.1109/VTCFall.2019.8891231, URL https://ieeexplore. ieee.org/document/8891231

Molisch AF, Balakrishnan K, Chong CC, Emami S, Fort A, Karedal J, Kunisch J, Schantz H, Schuster U, Siwiak K (2004) IEEE 802.15.4a channel model-final report. IEEE P802 15(04):0662, URL https://www.ieee802.org/15/pub/04/15-04-0662-02-004a-channel-model-final-report-r1.pdf

Moll I (2021) The myth of the fourth industrial revolution. Theoria 68(167):1 – 38, DOI https://doi. org/10.3167/th.2021.6816701, URL https://www.berghahnjournals.com/view/journals/theoria/ 68/167/th6816701.xml

Moran B (2021) A summary of security-enabling technologies for IoT device. Internet-Draft draft-moran-iot-nets-00, Internet Engineering Task Force, URL https://datatracker.ietf.org/doc/html/draft-moran-iot-nets-00, work in Progress

Muhati E, Rawat DB, Sadler BM (2022) A new cyber-alliance of artificial intelligence, internet of things, blockchain, and edge computing. IEEE Internet of Things Magazine 5(1):104–107, URL https://doi.org/10.1109/IOTM.001.2100181

Mukherjee M, Kumar S, Shojafar M, Zhang Q, Mavromoustakis CX (2019) Joint task offloading and resource allocation for delay-sensitive fog networks. In: IEEE International Conference on Communications (ICC), pp 1–7, DOI https://doi.org/10.1109/ICC.2019.8761239, URL https://ieeexplore.ieee.org/document/8761239

Murphy MJ, Tveito Ø, Kleiven EF, Raïs I, Soininen EM, Bjørndalen JM, Anshus O (2021) Experiences building and deploying wireless sensor nodes for the arctic tundra. In: IEEE/ACM 21st International Symposium on Cluster, Cloud and Internet Computing (CCGrid), pp 376–385, DOI https://doi.org/10.1109/CCGrid51090.2021.00047, URL https://ieeexplore.ieee.org/document/9499357

Negash B, Westerlund T, Tenhunen H (2019) Towards an interoperable internet of things through a web of virtual things at the fog layer. Future Generation Computer Systems 91:96–107, DOI https://doi.org/10.1016/j.future.2018.07.053, URL https://www.sciencedirect.com/science/article/pii/S0167739X18308859

Nkomo M, Hancke GP, Abu-Mahfouz AM, Sinha S, Onumanyi AJ (2018) Overlay virtualized wireless sensor networks for application in industrial internet of things: A review. Sensors 18(10), DOI https://doi.org/10.3390/s18103215, URL https://www.mdpi.com/1424-8220/18/10/3215

OpenFog Consortium (2018) IEEE Std 1934–2018: IEEE Standard for Adoption of OpenFog Reference Architecture for Fog Computing. IEEE, URL https://ieeexplore.ieee.org/document/8423800

Palattella MR, Accettura N, Vilajosana X, Watteyne T, Grieco LA, Boggia G, Dohler M (2013) Standardized protocol stack for the internet of (important) things. IEEE Communications Surveys & Tutorials 15(3):1389–1406, DOI https://doi.org/10.1109/SURV.2012.111412.00158, URL https://ieeexplore.ieee.org/document/6380493

Pallewatta S, Kostakos V, Buyya R (2022) QoS-aware placement of microservices-based IoT applications in fog computing environments. Future Generation Computer Systems 131:121–136, DOI https://doi.org/10.1016/j.future.2022.01.012, URL https://www.sciencedirect.com/science/article/pii/S0167739X22000206

Paravizo E, Chaim OC, Braatz D, Muschard B, Rozenfeld H (2018) Exploring gamification to support manufacturing education on industry 4.0 as an enabler for innovation and sustainability. Procedia Manufacturing 21:438–445, DOI https://doi.org/10.1016/j.promfg.2018.02.142, URL https://www.sciencedirect.com/science/article/pii/S2351978918301811, 15th Global Conference on Sustainable Manufacturing

Park S (2017) OCF: A new open IoT consortium. In: 31st International Conference on Advanced Information Networking and Applications Workshops (WAINA), pp 356–359, DOI https://doi.org/10.1109/WAINA.2017.86, URL https://ieeexplore.ieee.org/document/7929703

Patel P, Ali MI, Sheth A (2018) From raw data to smart manufacturing: AI and semantic web of things for industry 4.0. IEEE Intelligent Systems 33(4):79–86, DOI https://doi.org/10.1109/MIS.2018.043741325, URL https://ieeexplore.ieee.org/document/8497012

Patsavellas J, Salonitis K (2019) The carbon footprint of manufacturing digitalization: critical literature review and future research agenda. Procedia CIRP 81:1354–1359, DOI https://doi.org/10.1016/j.procir.2019.04.026, URL https://www.sciencedirect.com/science/article/pii/S2212827119306407, 52nd CIRP Conference on Manufacturing Systems (CMS), Ljubljana, Slovenia, June 12–14, 2019

Pereira C, Pinto A, Aguiar A, Rocha P, Santiago F, Sousa J (2016a) IoT interoperability for actuating applications through standardised M2M communications. In: IEEE 17th International Symposium on A World of Wireless, Mobile and Multimedia Networks (WoWMoM), pp

1–6, DOI https://doi.org/10.1109/WoWMoM.2016.7523564, URL https://ieeexplore.ieee.org/document/7523564

Pereira C, Rodrigues J, Pinto A, Rocha P, Santiago F, Sousa J, Aguiar A (2016b) Smartphones as M2M gateways in smart cities IoT applications. In: 23rd International Conference on Telecommunications (ICT), pp 1–7, DOI https://doi.org/10.1109/ICT.2016.7500481, URL https://ieeexplore.ieee.org/document/7500481

Piccarozzi M, Aquilani B, Gatti C (2018) Industry 4.0 in management studies: A systematic literature review. Sustainability 10(10), DOI https://doi.org/10.3390/su10103821, URL https://www.mdpi.com/2071-1050/10/10/3821

Pilloni V (2018) How data will transform industrial processes: Crowdsensing, crowdsourcing and big data as pillars of industry 4.0. Future Internet 10(3), DOI https://doi.org/10.3390/fi10030024, URL https://www.mdpi.com/1999-5903/10/3/24

Platform Industrie 40 (2019) Which criteria do industrie 4.0 products need to fulfil? - guideline. Tech. rep., Platform Industrie 4.0 & ZVEI, URL https://www.plattform-i40.de/IP/Redaktion/EN/Downloads/Publikation/criteria-industrie-40-products.pdf?__blob=publicationFile&v=5

Potocan V, Mulej M, Nedelko Z (2021) Society 5.0: balancing of industry 4.0, economic advancement and social problems. Kybernetes 50:794–811, URL https://www.emerald.com/insight/content/doi/10.1108/K-12-2019-0858/full/html

Pradhan M, Suri N, Fuchs C, Bloebaum TH, Marks M (2018) Toward an architecture and data model to enable interoperability between federated mission networks and IoT-enabled smart city environments. IEEE Communications Magazine 56(10):163–169, DOI https://doi.org/10.1109/MCOM.2018.1800305, URL https://ieeexplore.ieee.org/document/8493137?denied=

Pramukantoro ES, Yahya W, Bakhtiar FA (2017) Performance evaluation of IoT middleware for syntactical interoperability. In: International Conference on Advanced Computer Science and Information Systems (ICACSIS), pp 29–34, DOI https://doi.org/10.1109/ICACSIS.2017.8355008, URL https://ieeexplore.ieee.org/document/8355008

Pramukantoro ES, Andri Bakhtiar F, Aji B, Pratama R (2018) Middleware for network interoperability in IoT. In: 5th International Conference on Electrical Engineering, Computer Science and Informatics (EECSI), pp 499–502, DOI https://doi.org/10.1109/EECSI.2018.8752917, URL https://ieeexplore.ieee.org/document/8752917

Praveen Kumar D, Amgoth T, Annavarapu CSR (2019) Machine learning algorithms for wireless sensor networks: A survey. Information Fusion 49:1–25, DOI https://doi.org/10.1016/j.inffus.2018.09.013, URL https://www.sciencedirect.com/science/article/pii/S156625351830277X

Qadir Z, Le KN, Saeed N, Munawar HS (2022) Towards 6G internet of things: Recent advances, use cases, and open challenges. ICT Express DOI https://doi.org/10.1016/j.icte.2022.06.006, URL https://www.sciencedirect.com/science/article/pii/S2405959522000959

Qin J, Liu Y, Grosvenor R (2016) A categorical framework of manufacturing for industry 4.0 and beyond. Procedia CIRP 52:173–178, DOI https://doi.org/10.1016/j.procir.2016.08.005, URL https://www.sciencedirect.com/science/article/pii/S221282711630854X, the Sixth International Conference on Changeable, Agile, Reconfigurable and Virtual Production (CARV2016)

Qiu T, Chen N, Zhang S (2022) Future Research Directions, Springer Nature Singapore, Singapore, pp 201–214. URL https://doi.org/10.1007/978-981-16-9609-1_9

Ravina Ripoll R, Romero-Rodríguez LM, Ahumada-Tello E (2022) Guest editorial: Happiness management: key factors for sustainability and organizational communication in the age of industry 4.0. Corporate Governance: The International Journal of Business in Society 22(3):449–457, URL https://doi.org/10.1108/CG-05-2022-576

Ray PP, Thapa N, Dash D (2019) Implementation and performance analysis of interoperable and heterogeneous IoT-edge gateway for pervasive wellness care. IEEE Transactions on Consumer Electronics 65(4):464–473, DOI https://doi.org/10.1109/TCE.2019.2939494, URL https://ieeexplore.ieee.org/document/8823957

Robert J, Kubler S, Kolbe N, Cerioni A, Gastaud E, Främling K (2017) Open IoT ecosystem for enhanced interoperability in smart cities—example of Métropole De Lyon. Sensors 17(12), DOI https://doi.org/10.3390/s17122849, URL https://www.mdpi.com/1424-8220/17/12/2849

Rong K, Patton D, Chen W (2018) Business models dynamics and business ecosystems in the emerging 3D printing industry. Technological Forecasting and Social Change 134:234–245, DOI https://doi.org/10.1016/j.techfore.2018.06.015, URL https://www.sciencedirect.com/science/article/pii/S004016251731332X

Rufino J, Alam M, Ferreira J, Rehman A, Tsang KF (2017) Orchestration of containerized microservices for iiot using docker. In: IEEE International Conference on Industrial Technology (ICIT), pp 1532–1536, DOI https://doi.org/10.1109/ICIT.2017.7915594, URL https://ieeexplore.ieee.org/document/7915594

Rupp M, Schneckenburger M, Merkel M, Börret R, Harrison DK (2021) Industry 4.0: A technological-oriented definition based on bibliometric analysis and literature review. Journal of Open Innovation: Technology, Market, and Complexity 7(1), DOI https://doi.org/10.3390/joitmc7010068, URL https://www.mdpi.com/2199-8531/7/1/68

Sah DK, Amgoth T (2020) Renewable energy harvesting schemes in wireless sensor networks: A survey. Information Fusion 63:223–247, DOI https://doi.org/10.1016/j.inffus.2020.07.005, URL https://www.sciencedirect.com/science/article/pii/S156625352030316X

Sanislav T, Mois GD, Zeadally S, Folea SC (2021) Energy harvesting techniques for internet of things (iot). IEEE Access 9:39530–39549, DOI https://doi.org/10.1109/ACCESS.2021.3064066, URL https://ieeexplore.ieee.org/document/9370135

Sari A, Lekidis A, Butun I (2020) Industrial Networks and IIoT: Now and Future Trends, Springer International Publishing, pp 3–55. URL https://doi.org/10.1007/978-3-030-42500-5_1

Sarkar I, Adhikari M, Kumar N, Kumar S (2022) Dynamic task placement for deadline-aware IoT applications in federated fog networks. IEEE Internet of Things Journal 9(2):1469–1478, DOI https://doi.org/10.1109/JIOT.2021.3088227, URL https://ieeexplore.ieee.org/document/9451209

Schwab K (2016) The Fourth Industrial Revolution. World Economic Forum, Geneva, URL https://www.weforum.org/about/the-fourth-industrial-revolution-by-klaus-schwab

Schwab K (2017) The Fourth Industrial Revolution. Crown Publishing Group, USA

Sedlmeir J, Buhl HU, Fridgen G, Keller R (2020) The energy consumption of blockchain technology: Beyond myth. Business & Information Systems Engineering 62(6):599–608, URL https://doi.org/10.1007/s12599-020-00656-x

Sharma C, Gondhi NK (2018) Communication protocol stack for constrained IoT systems. In: 3rd International Conference On Internet of Things: Smart Innovation and Usages (IoT-SIU), pp 1–6, DOI https://doi.org/10.1109/IoT-SIU.2018.8519904, URL https://ieeexplore.ieee.org/document/8519904

Silva M, Lepikson H (2022) Resilience evaluation of cyber risks in industrial internet of things. In: IEEE International IOT, Electronics and Mechatronics Conference (IEMTRONICS), pp 1–6, DOI https://doi.org/10.1109/IEMTRONICS55184.2022.9795792, URL https://ieeexplore.ieee.org/document/9795792

Spachos P, Plataniotis K (2020) BLE beacons in the smart city: Applications, challenges, and research opportunities. IEEE Internet of Things Magazine 3(1):14–18, DOI https://doi.org/10.1109/IOTM.0001.1900073, URL https://ieeexplore.ieee.org/document/9063401

Tournier J, Lesueur F, Mouël FL, Guyon L, Ben-Hassine H (2020) IoTMap: A protocol-agnostic multi-layer system to detect application patterns in IoT networks. In: 10th International Conference on the Internet of Things, Association for Computing Machinery, New York, NY, USA, IoT '20, URL https://doi.org/10.1145/3410992.3411007

Tournier J, Lesueur F, Le Mouël F, Guyon L, Ben-Hassine H (2021) A survey of IoT protocols and their security issues through the lens of a generic IoT stack. Internet of Things Journal p 100264, DOI https://doi.org/10.1016/j.iot.2020.100264, URL http://www.le-mouel.net/Research/Publications/Journals/2020/IEEEIOT2020.pdf

Vaiyapuri T, Sbai Z, Alaskar H, Alaseem NA (2021) Deep learning approaches for intrusion detection in IIoT networks–opportunities and future directions. International Journal of Advanced Computer Science and Applications 12(4), URL https://thesai.org/Publications/ViewPaper?Volume=12&Issue=4&Code=IJACSA&SerialNo=11

Valtolina S, Ferrari L, Mesiti M (2019) Ontology-based consistent specification of sensor data acquisition plans in cross-domain IoT platforms. IEEE Access 7:176141–176169, DOI https://doi.org/10.1109/ACCESS.2019.2957855, URL https://ieeexplore.ieee.org/document/8924726

Vasudev H, Deshpande V, Das D, Das SK (2020) A lightweight mutual authentication protocol for V2V communication in internet of vehicles. IEEE Transactions on Vehicular Technology 69(6):6709–6717, DOI https://doi.org/10.1109/TVT.2020.2986585, URL https://ieeexplore.ieee.org/document/9064651

Verbraeken J, Wolting M, Katzy J, Kloppenburg J, Verbelen T, Rellermeyer JS (2020) A survey on distributed machine learning. ACM Computing Surveys 53(2), URL https://doi.org/10.1145/3377454

Viriyasitavat W, Xu LD, Bi Z, Hoonsopon D (2019) Blockchain technology for applications in internet of things—mapping from system design perspective. IEEE Internet of Things Journal 6(5):8155–8168, DOI https://doi.org/10.1109/JIOT.2019.2925825, URL https://ieeexplore.ieee.org/document/8752029

Vitturi S, Zunino C, Sauter T (2019) Industrial communication systems and their future challenges: Next-generation ethernet, IIoT, and 5G. Proceedings of the IEEE 107(6):944–961, DOI https://doi.org/10.1109/JPROC.2019.2913443, URL https://ieeexplore.ieee.org/document/8715451

Wang Le, Bai Y, Jiang Q, C M Leung V, Cai W, Li X (2021) Beh-Raft-Chain: A behavior-based fast blockchain protocol for complex networks. IEEE Transactions on Network Science and Engineering 8(2):1154–1166, DOI https://doi.org/10.1109/TNSE.2020.2984490, URL https://ieeexplore.ieee.org/document/9055192

Wang W, Capitaneanu SL, Marinca D, Lohan ES (2019) Comparative analysis of channel models for industrial IoT wireless communication. IEEE Access 7:91627–91640, DOI https://doi.org/10.1109/ACCESS.2019.2927217, URL https://ieeexplore.ieee.org/document/8756193

Wang Y (2020) Enhancing interoperability for IoT based smart manufacturing : An analytical study of interoperability issues and case study. Master's thesis, KTH, Communication Systems, CoS, URL https://www.diva-portal.org/smash/record.jsf?pid=diva2:1411144

Weyrich M, Ebert C (2016) Reference architectures for the internet of things. IEEE Software 33(1):112–116, DOI https://doi.org/10.1109/MS.2016.20, URL https://ieeexplore.ieee.org/document/7367994

de Wolff D (2021) The future of the IoT (batteries not required). URL https://news.mit.edu/2021/future-iot-batteries-not-required-0521

Wu Z, Meng Z, Gray J (2017) IoT-based techniques for online M2M-interactive itemized data registration and offline information traceability in a digital manufacturing system. IEEE Transactions on Industrial Informatics 13(5):2397–2405, DOI https://doi.org/10.1109/TII.2017.2704613, URL https://ieeexplore.ieee.org/document/7931573

Xiao G, Guo J, Xu LD, Gong Z (2014) User interoperability with heterogeneous IoT devices through transformation. IEEE Transactions on Industrial Informatics 10(2):1486–1496, DOI https://doi.org/10.1109/TII.2014.2306772, URL https://ieeexplore.ieee.org/document/6742587

Xiong J, Hsiang EL, He Z, Zhan T, Wu ST (2021) Augmented reality and virtual reality displays: emerging technologies and future perspectives. Light: Science & Applications 10(1):216, DOI https://doi.org/10.1038/s41377-021-00658-8, URL https://doi.org/10.1038/s41377-021-00658-8

Yang S, Wei R (2019) Tabdoc approach: An information fusion method to implement semantic interoperability between IoT devices and users. IEEE Internet of Things Journal 6(2):1972–1986, DOI https://doi.org/10.1109/JIOT.2018.2871274, URL https://ieeexplore.ieee.org/document/8468004

Zezulka F, Marcon P, Bradac Z, Arm J, Benesl T, Vesely I (2018) Communication systems for industry 4.0 and the IIoT. IFAC-PapersOnLine 51(6):150–155, DOI https://doi.org/10.1016/j.ifacol.2018.07.145, URL https://www.sciencedirect.com/science/article/pii/S2405896318308899, 15th IFAC Conference on Programmable Devices and Embedded Systems PDeS 2018

Zhang Z, Wu C, Cheung DW (2013) A survey on cloud interoperability: Taxonomies, standards, and practice. SIGMETRICS Performance Evaluation Review 40(4):13–22, URL https://doi.org/10.1145/2479942.2479945

PIS:
Interoperability and Decision-Making Process—A Review

Juliana Fernandes, Lucas Oliveira, Valdemar Vicente Graciano Neto,
Rodrigo Pereira dos Santos, Rafael Angarita, Sonia Guehis,
and Yudith Cardinale

1 Introduction

Modern organizations are recurrently pressured to collaborate to both sustain themselves in the market and form synergistic alliances that benefit the involved

The original version of the chapter has been revised. A correction to this chapter can be found at
https://doi.org/10.1007/978-3-031-18176-4_8

Lucas Oliveira, Valdemar Vicente Graciano Neto, Rodrigo Pereira dos Santos, Rafael Angarita,
Sonia Guehis, and Yudith Cardinale contributed equally to this work.

J. Fernandes (✉)
Federal Institute of Piauí, Campo Maior, Piauí, Brazil
e-mail: juliana.fernandes@ifpi.edu.br

L. Oliveira · R. P. dos Santos
Department of Applied Informatics, UNIRIO, Rio de Janeiro, Brazil
e-mail: oliveira.l.s@edu.unirio.br; rps@uniriotec.br

V. V. Graciano Neto
Federal University of Goiás, Goiânia, Goiás, Brazil
e-mail: valdemarneto@ufg.br

R. Angarita
LISITE, ISEP, Paris, France
e-mail: rafael.angarita@isep.fr

S. Guehis
AMSADE CNRS UMR 7243, Paris Dauphine University, PSL Research University, Paris, France
e-mail: sonia.guehis@dauphine.fr

Y. Cardinale (✉)
Grupo de Investigación en Ciencia de Datos (GRID), Universidad Internacional de Valencia,
Valencia, Spain
Universidad Simón Bolívar, Caracas, Venezuela
e-mail: yudith.cardinale@campusviu.es

M. Kirsch Pinheiro et al. (eds.), *The Evolution of Pervasive Information Systems*,
https://doi.org/10.1007/978-3-031-18176-4_7

enterprises. Amazon, for instance, has created a large ecosystem involving several other companies to expand their portfolio and sell products from other companies[1]. However, each time a set of companies aim to join business agreements, they face the recurrent challenge of interoperating their information systems (IS) to enable their business processes to be connected and, for instance, to sell a product offered, delivered, and even paid to another company (i.e., it has an impact in the decision-making processes of companies involved House et al. 2014). The IEEE defines interoperability as "the ability of two or more systems or components to exchange information and to use the information that has been exchanged" (IEEE 1990). However, achieving interoperability among IS that are managerially and operationally independent is a challenging task.

Over the years, researchers have looked for interoperability solutions from different perspectives: (i) *the software architecture perspective* to build connectors to allow the interaction of different software components; (ii) *the middleware perspective* decouple applications and services from each others by implementing common communication systems such as a service bus; (iii) the *formal methods perspective* to analyse the behavior of participating components and compute controllers to allow interoperability; and (iv) the *semantic web perspective* that focuses on providing shared ontologies describing the meaning of informatione (Bennaceur 2013). Furthermore, increasing the interoperation of different types of systems has led to the emergence of Pervasive Information Systems (PIS) conformed by IS deployed everywhere, going beyond the traditional frontiers of organizations. PIS can be seen as Systems-of-Information Systems (SoIS)[2] (Fernandes et al. 2018, 2020; Motta et al. 2017), which comprise a dynamic set of independent IS interoperating for addressing the convergent need for collaboration among enterprises and, at the same time, operating for their individual purposes. Different from subsystems context, this scenario should led IS research community and practitioners to promote interoperability, while still preserving the independence and supporting the decision-making processes of the IS involved.

The establishment of interoperability among IS is not a trivial activity and impose a diversity of requirements, such as the needs to: (i) enable spontaneous interoperability among IS, i.e., enabling temporary (or longer) cooperation links among a set of companies joined together; (ii) deal with several types of heterogeneities, namely data format and representation, hardware and software differences, and even cultural and business differences; and (iii) address the independence of constituent IS in a PIS, seen as SoIS, which allows them to join or leave the alliance at their convenience, which can make some of the interoperability links to be ephemeral. Then, PIS should not only manage the accomplishment of their main goals but also the impact of its changing nature due to the accomplishment of the goal from companies involved, which makes part of the decision-making processes.

---

[1] https://www.bloomberg.com/graphics/2019-amazon-reach-across-markets/?leadSource=uverify%20wall.

[2] Henceforth, the acronyms PIS and SoIS will be interchangeably used to express both singular and plural forms.

There have been significant research efforts to provide interoperability solutions among IS, especially in the field of complex systems. However, we observed that a static and focused view only on technical solutions limits the understanding of which factors and how they can solve or produce conflicts on arrangements of independent IS in SoIS. In order to address these gaps, our aim is to report the results of an investigation on the factors (i.e., technical, human, and organizational) that can answer the research question: *"Which and how factors influence interoperability in the PIS/SoIS context?"*. We build upon the analysis over these three aspects following the classic triad of factors that compose any IS, as prescribed by Laudon and Laudon (Laudon and Laudon 1998), Soares and Amaral (Soares and Amaral 2014), and also the modern perspective of business ecosystems (Luz et al. 2020). We surveyed the literature over the period 1992–2022 on influence factors that can apply to interoperability among IS through a systematic mapping study method. The survey also covers a diversity of complex systems types that could be formed by IS, such as Systems-of-Systems (SoS), Heterogeneous Systems, Large-Scale Systems, and Adaptive Systems.

From more than 5000 studies retrieved, 81 were included for extracting and discussing a set of ten factors that may influence interoperability in the SoIS domain, as well as their impact in decision-making process. These factors address since the provision of technical information about IT elements (technical factor), human thinking and perceptions (human factor) until the need for harmonized business strategies (organizational factor), because management teams have to deal with a diversity of technological, human, and managerial aspects to result in an efficient communication, towards better and smart decision-making, in complex arrangements as PIS and SoIS. We present these factors as potential issues to explain how practices around interoperability need a synergy of efforts beyond technical decisions and propose some guidelines for the design of interoperability links in PIS, seen as SoIS. These interoprability factors crosscut and surpass the enterprises boundaries to create complex networks of IS combining their business processes to achieve more complex decision-making and deliver more robust services.

2 Background and Related Reviews

Pervasive Information Systems (PIS) is the result of the massive introduction of current IT trends and technologies into the evolving IS. Since the emergence of technologies, such as Internet of Things (IoT), Cloud Computing, Fog/Edge Computing, Big Data, and Machine Learning, the number of smart ubiquitous computing environments has increased. These ubicomp environments are complex, heterogeneous, and mobile (Hauser et al. 2017; Kourouthanassis and Giaglis 2008). As a set of IS, PIS can be seen as SoIS. SoIS is a class of complex systems formed by an arrangement of IS, whose pervasiveness is evident, since nowadays the IT evolution makes the ubiquitous computing be present in any organization. Hence, in this chapter we treat PIS as SoIS, named PIS/SoIS.

SoIS are currently defined as *an alliance among several organizations that bring their IS together to accomplish a set of goals, sharing benefits from this consortium* (Fernandes et al. 2019; Saleh et al. 2015). PIS/SoIS are complex systems according to the Systems Engineering Body of Knowledge (SEBoK), since they are formed by multiple independent IS working collaboratively to achieve a mutual goal (Cloutier and NJ 2017).

SoIS is a specific type of SoS (Teixeira et al. 2019) and inherits SoS characteristics (Boardman and Sauser 2006; Fernandes et al. 2020), such as: (i) **autonomy**, which is related to how a system is governed by its own rules despite external influences; (ii) **evolutionary development**, meaning the SoIS evolves as constituent IS evolve as well; (iii) **emergent behavior**, which results from the synergistic collaboration among constituent IS and from the combination of the capabilities offered to form global behaviors; (iv) **connectivity**, since constituent IS are dispersed and depend on connectivity mechanisms for communication and information sharing; (v) **interdependence**, i.e., the mutual dependence between constituent IS to accomplish goals; (vi) **diversity**, once SoIS involves different technologies, data formats, people, processes, protocols, and even interpretations and purposes; (vii) **dynamicity**, which is characterized by the ability of a SoIS to modify its own structure and composition; and (viii) **belonging**, that represents the constituent IS perception of mutual benefit among the parts. All these characteristics are commonly considered in the literature approaching PIS as well (Najar et al. 2014; Raychoudhury et al. 2013).

Dynamicity (aka dynamic or evolutionary architecture), one of the main characteristics of PIS/SoIS, considerably increases the complexity for designing and managing interoperability, once the management of interoperability links can become dynamic and transitory, impacting on the services provided by the PIS/SoIS (Neto et al. 2017). Moreover, a PIS/SoIS should also cope with *full interoperability*, which comprises the spontaneity of forming a PIS/SoIS according to needs that emerge, in a transparent manner for the user, abstracting issues, such as middleware, network, data exchange (representation and transport), and communication support details (Maciel et al. 2017; Neto et al. 2017). To achieve this, the IS should support an instantaneous interoperability with any other type of available system, exchanging information between themselves, and being able to contribute to the accomplishment of missions, i.e., main goals and subgoals (Fernandes et al. 2019).

Interoperability is usually understood from the perspective of dimensions, i.e., levels or layers, established to provide some guidance for achieving it (Kubicek and Cimander 2009; Maciel et al. 2017). The classification around these perspectives refers to what should be provided and by which technical means interoperability should be established (Kubicek and Cimander 2009). The dimensions of interoperability most commonly addressed in the literature are: (i) the **legal interoperability**, which deals with agreements or legislation by which organizations are subject to interoperate their IS; (ii) the **organizational interoperability**, which deals with why interoperating is needed; (iii) **the pragmatic**, which has been highlighted as a key requirement to enhance collaboration; (iv) the **semantic**, which deals with what is interoperating; and (v) the **technical and syntactic**, which deals with the means with which are interoperating (Kubicek and Cimander 2009; Leal 2019; Maciel et al. 2017).

Since PIS/SoIS is composed of IS, the phenomenon of "information systems interoperability" must be also perceived, implemented, managed, and studied in a sociotechnical perspective (Soares and Amaral 2014), instead of only focusing on the technical aspects of interoperability. Thus, in this chapter, we also consider three aspects on the classic triad of factors (i.e., technical, human, and organizational) that compose any IS, as prescribed by Laudon and Laudon (Laudon and Laudon 1998), Soares and Amaral (Soares and Amaral 2014), and also the modern perspective of business ecosystems (Luz et al. 2020). As *technical factors*, we can consider elements associated with hardware and software components, networks and devices that facilitate machine-to-machine communication. As *human factors*, we consider the relationships that affect collaboration among operators who interact in technological environments (Brown 2010; Handley 2014). Finally, as *organizational factors* we consider inter- or intra-organizational connections, including interoperation of business processes for forming alliances and providing new services (Cagnin and Nakagawa 2021; Luz et al. 2020; Soares and Amaral 2014).

Over the years, studies have addressed specific aspects of interoperability in different sorts of arrangements of systems especially investigating technical interoperability. Leal (2019) present a literature review to study existing Interoperability Assessment (INAS) approaches which serve to identify potential interoperability problems and possible solutions. The key finding of this work are the following: the lack of INAS approaches addressing the performance of interoperation; the lack of INAS approaches taking into account multiple layers and concerns of the enterprise; the lack of best practices to improve interoperability based on the INAS results; and the lack of digital tools for supporting the whole or part of the assessment process. To do this analysis, Leal (2019) consider the semantic layer of interoperability concerning the format and semantics of information, the technical layer that covers applications and infrastructures; the organisational layer referring to the way in which systems align their processes, responsibilities and expectations; and the legal layer englobing legislations.

House et al. (2014) bring discussions beyond technical concerns. The work presents inherent complexity and dynamic nature of the major incident task environment. They discuss about different organisations that have different cultures and values that need to interoperate to deal with major incident environment. In this case, they suggest research on the factors of diversity that impact emergency organisations' social identity is lacking and further understanding needs to be developed on network governance of crisis events.

How decision-making processes benefit from interoperability has been analysed by some studies. Rezaei et al. (2014) group the interoperability factors into four granularity levels to compare e-business interoperability frameworks. The first granularity level of interoperability includes data, process, rules, objects, software systems, and cultural interoperability. The second level considers knowledge, services, social networks, and electronic identify interoperability. The third and fourth granularity levels are dedicated to cloud interoperability and ecosystem interoperability, respectively. In their comparative study, they highlight that technical, syntactic, semantic, and organizational levels of interoperability are the most considered in the revised frameworks, whose issues belong to the first and second granularity levels. Indeed, decision models in these frameworks are mainly defined in terms of data, knowledge, communication process, rules, and software systems. The interoperability issues in the third (cloud interoperability) and fourth (ecosystems interoperability) granularity levels have not been supported in these ancient frameworks, but in more recent works they play an important roll, since they could have a positive impact in the decision-making process in PIS/SoIS.

Fernandes et al. (2018) bring some factors that may affect interoperability in SoIS to discuss technical, human, and organizational factors that influence interoperability. However, the study presented in Fernandes et al. (2018) does not explore the real influence of factors in the SoIS interoperability in depth. On our study, we transcend the discussion on interoperability in complex systems by discussing not only technical aspects that influence on the establishment of interoperability links among IS but also human, and organizational factors that influence the interoperability in PIS/SoIS, and the impact on the decision-making processes. Such triad comply with the traditional view of IS and advances the state of the art by gathering the existent evidence on technical factors and also adding other factors. That is the main difference among the works. Next section discusses the research method.

3 Systematic Research Process

The research method we applied to perform the review follows the protocol based on the guidelines of Kitchenham and Charters (2007) for systematic mapping studies (SMS). Three phases were followed to perform this mapping: (1) planning; (2) conduction; and (3) analysis of the results. The research goal of this Goal-Question-Metric (GQM) (Basili 1992) mapping was defined as: *analyze* interoperability *with the purpose of* characterizing *with respect to* influence factors *from the point of view of* researchers *in the context of* complex software-intensive systems, as PIS/SoIS. The main research question (RQ) that drives this research is: *"Which and how factors influence interoperability in the PIS/SoIS context?"*. Other derived questions also compose this research in order to answer the main question. The rationale is the need of identifying Information Technology (IT) artifacts that are commonly used for providing interoperability and can apply in PIS/SoIS domain. Artifacts mean constructs (vocabulary and symbols), models (abstractions and representations), methods (algorithms and practices), and instances (implemented and prototype systems) (Hevner et al. 2008). Figure 1 presents a research protocol summary. The scientific libraries used to search for the studies were *Scopus*[3], *ScienceDirect*[4], *ISI*

---

[3] http://www.scopus.com.

Research questions	(RQ1) Which has been done to address interoperability that may be used in PIS/SoIS?	
	(RQ2) Which technical, human and organizational factors influence interoperability in the PIS/SoIS context?	
	(RQ3) How do technical factors influence interoperability and may affect the PIS/SoIS context?	
	(RQ4) How do human factors influence interoperability and may affect the PIS/SoIS context?	
	(RQ5) How do organizational factors influence interoperability and may affect the PIS/SoIS context?	
	(RQ6) How interoperability and decision-making are related in the PIS/SoIS context?	
Search string	Population	("interop* AND decision-making") AND
	Intervention	("systems of system*" OR "systems-of-system*" OR "system of information system*" OR "system-of-information-system*" OR "systems of information system*" OR "systems-of-information-system*" OR "Heterogeneous System*" OR "Large Scale System*" OR "Adaptive System*" OR "Pervasive Information Systems")
Search strategy	Scopus, ScienceDirect, ISI Web of Science, IEEE, Engineering Village, ACM + Snowballing (backward)	
Inclusion criteria	- to discuss factors that influence on interoperability; OR to propose or applies a solution for interoperability in **intervention**; OR to discuss how interoperability and decision making are related.	
Exclusion criteria	- is secondary study; OR is similar study to another reporting the same results, in which the most recent was chosen for the analysis; OR is specific about interoperability between database systems, specific components or network protocols AND not between different IS; OR mentions interoperability, but the approach is not specifically focused on it; OR is not accessible, the authors did not respond to the study request, or the researchers' institutional IP does not give access to the library; OR is not written in English; OR is not directed related to the state-of-the-art of interoperability; OR proposes only solutions for subsystems; OR is an erratum (Corrigendum); OR is a conference preface; OR is an editorial preface.	
Study type	Primary Studies.	

Fig. 1 Protocol summary

Web of Science[5], *IEEE*[6], *Engineering Village*[7], and *ACM Digital Library*[8]. They are the most important repositories for research in computer science (Afonso et al. 2020). In addition, these digital libraries also encompass studies relevant to IS domain.

On step 1, the electronic search was run using search string. The retrieved studies were stored in Parsifal.[9] Adaptations for each library can be checked on a report generated by Parsifal tool.[10] On step 2, Parsifal supported us to remove duplicate studies. On step 3, the first filter was applied, i.e., inclusion and exclusion criteria after reading titles, abstracts, and keywords. On step 4, we applied the second filter by reading introduction and conclusion. On step 5, the backward snowballing technique was applied to complete the search (Wohlin 2014). Inclusion and exclusion criteria were applied to the studies retrieved in steps 3 to 5 of the selection process. On step 6, the third filter (reading of full text) was applied on the selected studies. Finally, on step 7, data was extracted from the selected studies. The number of included and excluded studies at each step is shown in Fig. 2.

We based our analysis procedure to investigate influence factors on textual analysis following a method of four steps: (1) define the theoretical lens; (2) define the categorization; (3) analyze the discussions of the studies; and (4) identify and

---

[4] http://www.sciencedirect.com.

[5] http://www.isiknowledge.com.

[6] http://ieeexplore.ieee.org.

[7] http://www.engineeringvillage.com.

[8] https://dl.acm.org/.

[9] https://parsif.al/.

[10] http://bit.ly/Report-SMS-2020.

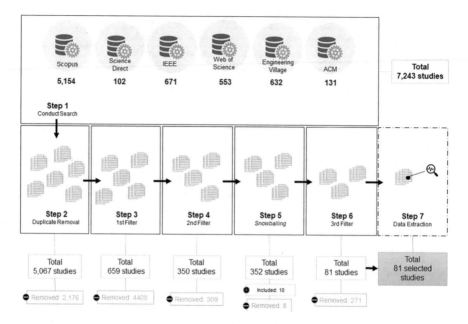

Fig. 2 Number of included and excluded papers during the selection process

extract the factors and identify if the studies address interoperability and decision-making. In order to identified factors and decision-making issues, we investigate the analysis and discussion sections from the included studies. The rationale for this decision is that generally in those sections authors often expose details about the application of the solutions reported in the research. We based our textual analysis using codes to assign factors of each relevant quote, expression, phrase or word from the extracted data, based on the open coding procedures for qualitative analysis (Corbin and Strauss 2014).

Data were extracted from the 81 selected primary studies. This study recovered publications from 1992 to 2022 regarding it. RQs were answered from data extracted from the selected published studies.

4 IT Artifacts for Interoperability and Their Implications in PIS/SoIS

Obtained results help us to answer RQ1 (*Which has been done to address interoperability that may be used in PIS/SoIS?*). The research field about interoperability has popularity in the literature. Indeed, the number of publications recovered in the first stages of this study can confirm our perception (7,243 publications, see Fig. 2). However, researches specific about PIS/SoIS domain are still incipient, ratifying the result of the study conducted by Teixeira et al. (2019) on the status quo of

PIS/SoIS. As such, we seek to recover similar types of complex systems structures to find artifacts that are commonly used for providing interoperability that can be extended for PIS/SoIS. We analysed the artifacts considering IS characteristics in a PIS/SoIS (autonomy, evolutionary development, emergent behavior, connectivity, interdependence, diversity, dynamicity, and belonging—see Sect. 2). In the IS interoperability scenario, despite involved entities should be able to operate together to promote the image of a whole, their independence and autonomy should be maintained (Lueders 2005); thus, allowing them to preserve their own identity and way of working (Lueders 2005; Soares and Amaral 2014). Based on these reflections, if we consider a PIS/SoIS, we have to be critical of artifacts that have a tightly coupled nature because the constituent IS in a SoIS can belong to different organizations. Even if the artifact has a loosely coupled nature, it is necessary to check if its manager agrees to follow some recommendations for interoperability of the PIS/SoIS arrangement. In Table 1, we summarize the identified artifacts, their sources (studies), level of interoperability they can provide, and if the artifacts can be extended for supporting interoperability in PIS/SoIS.

We provide an additional view about artifacts identified by categorizing them according to the strategies to provide some level of interoperability for the PIS/SoIS context (Fig. 3). Such strategies can be used for the production of knowledge, such as (i) **conceptual** and (ii) **descriptive**; and also for (iii) **software production**, which can directly **affect the decision-making processes**. The production of knowledge through some approach or paradigm can nourish the design of **conceptual** artifacts, such as architectural models, meta-model, conceptual or reference model, business process. Conceptual artifact represents the idea of what we aim to build technically. The **descriptive** artifacts includes framework, guidelines, recommendations, set of indicators or techniques. A descriptive artifact represents conceptual elements that can be prototyped through software-intensive solutions. **Software production** represents the final product developed to accomplish real business demands.

Each type of artefact allows some level of interoperability to be established. Inter-operability levels are represented in this study through the dimensions discussed in Sect. 2, which are also known as layers. Software production with its technological artifacts feeds the syntactic and technical dimensions. On the other hand, descriptive and conceptual artifacts are able to feed more than one dimension. Both can feed the semantic and intra/inter-organizational interoperability dimension directly or feed them through the pragmatic layer. In conjunction, these artifacts become essential for "anytime, anywhere" decision-making processes of IS implemented "everywhere", as in PIS/SoIS.

5 Ten Factors Influencing PIS/SoIS Interoperability

In this section, we answer RQ2 (*Which technical, human, and organizational factors influence interoperability in the PIS/SoIS context?*). We identified 10 technical, human, and organizational factors (Fig. 4). We present these factors discussing how

Table 1 Identified artifacts and their source, level of interoperability, and if they can be extended for supporting interoperability in PIS/SoIS

Artifact identified	Source (included publication)	Level of interoperability	Can be extended for PIS/SoIS?
Agent-based platform	Mendes et al. (2018), Papageorgiou et al. (2021)	Technical and syntactic	✓
Mediator system	Benaben et al. (2018), Touzi et al. (2008)	Technical	✓
Prototype application	Agostinho and Jardim-Goncalves (2015)	Technical	✓
Architectural model	Bicocchi et al. (2018), Vargas et al. (2018), Mazzetti and Nativi (2012), Song et al. (2011), Zarour et al. (2011), Kuehn et al. (2011), Diallo et al. (2010), Neaga and Henshaw (2010), Mantzana and Koumaditis (2010), Dividino et al. (2018), Buhalis and Leung (2018), Dolk et al. (2012), Kazemzadeh et al. (2010)	Semantic	✓
Meta-model	Chapurlat and Daclin (2012), Jardim-Goncalves et al. (2010), Chen et al. (2008), Rosener et al. (2004)	Semantic	✓
Conceptual model	Zeinali et al. (2016), Soares and Amaral (2014), Athanasopoulos et al. (2006)	Semantic	✓
Maturity model	Guédria et al. (2015)	Organizational	
Macro-process model	Fouletier et al. (1997)	Organizational	✓
Reference model	Jamoussi et al. (2017), Marlowe et al. (2012), Jardim-Goncalves et al. (2012)	organizational	✓

	References		
Framework	Espadinha-Cruz and Grilo (2019), Mordecai et al. (2016), Zacharewicz et al. (2017), Zdravković et al. (2017), Coutinho et al. (2016), Weichhart et al. (2016), Chalmeta and Pazos (2015), Cuenca et al. (2015), Li et al. (2013), Ostadzadeh et al. (2015), Tripathi et al. (2013), Wang et al. (2010), Camara et al. (2010), Widergren et al. (2010), Qureshi et al. (2010), Pyarelal et al. (2004), Chituc et al. (2009), Wang et al. (2009), Barchetti et al. (2009), Yahia et al. (2009), Agostinho and Jardim-Goncalves (2009), Bittencourt et al. (2009), Ullberg et al. (2009), Ambrosio and Widergren (2007), Whitman and Panetto (2006), Hollenbach and Alexander (1997), Hollenbach and Alexander (1997), Mazzetti et al. (2022), Buhalis and Leung (2018), Kalatzis et al. (2019)	Technical, semantic, organizational	✓
Guidelines/ recommendations	Yahia et al. (2009), Chen et al. (2008), Arakelian et al. (2022), Kalatzis et al. (2019)	Semantic	✓
Methods	Giachetti et al. (2019), Ullberg et al. (2012), Cornu et al. (2012), Naudet et al. (2010), Ford et al. (2009), Perrone and Finkelstein (2007), Rhodes and Wilson (1992)	Organizational	
Methodologies	Daclin et al. (2016), Deniaud et al. (2012), Agostinho et al. (2011)	Organizational	
Ontology	Rosener et al. (2004), Mazzetti et al. (2022), Lima et al. (2022), Dividino et al. (2018)	Semantic	✓
Set of indicators	Billaud et al. (2015), Muller (2009)	Technical, organizational	✓
Set of strategies	Agostinho et al. (2016), Klischewski et al. (2011), Lewis et al. (2008), Mills and Ruston (1990)	Organizational	✓
Set of techniques	Anderson and Boxer (2008)	Organizational	✓
Thesaurus/vocabulary	Naudet et al. (2008), Yaacoubi et al. (2006), Navigli and Velardi (2005)	Semantic	✓

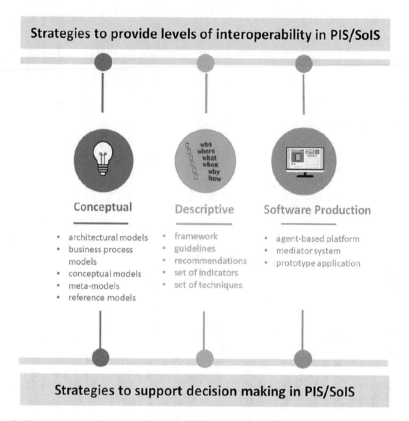

Fig. 3 Strategies to provide levels of interoperability in PIS/SoIS

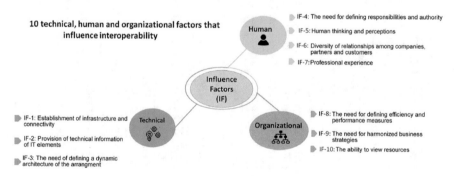

Fig. 4 Set of influence factors for interoperability in PIS/SoIS

each one influences interoperability in SoIS, more especifically in RQ3, RQ4, and RQ5 (*How technical, human, and organizational factors influence interoperability in PIS/SoIS?*).

5.1　Technical Factors

The first factor is **establishment of infrastructure and connectivity (IF-1)** (Ambrosio and Widergren 2007; Athanasopoulos et al. 2006; Chapurlat and Daclin 2012; Chen et al. 2008; Chituc et al. 2009; Diallo et al. 2010; Espadinha-Cruz and Grilo 2019; Giachetti et al. 2019; Hollenbach and Alexander 1997; Jardim-Goncalves et al. 2012; Klischewski et al. 2011; Muller 2009; Naudet et al. 2010; Neaga and Henshaw 2010; Ostadzadeh et al. 2015; Ullberg et al. 2012; Wang et al. 2010; Zarour et al. 2011; Zeinali et al. 2016). This factor includes structural aspects (Ullberg et al. 2012) as a platform (Chituc et al. 2009; Klischewski et al. 2011; Mazzetti and Nativi 2012) or system (Klischewski et al. 2011). An infrastructure for interoperability is often composed of physical connectivity (Ambrosio and Widergren 2007; Buhalis and Leung 2018; Dolk et al. 2012; Kalatzis et al. 2019; Muller 2009; Papageorgiou et al. 2021), such as cables, connectors (Ambrosio and Widergren 2007; Muller 2009), network connectors, and protocols for communication links. Studies indicate the use of protocols, such as SOAP[11] or REST[12] (Benaben et al. 2018; Ullberg et al. 2012; Wang et al. 2010). The type of interface that will be used is a relevant aspect for the connectivity of the arrangement (Chapurlat and Daclin 2012; Chituc et al. 2009; Mantzana and Koumaditis 2010; Mordecai et al. 2016; Naudet et al. 2010; Neaga and Henshaw 2010; Song et al. 2011; Vargas et al. 2018; Weichhart et al. 2016). In this case, layers of user interface and web services have been identified as ways to facilitate interoperations (Lima et al. 2022; Song et al. 2011; Weichhart et al. 2016).

In addition, some type of definition of common operating environments was discussed as an aspect of influence for interoperability (Athanasopoulos et al. 2006; Billaud et al. 2015; Touzi et al. 2008; Wang et al. 2010). This is because it can facilitate automated data exchange between heterogeneous platforms in terms of operating systems or hardware systems and programming languages (Chen et al. 2008; Rosener et al. 2004; Wang et al. 2010). This factor is important so that some level of technological compatibility can be established when a more automated level of technical interoperability is desired.

Technical interoperability supports electronic interaction between constituent systems, capitalizing on hardware, software, and firmware infrastructure (Buhalis and Leung 2018; Espadinha-Cruz and Grilo 2019; Mordecai et al. 2016). Therefore, **IF-1** influences interoperability by treating the interconnectivity layer of the systems through the interfaces that enable the use of services (Agostinho et al. 2011; Bicocchi et al. 2018; Billaud et al. 2015; Camara et al. 2010; Chituc et al. 2009; Cuenca et al. 2015; Diallo et al. 2010; Guédria et al. 2015; Jardim-Goncalves et al. 2010; Klischewski et al. 2011; Navigli and Velardi 2005; Ostadzadeh et al. 2015; Touzi et al. 2008; Whitman and Panetto 2006; Yaacoubi et al. 2006).

---

[11] SOAP (Simple Object Access Protocol) is a network protocol for exchanging structured data among nodes.

[12] REST (Representational State Transfer) defines characteristics for building web applications.

Provision of technical information of IT elements (IF-2) Mordecai et al. (2016), Vargas et al. (2018), Weichhart et al. (2016), Chapurlat and Daclin (2012), Song et al. (2011), Neaga and Henshaw (2010), Mantzana and Koumaditis (2010), Naudet et al. (2010), Chituc et al. (2009), Mills and Ruston (1990) include metadata information (e.g., structural, syntactic, and semantic data formats) that facilitate the integration of information around the heterogeneity of data models (Chituc et al. 2009; Cornu et al. 2012; Diallo et al. 2010; Kalatzis et al. 2019; Kazemzadeh et al. 2010; Wang et al. 2010), ontologies (Dividino et al. 2018; Lima et al. 2022; Mazzetti et al. 2022; Zarour et al. 2011), meta-model (Cornu et al. 2012), and frameworks (Anderson and Boxer 2008; Mazzetti et al. 2022). However, for this information supply to be carried out with better precision, some studies defend the need for technical functions and procedures by which the responsible professionals can benefit (Agostinho and Jardim-Goncalves 2009; Billaud et al. 2015; Chapurlat and Daclin 2012; Chen et al. 2008; Chituc et al. 2009; Mordecai et al. 2016; Muller 2009; Soares and Amaral 2014; Zeinali et al. 2016). This factor is related to media exchange and standardization procedures when exchanging and analyzing functional compatibility or requirements (Billaud et al. 2015; Fouletier et al. 1997). Hence, the need for articulation among IS comes as an aspect that directly assists the need to reconfigure components so that there is adaptability (Deniaud et al. 2012; Jardim-Goncalves et al. 2012) and conformity (Muller 2009) among systems. of an arrangement.

In turn, providing of technical information from the IT elements (**IF-2**) involved in the interoperation influences decisions about design of interoperability links by considering information, such as data structures, i.e., attributes and formats (Giachetti et al. 2019). An arrangement of PIS/SoIS being subject to changing formation implies that new data formats, semantics, procedures, and technologies are continuously adopted (Billaud et al. 2015; Fouletier et al. 1997; Soares and Amaral 2014), such as data anonymization for preserving the privacy of patients in the context of health IS (Lima et al. 2022). The existence of functions and technical procedures that support the emergence demands of PIS/SoIS is one way.

The third factor is related to the **need of defining a dynamic architecture of the arrangement (IF-3)** (Agostinho et al. 2016; Billaud et al. 2015; Buhalis and Leung 2018; Camara et al. 2010; Chen et al. 2008; Giachetti et al. 2019; Ullberg et al. 2009). In this case, types of model-oriented architecture (MDA, i.e., model-driven architecture) or high-level architecture (HLA, i.e., high-level architecture) were mentioned by Barchetti et al. (2009) and Touzi et al. (2008). Also, a list of negative technical factors has been identified in some publications. In Kuehn et al. (2011), authors highlight as critical points: (i) lack of redundancy in system arrangements; (ii) limited resistance of equipment during emergencies that hinder the execution of the arrangement; and (iii) lack of coordinated planning or contingency plans to deal with disaster situations that may require the full operation of an interoperable systems arrangement.

In (Agostinho et al. 2016), the definition of architecture is seen as one of the pillars that sustain the achievement of business and sustainable interoperability. In this case, the need of defining the dynamic arrangement architecture (**IF-3**) is a factor that influences interoperability in the context of PIS/SoIS given the the need of a loosely coupled IS design (Klischewski et al. 2011). If, on the one hand, the use of common environments/interfaces favors the desired stability in the context of interoperability (Billaud et al. 2015), in PIS/SoIS it is necessary to pay attention to the fact that, depending on the belonging characteristic of the IS to SoIS, the use of common environments can cause harm.

5.2 Human Factors

One of human factors identified is regarding to the **need for defining responsibilities and authority (IF-4)** (Chen et al. 2008; Espadinha-Cruz and Grilo 2019; Mills and Ruston 1990) especially to manage the operation of the system arrangements that are formed to achieve a greater objective. This definition is related to the roles or functions that members of a technical team can play to interoperate systems. Someone responsible for specifying tasks or rules to fulfill a mission, goal or objective is an example of a definition of responsibility (Arakelian et al. 2022; Benaben et al. 2018; Chalmeta and Pazos 2015; Chen et al. 2008; Daclin et al. 2016; Mazzetti et al. 2022; Mills and Ruston 1990). It was observed that there are studies that envision the importance of establishing roles for the stakeholders involved in the formation of systems arrangements that need to interoperate (Chituc et al. 2009; Mendes et al. 2018; Mordecai et al. 2016; Vargas et al. 2018; Wang et al. 2009). According to the study presented in Rhodes and Wilson (1992), it is important to stress that the overall performance of a supersystem such as this relies just as much on human actions as it does upon the performance of its technical components and in the final analysis the effectiveness can only be judged by the extent to which the operators manage to coordinate their activities (Rhodes and Wilson 1992). Some roles have been identified in publications on SoS and may contribute to discussions in the PIS/SoIS domain, such as constituent IS owners, beneficiaries, operators, and SoS users (Mendes et al. 2018; Mordecai et al. 2016; Vargas et al. 2018); SoS manager (Mendes et al. 2018); and SoS developer (Vargas et al. 2018).

Interoperability can be seen or simplified by some researchers or practitioners as an integration question. However, this study shows us this is just one of the concern for being considered. The human level is discussed in literature by Soares and Amaral on the Information Systems interoperability (ISI) domain (Soares and Amaral 2014). For ISI, the human perspective should be considered when designing, implementing, and managing interoperability (Soares and Amaral 2014). As such, human factors may influence interoperability in the PIS/SoIS domain.

The need for defining **responsibilities and authority (IF-4)** influences interoperability in PIS/SoIS as the relationships among stakeholders that hold IS that are interoperating (or that will interoperate) come from diverse organizational contexts and cultures. The definition of responsibilities and roles in a PIS/SoIS is valid both for the management team (authority that will benefit from the formation of the arrangement) and for the technical team allocated to operationalize the formed

SoIS. Definition of an authority also directly influences the type of SoIS that will be formed (Directed or Acknowledged). In this case, depending on the power exercised by the authority, a PIS/SoIS will be more or less subject to unwanted emerging behaviors.

We noticed that the aspects related to **human thinking and perceptions (IF-5)** are commonly discussed in the theories of human communication (Littlejohn and Foss 2010). This factor is related to the expectations and feelings that stakeholders have when making IS available to collaborate in an arrangement (Chen et al. 2008).

On the other hand, **human thinking and perceptions (IF-5)** influence interoperability because it is generally planned in business scenarios based on the expectations of the stakeholders of a SoIS and each stakeholders of constituent IS (Buhalis and Leung 2018). The main objective of a PIS/SoIS is driven by the perception of a person or management team about the capabilities that a set of existing constituent IS can offer to the arrangement (Lima et al. 2022).

Diversity of relationships among companies, partners and customers (IF-6) is a factor of influence existing in the context of interoperability (Hollenbach and Alexander 1997). This diversity is related to how people, processes, technologies, and operational demands are orchestrated in a context of interoperability (Anderson and Boxer 2008; Arakelian et al. 2022; Mazzetti et al. 2022). Aspects related to human communication and the way in which collaborations among members of technical teams, companies, partners, and customers or users are materialized tend to be in the concerns of diverse business domains (Agostinho and Jardim-Goncalves 2015; Agostinho et al. 2011, 2016; Benaben et al. 2018; Bittencourt et al. 2009; Chalmeta and Pazos 2015; Chituc et al. 2009; Diallo et al. 2010; Guédria et al. 2015; Klischewski et al. 2011; Kuehn et al. 2011; Mordecai et al. 2016; Muller 2009; Naudet et al. 2010; Navigli and Velardi 2005; Pyarelal et al. 2004; Qureshi et al. 2010; Touzi et al. 2008; Zdravković et al. 2017; Zeinali et al. 2016).

Aspects of human communication involve communication among individuals and groups (Agostinho et al. 2011), as interactions of people at intra or inter-organizational boundaries (Bittencourt et al. 2009; Diallo et al. 2010; Muller 2009; Naudet et al. 2010; Neaga and Henshaw 2010). In turn, aspects of collaboration among stakeholders (Klischewski et al. 2011) expose diversity of relationships that may arise from social behavior that influences how the articulations between IS will be made (Agostinho et al. 2016; Soares and Amaral 2014; Ullberg et al. 2009). Aspects of culture, such as language differences (Agostinho et al. 2016; Marlowe et al. 2012; Ostadzadeh et al. 2015; Soares and Amaral 2014) between technical or managerial teams can hinder or facilitate aspects of human communication and collaboration.

The nature of PIS/SoIS contemplates interorganizational aspects formed by the diversity of relationships among companies, partners, and customers **(IF-6)** (Hollenbach and Alexander 1997). This factor influences interoperability as the communication aspects and human collaboration are coordinated. This coordination should favor the process of knowledge and understanding related to the data and information to be exchanged. This knowledge in IS interoperability is obtained based on the meanings provided by a human being (Zdravković et al. 2017).

Another influencing factor for interoperability in PIS/SoIS is related to **professional experience (IF-7)** (Agostinho et al. 2016; Chapurlat and Daclin 2012; Coutinho et al. 2016). This factor is related to the competence of people who work with interoperability (Agostinho et al. 2011; Guédria et al. 2015). In general, managers expect professionals to have the ability to use the information exchanged, that is, operate it, interpret it, transform it, and extract stakeholder requirements (Billaud et al. 2015; Ullberg et al. 2012). The desirable experience involves the ability to interpret data for semantic understanding (Agostinho et al. 2011; Ambrosio and Widergren 2007; Lewis et al. 2008), as well as for the extraction and formalization of domain knowledge expressed by specialists (Navigli and Velardi 2005).

On the other hand, professional expertise **(IF-7)** influences interoperability in PIS/SoIS as the quality of the services provided by the arrangement depends on the professional profile of the management (or technical) team developed throughout the career. An example of this influence is the inconsistencies that must be noticed and corrected by professionals when checking, reevaluating, or redesigning the interoperability links (Navigli and Velardi 2005). Furthermore, as semantic understanding is important for the context of interoperability, this factor can influence rules that govern the definition of concepts and the relationships between multiple IS (Ambrosio and Widergren 2007).

5.3 Organizational Factors

We identified organizational factors regarding the **need for defining measures of effectiveness and performance (IF-8)** (Billaud et al. 2015; Chen et al. 2008; Giachetti et al. 2019; Ullberg et al. 2009; Zacharewicz et al. 2017). Measures can be formed by metrics or indicators, but they are not limited to that. Studies indicate that performance measures may include the duration/time of interoperation (Agostinho et al. 2016; Billaud et al. 2015; Camara et al. 2010; Chen et al. 2008), cost of interoperation (Agostinho et al. 2016; Chen et al. 2008), integrity (Billaud et al. 2015), quality of interoperation (Billaud et al. 2015), data latency (Camara et al. 2010), and meeting IT requirements (Ullberg et al. 2009).

The need for defining **efficiency and performance measures (IF-8)** influences interoperability given that the purpose of identifying measures as part of the interoperability analysis is to determine whether the interoperability is sufficient to support missions in the context of SoS/PIS/SoIS (Giachetti et al. 2019). In turn, performance measures are commonly used in corporate cultures as a business strategy to improve results. Thus, defining performance measures influences interoperability because this type of information can help to measure the ability to maintain an adaptable arrangement to the mutations to which an environment such as SoS/PIS/SoIS is subject (Billaud et al. 2015). These mutations are related to inputs and outputs of constituent IS that make up a SoIS.

The **need for harmonized business strategies (IF-9)** (Cuenca et al. 2015; Espadinha-Cruz and Grilo 2019; Kuehn et al. 2011; Ostadzadeh et al. 2015; Ullberg et al. 2009) is a factor that influences decisions on interoperability if considered in the design of systems arrangements (Cuenca et al. 2015; Espadinha-Cruz and Grilo 2019; Kuehn et al. 2011; Ostadzadeh et al. 2015; Ullberg et al. 2009). Issues involving differences in organizational policies and practices pose challenges in the orchestration of business (Marlowe et al. 2012; Zarour et al. 2011). Policies and practices depend on organizational cultures (Anderson and Boxer 2008; Bittencourt et al. 2009; Chituc et al. 2009; Cuenca et al. 2015; Ford et al. 2009; Klischewski et al. 2011; Navigli and Velardi 2005; Touzi et al. 2008; Ullberg et al. 2009) that are influenced by the diversity of nationalities, languages, and linguistics. These diverse aspects also generate challenges in semantic dimension (Cuenca et al. 2015; Touzi et al. 2008). In view of the technical and human diversity involved (IF-2 and IF-6) and to deal with this organizational factor, the harmonization of the business network aiming at collaboration among companies or organization units should be sought (Agostinho et al. 2011; Chituc et al. 2009; Jardim-Goncalves et al. 2010; Touzi et al. 2008). In addition, we observed that this factor (IF-9) creates challenges related to the right of access and right to ownership of information (Chituc et al. 2009; Ullberg et al. 2009). Therefore, the definition and specification of inter-organizational collaborative activities is necessary (Chituc et al. 2009). On the other hand, political aspects also influence interoperability because it involves economics, regulation, and the need to seek compliance with legislation (Ambrosio and Widergren 2007; Chapurlat and Daclin 2012; Chituc et al. 2009; Espadinha-Cruz and Grilo 2019; Kuehn et al. 2011; Pyarelal et al. 2004; Ullberg et al. 2009; Widergren et al. 2010).

The factor related to the **need for harmonized business strategies (IF-9)** can both influence business-to-business connectivity **(IF-1)** and can assist in obtaining better performance of the arrangement **(IF-3)** (Navigli and Velardi 2005). SoIS can present complex interorganizational relationships due to the diversity of organizational cultures to which it is subject. Therefore, harmonized strategies can influence an organization's interest in maintaining or not its IS participating in a formed arrangement.

We identified that the **ability to view resources (IF-10)** is an influencing factor because the management team may not have control over technical or human resources to be allocated to achieve interoperability (Benaben et al. 2018; Cuenca et al. 2015; Perrone and Finkelstein 2007; Ullberg et al. 2009; Widergren et al. 2010). This happens due to the managerial and operational autonomy of the IS that make up a PIS/SoIS. In this sense, care must be taken to ensure that the specification and allocation of interoperability requirements is performed properly (Agostinho et al. 2011; Ambrosio and Widergren 2007; Camara et al. 2010; Cuenca et al. 2015; Daclin et al. 2016; Giachetti et al. 2019; Jamoussi et al. 2017; Neaga and Henshaw 2010; Ostadzadeh et al. 2015; Tripathi et al. 2013; Widergren et al. 2010). This factor influences interoperability in PIS/SoIS by including programmatic aspects (Ostadzadeh et al. 2015), such as: aligned operations and procedures, analysis activities and definition of missions, goals, objectives (Camara et al. 2010;

Cuenca et al. 2015; Espadinha-Cruz and Grilo 2019; Ostadzadeh et al. 2015; Perrone and Finkelstein 2007), and business needs (Agostinho et al. 2011; Ambrosio and Widergren 2007; Bicocchi et al. 2018; Cuenca et al. 2015; Daclin et al. 2016; Jamoussi et al. 2017; Neaga and Henshaw 2010; Ostadzadeh et al. 2015; Tripathi et al. 2013; Weichhart et al. 2016; Widergren et al. 2010).

In addition, we identified a list of negative organizational factors on some publications. The lack of mediation results in difficulty in solving problems produces degrees of uncertainty or low levels of confidence around interoperations (Cuenca et al. 2015). Another negative point is the constant occurrence of new restrictions of products and processes to the IS because they cause the need for interference in the interoperability links (Marlowe et al. 2012). Moreover, non-transparent processes between organizations participating in an arrangement cause incompatibilities ranging from techniques issues to business interests (Athanasopoulos et al. 2006; Pyarelal et al. 2004).

The ability to view resources (IF-10) influences interoperability in SoIS as a manager or management team in this domain may not have full access to the resources of all the IS involved. Thus, the specification and allocation of interoperability requirements (Perrone and Finkelstein 2007; Ullberg et al. 2009) requires SoIS management to be able to collect information with semantic understanding (Athanasopoulos et al. 2006; Ullberg et al. 2009; Widergren et al. 2010). Through this understanding, one or more business models are produced (Zarour et al. 2011) and strategic alignment can be achieved (Klischewski et al. 2011).

5.4   Impact of Interoperability Factors in the Decision-making Processes

The expansion of IS beyond the traditional frontiers of organizations, thus deployed everywhere, has fostered the creation of complex systems as PIS/SoIS. Such unbounded deployment represents the possibility of enlarging decision-making processes beyond traditional IS and the possibility of deeply observing the impact of technical, human, and organizational factors in which such processes occur. Hence, this new "anytime, anywhere" perspective for decision-making processes makes interoperability from the three perspectives discussed in the previous sections a key aspect to consider. Most studies revised, implicitly state the need of considering decision-making and dependencies among interoperability perspectives. Some of them, explicitly detail which specific interoperability factors directly impact on decision-making processes. In this section, we respond the RQ6 (*How interoperability and decision-making are related in PS/SoIS context?*).

Technical factors, as **establishing infrastructure and connectivity (IF-1)** are considered to provide interoperability to support decision-making. The studies presented in Jardim-Goncalves et al. (2010) and Agostinho and Jardim-Goncalves (2009) provide an interconnectivity layer of systems through the interfaces that enable the use of services, for monitoring and decision support. The proposal presented in Rosener et al. (2004) facilitates automated data exchange by integrating a decisional model and a technical aspects model that includes persistence, communication, security, etc. In Papageorgiou et al. (2021), it is proposed an interoperability approach to support the interactions among unmanned aerial vehicles by the context of airborne radar surveillance to support decision-making during missions, operations, and analysis. In Buhalis and Leung (2018), authors propose an architecture of smart hospitality systems supported on big data analytics, artificial intelligence, cloud services, sensors, and ambient ecosystem. The study described by Kalatzis et al. (2019) treats the semantic interoperability for IoT platforms in support of decision making. In Dolk et al. (2012), authors propose a Global Information Network Architecture, a smart mobile systems deployed in support of organizational decision-making objectives, based on a model-based architecture and component-based development. In Zarour et al. (2011), authors propose a P2P-based architecture to allow interoperability among distributed heterogeneous systems, and the sharing of information towards decision making. In Mazzetti and Nativi (2012), authors propose a Service Oriented Architecture (SOA) towards the interoperability of Earth Observation Systems, which include sensors providing real-time information.

For decision-making, data, information, and knowledge are key elements that must provide high levels of interoperability. Semantic and pragmatic information help to reduce the gap between data and policy- and decision-making goals that are actionable knowledge for decision-makers. Thus, the goal of linking the data managed by the constituent IS is to provide comprehensive data summaries and visualisations that can support technicians, professionals, managers, politicians, etc., in their decision-making process. Thus, formal representation of knowledge, as ontologies have been developed to provide **technical information of the IT elements involved (IF-2)** that support decisional models (Agostinho and Jardim-Goncalves 2009; Dividino et al. 2018; Jardim-Goncalves et al. 2010; Kalatzis et al. 2019; Kazemzadeh et al. 2010; Lima et al. 2022; Mazzetti et al. 2022; Rosener et al. 2004; Weichhart et al. 2016; Zarour et al. 2011). In Weichhart et al. (2016) and Zarour et al. (2011), authors propose approaches based on agents, an ontology of concepts and relations allowing organizational interoperability, and a P2P-based architecture to allow the interoperability among distributed heterogeneous systems, and the sharing of information towards decision making. The core component of the sustainable interoperability framework proposed in Jardim-Goncalves et al. (2010) and Agostinho and Jardim-Goncalves (2009) is a knowledge base supported on harmonized ontologies that represent environmental knowledge and human preferences. A model-based ontology of interoperabilty problems in IS is presented in Rosener et al. (2004), which integrates a decisional model and technical aspects model. In Mazzetti et al. (2022), authors propose an ontology for annotating resources with their type, role, and relations in the knowledge generation process for decision-making. In Lima et al. (2022), an approach towards data integration and sharing among health IS to support the construction of evidence-based decision making tools is proposed; this approach is based on web services and on an ontology considering clinical concepts, the multiple existing IS, and concepts related to diseases, diagnostics, therapies, and patients with an emphasis on data anonymization for preserving their privacy.

In Dividino et al. (2018), it is defined an ontology for ocean-related decision-making in military environments, in which data comes in the form of continuous streams from multiple IS; this ontological data architecture is used for real-time data representation, integration, and querying over a multitude of heterogeneous data streams and visualisations. Authors in Kalatzis et al. (2019) treat the semantic interoperability for IoT platforms in support of decision making, by providing a solution towards the support of uniform data exchange and adapts, extends data model, API standards enabling, and the use of IoT data analytics and intelligent decision making. In Kazemzadeh et al. (2010), authors present a proposition of a novel knowledge management framework for a Clinical Decision Support System. They address the issues of data and knowledge interoperability by adopting health-care and data mining modeling standards in order to assist healthcare personnel to improve the quality of clinical practice.

Novel technologies, such as big data analytics, artificial intelligence, and cloud computing are being included to achieve smart decision-making systems supported in **dynamic architecture of the arrangement (IF-3)**, as in Klischewski et al. (2011), Buhalis and Leung (2018), and Kalatzis et al. (2019). In Klischewski et al. (2011), authors propose a SOA to provide the government with improved data about the population for decision making purposes.

Multiple studies focused on interoperability and decision-making coincide in considering the three human factors—i.e., **defining responsibilities and authority (IF-4)** (Arakelian et al. 2022; Espadinha-Cruz and Grilo 2019; Mazzetti et al. 2022), **human thinking and perceptions (IF-5)** (Chen et al. 2008; Lima et al. 2022), and **diversity of relationships among companies, partners, and customers (IF-6)** (Arakelian et al. 2022; Klischewski et al. 2011; Marlowe et al. 2012; Mazzetti et al. 2022).

In Espadinha-Cruz and Grilo (2019), authors propose a business interoperability decomposition framework to support the analysis of interoperability conditions in buyer- supplier dyads. Authors in Chen et al. (2008) highlight the importance of considering expectations and feelings of stakeholders in the decisional models of IS available to collaborate in an arrangement. Authors in Mazzetti et al. (2022) acknowledge that achieving complete interoperability towards policy- and decision-making goals requires a dialogue among the different worlds inhabited by different people. In Arakelian et al. (2022), authors study the obstacles to interoperability in the context of Human Resource IS (HRIS) with a focus on the use case of the Uganda HRIS; they map existing HRIS and the administrative processes and data flows of three decision-making use cases (recruitment and deployment of health workers, salary payments, and performance management) and suggest some directions to tackle the HRIS interoperability barriers, such as sharing and integration among HRSI that enables decision-making with a focus on preserving user privacy. In Lima et al. (2022), authors highlight the need to address interoperability from a socio-technical perspective in the sense of engaging different actors, such as users and developers into the conception of new solutions and strategies, remaining in the domain of user experience regarding the final solution. In Marlowe et al. (2012), authors state that, since decision making mechanisms are typically oriented towards reaching consensus, interoperability becomes a matter of how to interact instead of just linking entities and operations, thus, collaborating entities must focus on semantic and personal features to facilitate those interactions and improve decision making processes.

Since decision-making implies the aggregation of business, managers, and technical goals, in some how, all studies analysing the influence of interoperability on decision-making consider the organizational factors: the need for defining **efficiency and performance measures (IF-8)** (Buhalis and Leung 2018; Daclin et al. 2016; Dolk et al. 2012; Jamoussi et al. 2017; Kalatzis et al. 2019; Mazzetti et al. 2022; Rosener et al. 2004), the need for **harmonized business strategies (IF-9)** (Agostinho and Jardim-Goncalves 2009; Espadinha-Cruz and Grilo 2019; Jardim-Goncalves et al. 2010; Klischewski et al. 2011; Lima et al. 2022; Marlowe et al. 2012; Rosener et al. 2004; Zarour et al. 2011), and the **ability to view resources (IF-10)** (Daclin et al. 2016; Kazemzadeh et al. 2010; Klischewski et al. 2011; Mazzetti et al. 2022; Rosener et al. 2004; Tripathi et al. 2013; Zarour et al. 2011). In Espadinha-Cruz and Grilo (2019), it is proposed a framework that generates new scenarios, proposed to decision-makers, in order to scale-up cooperation between buyer and supplier, achieve optimal interoperability, and increase performances. The study presented in Jamoussi et al. (2017) proposes a guidance-based approach for enhancing the e-government interoperability, by elaborating a Requirement Model (modeling e-government interoperability in business term) and after that modeling the satisfaction (align these specific requirements with the needs of requesters). From decision making's point of view, this approach allows ministries to identify their problems in terms of interoperability and select solutions adapted to their needs. Authors in Daclin et al. (2016) and Rosener et al. (2004) propose enterprise interoperability frameworks based on interoperability measurements, such as availability, scalability, feasibility, and cost, to select and combine solutions suitable to the enterprises involved. Similarly, the physical/empirical model of the proposed framework in Mazzetti et al. (2022) includes indicators and indices to allow decision makers to reduce the gap between data and goals.

In Tripathi et al. (2013), differences in organizational policies and practices are tackled by the implementation of a Multi Agent System to support the organizational, syntactic, and semantic interoperability. This harmonization via the collaboration and coordination of software agents provides the basis of common agreements and decision making. In Klischewski et al. (2011), the proposed SOA allows planning strategies towards implementing e-government interoperability, hence, multiple stakeholders with independent agendas can interact with top-down approaches to reach governing public information infrastructure. In Jardim-Goncalves et al. (2010) and Agostinho and Jardim-Goncalves (2009), the decision support system is a key component relayed on an ontological knowledge base to allow capturing the environment and relating human choices and preferences, towards the harmonized enterprise interoperability. In Marlowe et al. (2012), authors highlight the importance of complex and harmonized collaboration supported on interoperability; they propose a strategy interoperability level to help in the creation of high level goals and objectives of participating IS, aligned with the collaborative business plan in the context of decision-making. In Buhalis and Leung (2018), the use of big data and cloud computing allows the decisional support system to generate different scenarios for services in hotels, thus decision makers can adjust the services in real-time.

The decision engine proposed in Kalatzis et al. (2019) automatically assesses how critical an emergency situation is (early wildfire detection), based on a predefined scale (i.e., low, medium, high), supported on data interoperability of the IoT and social media services; it supports the cross application domain reasoning, through the homogenisation of information and automated identification of an emergency situation. In the healthcare domain, PIS/SoIS are common (Kazemzadeh et al. 2010; Lima et al. 2022; Zarour et al. 2011), in which interoperability must ensure a consistent interaction among the constituent IS, as well as providing facilities to visualise results, resources, in the support of decision-making.

6   Key Findings and Reflections

Given the current definition of SoIS, that also includes the definition of PIS (Fernandes et al. 2019; Motta et al. 2017), we can consider that one of the main challenges in the context is to coordinate interest in maintaining the arrangement formed to fulfill the main goal of PIS/SoIS, while the essence of each participant constituent IS is preserved. This concern makes us deal with interoperability in PIS/SoIS not only as an integration phenomenon. The integration phenomenon on interoperability of IS has been discussed by Soares and Amaral (2014). They point out that the existence of a high level of integration among IS may not be the most appropriate solution for any given business environment, since it may significantly compromise the agility or flexibility, and responsiveness of operations (Aubert et al. 2003; Lee and Myers 2004; Pavlou and Singletary 2002), especially when in the arrangement are involved IS from different organizations. From this point of view, this idea can be extended to the context of PIS/SoIS, given the need to preserve the autonomy of the constituent IS, to deal with the distribution of IS, the emerging behavior, evolutionary development, and dynamic architecture of PIS/SoIS.

The **establishment of infrastructure and connectivity (FI-1)** is a factor that affects interoperability in PIS/SoIS, because the **autonomy** of the constituent IS can limit the alternatives that a SoIS manager has to make the arrangement feasible. At this point, the establishment of infrastructure in PIS/SoIS must consider that the weak **belonging** that these IS may have in relation to the arrangement is a barrier to connectivity.

The technological **diversity** of the constituent IS resembles any arrangement of heterogeneous systems. However, unlike other arrangements, PIS/SoIS deals with **dynamism**, which causes an IS to leave the arrangement (Salado 2015).

In that case, the establishment of PIS/SoIS infrastructure and connectivity is not static as it would be in a formation of Federated Information Systems (FIS), for instance (Busse et al. 1999). This sort of arrangement does not prioritize the preservation of constituent autonomy. PIS/SoIS deals with the emergent behavior influenced by the evolutionary development of the IS that, when working to fulfill their particular objectives, they can not prioritize PIS/SoIS. The **interdependence** of the constituent IS in relation to the PIS/SoIS is weaker, because the arrangement must be designed by counting that an IS can leave the arrangement at the decision of the IS stakeholder.

Providing of technical information of the IT elements involved (IF-2) is a factor that affects interoperability in PIS/SoIS because the IS **autonomy** can make it difficult to fully understand the technical information. The fact that IS belonging to PIS/SoIS is not clear and mandatory as it happens in an Enterprise Resource Planning (ERP) may not be enough for the management of PIS/SoIS. For IF-1 to be efficient for the running of the arrangement, IF-2 is important for PIS/SoIS manager to have full knowledge in relation to the diversity of the IS involved. PIS/SoIS management also has the guarantee of IF-2 due to the dynamism of this arrangement.

The **need for defining a dynamic architecture (IF-3)** is a factor that affects interoperability, especially because the IS **autonomy** leads to the abandonment of the arrangement's constituents. In this sense, the architectural planning of a PIS/SoIS that takes into account the **diversity** of IS that initially make up the arrangement may be subject to constant changes. **Emerging behavior** and constant **evolutionary development** mean that IF-3 is adapted to dynamism necessary for this domain.

In PIS/SoIS, human influences on interoperability, such as **the need for defining responsibilities and authority (IF-4)**, represent a reality because the integration provided by a requirement is not a rule as occurs in the federation of systems. Defining responsibilities and authority becomes necessary in PIS/SoIS because the existence of an actor who acts for the governance of the arrangement can be a point of balance in relation to the **interdependence** of the IS that have autonomy.

Human thinking and perceptions (IF-5) is a factor that influences interoperability because it affects the design of interoperability links. We consider that thinking and perceptions direct the needs for formation of PIS/SoIS arrangements are forged. At this point, human perceptions go along with thoughts. This occurs from the moment that the way in which human beings abstract the real world, based on their personal experiences and experiences, can envision the formation of arrangements. **Connectivity** and **interdependence** of IS in a PIS/SoIS will be planned initially based on IF-5, since different constituent IS may not be directly related to the PIS/SoIS stakeholder. This factor can be considered as a guide for the desired **emerging behaviors** and **evolutionary development** to be a priority.

The **diversity of relationships among companies, partners and customers (IF-6)** affects interoperability in PIS/SoIS, as it is reflected in the **autonomy** of the constituent IS. PIS/SoIS **connectivity** must be planned considering the technological **diversity** of the IS that will be part of the arrangement. It may not be trivial for a PIS/SoIS stakeholder to deal with actors that cannot be predicted during the design of interoperability links, given the lack of prior knowledge of the relationships of partnerships and customers that are part of the IS universe. PIS/SoIS can be formed to serve a business domain as an educational one, for instance; however, they may need IS from other domains to achieve the main objective, such as urban mobility.

Professional experience (IF-7) is a factor that affects interoperability in the PIS/SoIS domain, as it makes the process of designing interoperability links more complex without a minimum experience in practical work with interoperability. In conventional contexts where an IT professional works in the sector development of an organization, interoperability occurs on demand. On the other hand, PIS/SoIS is a domain whose premise is interoperability. Therefore, professional knowledge about different approaches and technologies used for IS connectivity must exist so that IF-5 and IF-6 can lead the professional to forge arrangements.

The need for defining efficiency and performance measures (FI-8) affects the interoperability in PIS/SoIS due to the **diversity** and **autonomy** of the constituent IS. In this case, the governance of a dynamic arrangement as PIS/SoIS can be undermined without there being no way to measure the effectiveness and performance of the arrangement in fulfilling the mission. The entry and exit of the constituent IS within a PIS/SoIS can come spontaneously from the holders of these systems, although also due to the influence of PIS/SoIS management.

The need for harmonized business strategies (IF-9) is a factor that influences interoperability in PIS/SoIS, mainly because the management team has to deal with IF-6. Harmonized strategies are necessary because PIS/SoIS is a type of arrangement that may involve constituent IS from different domains that, in order to communicate, may require PIS/SoIS stakeholder interference.

The **ability to view resources (IF-10)** is a factor that affects interoperability in PIS/SoIS, especially if the design of interoperability links involves IS from different organizations. PIS/SoIS stakeholder may not have a direct relationship with the IS management team. Therefore, the ability to view all IS resources can be impaired. Having knowledge about the resources that an IS may be able to provide to PIS/SoIS is important, especially in the planning of emerging behavior and evolutionary development of the arrangement.

Most works acknowledge the key role of interoperability in decision making. Indeed, decision making in PIS/SoIS relies heavily on making sense of data coming from heterogeneous IS which offer interfaces that can differ regarding the names and types of the data they provide or consume, and the granularity and ordering of the operations they interface provide (**IF-1**); hence, semantic interoperability is a key aspect in this regard (**IF-2**). Some of the works we reviewed propose interoperability approaches based on ontologies, which can provide a precise description of all relevant concepts and relationships found in the involved IS. These ontologies can contain concepts regarding decision making such as data, decision criteria, and decision types. Domain experts are the ones who build and maintain ontologies, which can be efficient in IS that are more or less static, whose properties do not change continuously. There is still the need for researching how to build and maintain ontologies for decision making in PIS that continuously evolve and which properties emerge on-the-fly.

Moreover, decision making is a complex process that deserves to have more attention in the context of interoperability of PIS/SoIS . Indeed, decisions are required to be coherent, that is, by relying on common information and reaching consensus (particularly in the context of collective decisions) (**IF-3**); thus, PIS/SoIS should act as one confronted with different inputs and stimuli. This is challenging due to the complexity and dynamicity of PIS/SoIS and the multiple and heterogeneous technical, human, and organizational factors that influence interoperability, and hence, influence decision making processes.

Several fields have considered the importance of interoperability in the decision-making process: healthcare, airborne radar surveillance, smart hospitality systems, smart mobile systems, earth observation systems, military environment, clinical decision support, e-government, human resource IS, buyer-supplier relationship, real-time hotels services, critical emergency situation detection. The common decision-making strategies to all these fields are based mainly on frequently used terms: exchange, communication, knowledge generation, harmonized information, negotiation, dialogue, consensus, interaction between partners, a clear and homogenized representation of data, information and knowledge, security. New technologies as big data analytics, cloud computing, IoT, domain-specific ontologies, multi agent systems, artificial intelligence, social media services, real-time process and streaming data flow are solutions to strengthen communication and harmonize knowledge. All these aspects are directly related to the integration of all interoperabilty factors, emphasizing of course, human (**IF-4, IF-5, IF-6**) and organizational factors (**IF8, IF-9, IF-10**).

To finish, we propose some guidelines for the design of interoperability links in PIS/SoIS, and thus better support the decision-making processes, based on the influencing factors. The influence that technical, human, and organizational elements can have on the interoperability of complex systems, such as PIS/SoIS, is a determining factor in achieving good results regarding meeting the goals of forming an IS arrangement. A PIS/SoIS manager is an actor who provides the tools necessary for the team can successfully orchestrate the achievement of PIS/SoIS main goal, such as:

- *Clear and accurate planning of PIS/SoIS goals:* Increasing the chances of generating the expected results requires clear technical functions and procedures that converge towards the fulfillment of the purposes of a PIS/SoIS, that is, the main objective and secondary objectives. In this case, collect information IT elements (IF-2) helps this need;
- *Business strategy planning:* Human and organizational factors for PIS/SoIS management are important because they involve elements capable of guiding business strategies for establishing alliances, even if temporary. PIS/SoIS deal with inter-organizational alliances whose diversity of cultures may be present. Therefore, the search by harmonized business strategies (IF-9) is essential for the formation of inter-organizational alliances. This harmonization is a factor

that converges to the need to specify and allocate interoperability requirements. On the other hand, the complexity of inter or intra-organizational relationships may be linked to factors such as political aspects. In this case, managing these relationships is complex in itself. Factors such as the ability to view resources may be limited in an inter-organizational alliance (IF-10);

- *Interoperability links management:* To increase the chances of establishing connectivity among constituent IS in PIS/SoIS, an articulation around these IS is necessary. This connectivity depends on the use of appropriate types of interfaces to guarantee the autonomy of the constituent IS (IF-2). However, it is worth mentioning that the definition of the architecture of the arrangement in PIS/SoIS must take into account the dynamic (changeable) nature. Therefore, this factor requires that the provision of technical information from the IT elements involved and the existing technical functions and procedures for the operationalization of interoperability be reviewed;
- *Definition of performance and effectiveness measures:* In technical terms, the need for definition of the performance measures (IF-8) is an important factor in helping to measure the ability of an arrangement to remain viable or adaptable to emerging behaviors to which PIS/SoIS is subject. In business or organizational terms, the definition of effectiveness measures can influence the constituent IS stakeholders in decisions to interoperate or leave from the PIS/SoIS arrangement. Effectiveness measures such as costs, benefits or needs (Sobkowski and Freedman 2013) can be used to demonstrate to stakeholders the benefits of their IS collaborating in the PIS/SoIS arrangement.
- *Incorporate decisional models into the process of modeling interoperability:* Interoperability constitutes one methodological approach to achieve consistent enterprise-wide decision-making. Semantic features can be resolved with harmonized business strategies (IF-9) and domain-specific ontologies (IF-2). Big data, multi agent systems enhance the reconciliation of policies and practices (IF-2). Artificial intelligence and big data analysis can be solutions to knowledge generation and homogenized visualizations (IF-10). Service oriented architecture, social media services, real-time processing, and streaming data flow improve consensus and communication challenges.

In short, seeking to understand the human and organizational factors that are part of this domain can help who glimmer the formation of an arrangement PIS/SoIS seek answers on how best to conduct activities, create arrangement running strategies, or even increase assertiveness in the search for potential IS candidates to compose an arrangement.

7 Final Remarks and Future Directions

This chapter present a study of influence factors for interoperability in PIS, considered as SoIS (PIS/SoIS), and also provides theoretical and practical implications considering their impact in decision-making processes. We selected 81 studies for discussion and from them we identified ten technical, human, and organizational influence factors that affect interoperability, which in turn impact the decision-making process in the PIS/SoIS domain. The systematic mapping studies (SMS) protocol is another contribution because researchers can benefit from a schema for a research wide-open field as interoperability. In addition, this SMS brings a set of papers about the understanding of interoperability and its impact in decision-making processes in PIS/SoIS. The state-of-art of interoperability is been widely addressed in literature given the wide range of studies retrieved in the first steps, in this case, researchers can also use this chapter to conduct a tertiary study about interoperability and decision-making based on the literature revised in this chapter. The main aspects we extract from this study are summarized in the following points:

- Interoperability in PIS/SoIS characterizes as a capability to seek the synergy among constituents to accomplish the PIS/SoIS main goal (and subgoals), while the constituent IS keep their operation for the fulfillment of their own individual goals;
- Dealing with a PIS/SoIS domain calls us to notice which technical, human, and organizational factors that can influence the design or analysis of interoperability given its business nature;
- Each choice of technology (technical factor) will bump into a human factor that is important in an intra/inter-organizational context (organizational factor);
- Who glimmer the formation of a PIS/SoIS is exposed to the need to join the requirements necessary to form an interoperated PIS/SoIS arrangement considering that some concerns also may be inherited from different organizational contexts;
- Interoperability and decision-making are closely linked in the PS/SoIS context. The focus is on the harmonization of business-strategies as well as the exchange and the visualization of information, data and knowledge. Several technical, human, and organizational factors influence interoperability, and hence, influence decision making processes.

The results of this extensive investigation bring some implications for researchers. As such, results may be affected by incompleteness of study search, bias on study selection, inaccuracy of data extraction and data synthesis, high amount of publications recovered. Nevertheless, these results provide some impressions and common aspects in the literature reviewed that can be a good input to continue the research in this direction. We deduce for example that the immediate future hold for practitioners to deal with interoperability in PIS/SoIS should consider that although each influence factor (IF) is grouped into three categories to answer research questions, these factors are not dissociated on interoperability in this domain. We are conducting the analysis and discussions around surveys with industry practitioners on the frequent challenges of interoperability in practice and what has been done to mitigate the problems faced. Knowing the influence factors for interoperability provide to team manager recommendations in favor of reasonable technology support. In this light, PIS/SoIS interoperability among managerial and operationally independent IS can be better designed to yield impactful solutions for emergency demands or optimized business goals, supported on improved decision-making processes.

Acknowledgments This study was financed in part by the Coordenação de Aperfeiçoamento de Pessoal de Nível Superior - Brasil (CAPES) - Finance Code 001 and FAPERJ (Proc. 211.583/2019).

References

Afonso, A.T.Q., Chueri, L.V., d. Santos, R.P.: Business process management in digital and software ecosystems: A systematic mapping study. In: IEEE Internat. Conf. on Software Architecture Companion, pp. 226–233 (2020)

Agostinho, C., Jardim-Goncalves, R.: Dynamic business networks: a headache for sustainable systems interoperability. In: OTM Confederated International Conferences" On the Move to Meaningful Internet Systems", pp. 194–204 (2009). Springer

Agostinho, C., Jardim-Goncalves, R.: Sustaining interoperability of networked liquid-sensing enterprises: A complex systems perspective. Annual Reviews in Control 39, 128–143 (2015)

Agostinho, C., Jardim-Gonçalves, R., Steiger-Garcao, A.: Using neighboring domains towards setting the foundations for enterprise interoperability science. In: Symp. on Collaborative Enterprises (2011)

Agostinho, C., Ducq, Y., Zacharewicz, G., Sarraipa, J., Lampathaki, F., Poler, R., Jardim-Goncalves, R.: Towards a sustainable interoperability in networked enterprise information systems: trends of knowledge and model-driven technology. Computers in industry 79, 64–76 (2016)

Ambrosio, R., Widergren, S.: A framework for addressing interoperability issues. In: Power Eng. Society General Meet., pp. 1–5 (2007)

Anderson, W.B., Boxer, P.J.: Modeling and analysis of interoperability risk in systems of systems environments. In: The Journal of Defense Software Engineering (2008)

Arakelian, M., Brown, A.N., Collins, A., Gatt, L., Hyde, S., Oketcho, V., Olum, S., Schurmann, A., Siyam, A.: Getting human resource information systems right: A case presentation of uganda (2022)

Athanasopoulos, G., Tsalgatidou, A., Pantazoglou, M.: Interoperability among heterogeneous services. In: IEEE Internat. Conf. on Services Computing, pp. 174–181 (2006)

Aubert, B., Vandenbosch, B., Mignerat, M.: Towards the measurement of process integration. Cahier du GReSI no **3**(06) (2003)

Barchetti, U., Guido, A.L., Mainetti, L.: A conceptual framework for business driven integration. In: Internat. Conf. for Internet Technology and Secured Transactions,(ICITST), pp. 1–6 (2009). IEEE

Basili, V.R.: Software modeling and measurement: the goal/question/-metric paradigm. Technical report (1992)

Benaben, F., Truptil, S., Mu, W., Pingaud, H., Touzi, J., Rajsiri, V., Lorre, J.-P.: Model-driven engineering of mediation information system for enterprise interoperability. Internat. Journal of Computer Integrated Manufacturing **31**(1), 27–48 (2018)

Bennaceur, A.: Dynamic synthesis of mediators in ubiquitous environments. PhD thesis, Université Pierre et Marie Curie-Paris VI (2013)

Bicocchi, N., Cabri, G., Mandreoli, F., Mecella, M.: Dealing with data and software interoperability issues in digital factories. In: Trans disciplinary Engineering Methods for Social Innovation of Industry 4.0, pp. 13–22. IOS Press, New York (2018)

Billaud, S., Daclin, N., Chapurlat, V.: Interoperability as a key concept for the control and evolution of the system of systems (sos). In: Internat. IFIP Working Conf. on Enterprise Interoperability, pp. 53–63 (2015)

Bittencourt, I.I., Costa, E., Braz, L., Pacheco, H., Dicheva, D.: Supporting interoperability between web-based educational systems. In: IEEE Frontiers in Education Conf., pp. 1–6 (2009)

Boardman, J., Sauser, B.: System of systems - the meaning of 'of'. In: Internat. Conf. on System of Systems Engineering, pp. 1–6. IEEE, Los Angeles, USA (2006)

Brown, A.: Human interoperability and building partnership capacities: Introduction to human interoperability. Human interoperability and netcentric series (2010)

Buhalis, D., Leung, R.: Smart hospitality—interconnectivity and interoperability towards an ecosystem. Internat. Journal of Hospitality Management 71, 41–50 (2018)

Busse, S., Kutsche, R.-D., Leser, U., Weber, H.: Federated information systems: Concepts, terminology and architectures. Forschungsberichte des Fachbereichs Informatik **99**(9), 1–38 (1999)

Cagnin, M.I., Nakagawa, E.Y.: Towards dynamic processes-of-business processes: a new understanding. Business Process Management Journal **27**(5), 1545–1568 (2021)

Camara, M., Ducq, Y., Dupas, R.: Methodology for prior evaluation of interoperability. In: Working Conf. on Virtual Enterprises, pp. 697–704 (2010). Springer

Chalmeta, R., Pazos, V.: A step-by-step methodology for enterprise interoperability projects. Enterprise Infor. Systems **9**(4), 436–464 (2015)

Chapurlat, V., Daclin, N.: System interoperability: definition and proposition of interface model in mbse context. IFAC Proceedings Volumes **45**(6), 1523–1528 (2012)

Chen, D., Doumeingts, G., Vernadat, F.: Architectures for enterprise integration and interoperability: Past, present and future. Computers in Industry **59**(7), 647–659 (2008)

Chen, D., Vallespir, B., Daclin, N.: An approach for enterprise interoperability measurement. In: Internat. Workshop on Model Driven Information Systems Engineering: Enterprise, User and System Models, vol. 341, pp. 1–12 (2008)

Chituc, C.-M., Azevedo, A., Toscano, C.: A framework proposal for seamless interoperability in a collaborative networked environment. Computers in industry **60**(5), 317–338 (2009)

Cloutier, R.J., NJ, H.: The Guide to the Systems Engineering Body of Knowledge (SEBoK), v. 1.9.1. BKCASE Editorial Board. https://www.sebokwiki.org/ (2017)

Corbin, J., Strauss, A.: Basics of Qualitative Research: Techniques and Procedures for Developing Grounded Theory. Sage publications, (2014)

Cornu, C., Chapurlat, V., Quiot, J.-M., Irigoin, F.: Interoperability assessment in the deployment of technical processes in industry. IFAC Proceedings Volumes **45**(6), 1246–1251 (2012)

Coutinho, C., Cretan, A., Da Silva, C.F., Ghodous, P., Jardim-Goncalves, R.: Service-based negotiation for advanced collaboration in enterprise networks. Journal of Intelligent Manufacturing **27**(1), 201–216 (2016)

Cuenca, L., Boza, A., Ortiz, A., Trienekens, J.J.: Conceptual interoperability barriers framework (CIBF). In: Internat. Conf. on Enterprise Information Systems, vol. 2, pp. 521–531 (2015)

Daclin, N., Chen, D., Vallespir, B.: Developing enterprise collaboration: a methodology to implement and improve interoperability. Enterprise Information Systems **10**(5), 467–504 (2016)

Deniaud, I., Quiguer, S., Breuil, D., Le Maguet, P., Lecourt, J., Pourcel, C., Ruault, J.-R., Somat, A.: Interoperability dimensions for multimodal mobility management. IFAC Proceedings Volumes **45**(6), 1529–1536 (2012)

Diallo, S.Y., Padilla, J.J., Tolk, A.: Why is interoperability bad: towards a paradigm shift in simulation composition. In: Fall Simulation Interoperability Workshop, pp. 20–24 (2010)

Dividino, R., Soares, A., Matwin, S., Isenor, A.W., Webb, S., Brousseau, M.: Semantic Integration of Real-time Heterogeneous Data Streams for Ocean-related Decision Making. STO, NATO/OTAN (2018)

Dolk, D., Anderson, T., Busalacchi, F., Tinsley, D.: Gina: System interoperability for enabling smart mobile system services in network decision support systems. In: Hawaii Internat. Conf. on System Sciences, pp. 1472–1481 (2012)

Espadinha-Cruz, P., Grilo, A.: The business interoperability decomposition framework to analyse buyer-supplier dyads. Computers in Industry 109, 165–181 (2019)

Fernandes, J.C., Neto, V.V.G., Santos, R.P.D.: Interoperability in systems-of-information systems: A systematic mapping study. In: Brazilian Symposium on Software Quality, pp. 131–140 (2018). ACM

Fernandes, J., Ferreira, F., Cordeiro, F., Graciano Neto, V.V., Pereira dos Santos, R.: A conceptual model for systems-of-information systems. In: IEEE Internat. Conf. on Information Reuse and Integration for Data Science, pp. 364–371 (2019)

Fernandes, J., Ferreira, F., Cordeiro, F., Graciano Neto, V.V., Santos, R.: How can interoperability approaches impact on systems-of-informationsystems characteristics? In: Brazilian Symposium on Information Systems (2020)

Ford, T.C., Colombi, J.M., Jacques, D.R., Graham, S.R.: A general method of measuring interoperability and describing its impact on operational effectiveness. The Journal of Defense Modeling and Simulation 6(1), 17–32 (2009)

Fouletier, P., Park, K.H., Favrel, J.: An inter-organizational information system design for virtual enterprises. In: IEEE Internat. Conf. on Emerging Technologies and Factory Automation, pp. 139–142 (1997)

Giachetti, R., Wangert, S., Eldred, R.: Interoperability analysis method for mission-oriented system of systems engineering. In: Internat. Systems Conf., pp. 1–6 (2019). IEEE

Guédria, W., Naudet, Y., Chen, D.: Maturity model for enterprise interoperability. Enterprise Information Systems 9(1), 1–28 (2015)

Handley, H.A.: A network model for human interoperability. Human factors 56(2), 349–360 (2014)

Hauser, M.M., Günther, S.A., Flath, C., Thiesse, F.: Designing pervasive information systems: A fashion retail case study. In: ICIS (2017)

Hevner, A.R., March, S.T., Park, J., Ram, S.: Design science in information systems research. Management Information Systems Quarterly 28(1), 6 (2008)

Hollenbach, J.W., Alexander, W.L.: Executing the dod modeling and simulation strategy—making simulation systems of systems a reality. In: Conf. on Winter Simulation, pp. 948–954 (1997)

House, A., Power, N., Alison, L.: A systematic review of the potential hurdles of interoperability to the emergency services in major incidents: recommendations for solutions and alternatives. Cognition, technology & work 16(3), 319–335 (2014)

IEEE: IEEE Standard Glossary of Software Engineering Terminology. IEEE Std 610.12-1990, 1–84 (1990)

Jamoussi, Y., Al-Khanjari, Z., Kraiem, N.: A guidance based approach for enhancing the e-government interoperability. Journal of Information and Organizational Sciences 41(1), 35–56 (2017)

Jardim-Goncalves, R., Steiger-Garcao, A., Agostinho, C.: Sustainable systems' interoperability: A reference model for seamless networked business. In: Internat. Conf. on Systems, Man and Cybernetics, pp. 1785–1792 (2010). IEEE

Jardim-Goncalves, R., Agostinho, C., Steiger-Garcao, A.: A reference model for sustainable interoperability in networked enterprises: towards the foundation of ei science base. Internat. Journal of Computer Integrated Manufacturing 25(10), 855–873 (2012)

Kalatzis, N., Routis, G., Marinellis, Y., Avgeris, M., Roussaki, I., Papavassiliou, S., Anagnostou, M.: Semantic interoperability for iot platforms in support of decision making: An experiment on early wildfire detection. Sensors 19(3) (2019)

Kazemzadeh, R.S., Sartipi, K., Jayaratna, P.: A framework for data and mined knowledge interoperability in clinical decision support systems. Int. J. Heal. Inf. Syst. Informatics 5, 37–60 (2010)

Kitchenham, B., Charters, S.: Guidelines for performing systematic literature reviews in software engineering 2 (2007)

Klischewski, R.: Architectures for tinkering? contextual strategies towards interoperability in e-government. Journal of theoretical and applied electronic commerce research 6(1), 26–42 (2011)

Kourouthanassis, P.E., Giaglis, G.M.: Pervasive Information Systems. ME Sharpe, New York (2008)

Kubicek, H., Cimander, R.: Three dimensions of organizational interoperability. European Journal of ePractice 6, 1–12 (2009)

Kuehn, A., Kaschewsky, M., Kappeler, A., Spichiger, A., Riedl, R.: Interoperability and information brokers in public safety: an approach toward seamless emergency communications. Journal of theoretical and applied electronic commerce research 6(1), 43–60 (2011)

Laudon, K.C., Laudon, J.P.: Information Systems and the Internet. Harcourt College Publishers, (1998)

Leal, G.: Decision support for interoperability readiness in networked enterprises. PhD thesis, Université de Lorraine (2019)

Lee, J.-C., Myers, M.: The challenges of enterprise integration: cycles of integration and disintegration over time. ICIS, 75 (2004)

Lewis, G.A., Morris, E., Simanta, S., Wrage, L.: Why standards are not enough to guarantee end-to-end interoperability. In: Internat. Conf. on Composition-Based Software Systems, pp. 164–173 (2008)

Li, W., Liu, K., Liu, S.: Semiotics in interoperation for information systems working collaboratively. In: Internat. Joint Conf. on Knowledge Discovery, Knowledge Engineering, and Knowledge Management, pp. 370–386 (2013). Springer

Lima, V.C., Bernardi, F.A., Domingues, M., Kritski, A.L., Rijo, R.P.C.L., Alves, D.: A computational infrastructure for semantic data integration towards a patient-centered database for tuberculosis care. Procedia Computer Science 196, 434–438 (2022)

Littlejohn, S.W., Foss, K.A.: Theories of Human Communication. Waveland press, New Mexico (2010)

Lueders, H.: Interoperability and open standards for egovernment services. In: 1st Intern. Conf. on Interoperability of Enterprise Software-Applications, Switzerland (2005)

Luz, P.B.V., Fernandes, J., Valença, G., Santos, R.P.d.: Exploring sustainability in real cases of emerging small-to-medium enterprises ecosystems. In: Santos, R.P.d., Maciel, C., Viterbo, J. (eds.) Software Ecosystems, Sustainability and Human Values in the Social Web, pp. 42–59. Springer, Cham (2020)

Maciel, R.S.P., David, J.M.N., Claro, D.B., Braga, R.: Full interoperability: Challenges and opportunities for future information systems. I GranDSI-BR, 107 (2017)

Mantzana, V., Koumaditis, K., Themistocleous, M.: Is soa a solution to healthcare information systems interoperability? In: Internat. Conf. on Information Technology and Applications in Biomedicine, pp. 1–4 (2010). IEEE

Marlowe, T., Jastroch, N., Nousala, S., Kirova, V.: Complex collaboration, knowledge sharing and interoperability. In: Internat. ICE Conf. on Engineering, Technology and Innovation, pp. 1–10 (2012). IEEE

Mazzetti, P., Nativi, S.: Multidisciplinary interoperability for earth observations: some architectural issues. Journal of Selected Topics in Applied Earth Observations and Remote Sensing 5(3), 1054–1059 (2012)

Mazzetti, P., Nativi, S., Santoro, M., Giuliani, G., Rodila, D., Folino, A., Caruso, S., Aracri, G., Lehmann, A.: Knowledge formalization for earth science informed decision-making: The geoessential knowledge base. Environmental Science & Policy 131, 93–104 (2022)

Mendes, A., Loss, S., Cavalcante, E., Lopes, F., Batista, T.: Mandala: an agent-based platform to support interoperability in systems-of-systems. In: Internat. Workshop on Software Engineering for Systems-of-Systems, pp. 21–28 (2018)

Mills, J.A., Ruston, L.: The osca architecture: enabling independent product software maintenance. In: EUROMICRO Workshop on Real Time, pp. 64–70 (1990)

Mordecai, Y., Orhof, O., Dori, D.: Model-based interoperability engineering in systems-of-systems and civil aviation. IEEE Transactions on Systems, Man, and Cybernetics: Systems 48(4), 637–648 (2016)

Motta, R.C., De Oliveira, K.M., Travassos, G.H.: Rethinking interoperability in contemporary software systems. In: Joint Internat. Workshop on Software Engineering for Systems-of-Systems and Workshop on Distributed Software Development, Software Ecosystems and Systemsof-Systems, pp. 9–15 (2017). IEEE

Muller, G.: 3.1. 2 interoperability: a reliability challenge across systems and humans; illustrated by health care examples. In: INCOSE Internat. Symposium, vol. 19, pp. 368–377 (2009). Wiley Online Library

Najar, S., Pinheiro, M.K., Le Grand, B., Souveyet, C.: A user-centric vision of service-oriented pervasive information systems. In: Internat. Conf. on Research Challenges in Informat. Sc., pp. 1–12 (2014). IEEE

A systemic approach to interoperability formalization. IFAC Proceedings Volumes **41**(2), 11925–11930 (2008)

Naudet, Y., Latour, T., Guedria, W., Chen, D.: Towards a systemic formalisation of interoperability. Computers in Industry **61**(2), 176–185 (2010)

Navigli, R., Velardi, P.: Automatic acquisition of a thesaurus of interoperability terms. IFAC Proceedings Volumes **38**(1), 100–105 (2005)

Neaga, E.I., Henshaw, M.J.D.C.: Modeling the linkage between systems interoperability and security engineering. In: Internat. Conf. on System of Systems Engineering, pp. 1–6 (2010). IEEE

Neto, V.V.G., Oquendo, F., Nakagawa, E.Y.: Smart systems-ofinformation systems: Foundations and an assessment model for research development. Grand Research Challenges in Information Systems in Brazil 2016 - 2026 10, 1–12 (2017)

Ostadzadeh, S.S., Shams, F., Badie, K.: An architectural model framework to improve digital ecosystems interoperability. In: New Trends in Networking, Computing, E-learning, Systems Sciences, and Engineering, pp. 513–520. Springer, CHAM (2015)

Papageorgiou, A., Ölvander, J., Amadori, K., Jouannet, C.: Development of analysis and simulation models for evaluating airborne radar surveillance system of systems. In: AIAA Scitech Forum, p. 0303 (2021)

Pavlou, P., Singletary, L.: Empirical study of stakeholders perceived benefits of integration attributes for enterprise it applications. AMCIS, 358 (2002)

Perrone, V., Finkelstein, A.: Analyzing requirements for a large scale system for cancer research. In: IEEE Internat. Symposium on Computer-Based Medical Systems, pp. 103–108 (2007)

Pyarelal, S.: Interoperability framework for e-governance (ifeg)-strategic approach to evolve national standards. (2004). Informatics

Qureshi, N.A., Nguyen, C.D., Perini, A.: Analyzing interoperability requirements for adaptive service-based applications: A goal-oriented approach. In: Annual Computer Software and Applications Conf. Workshops, pp. 239–244 (2010). IEEE

Raychoudhury, V., Cao, J., Kumar, M., Zhang, D.: Middleware for pervasive computing: A survey. Pervasive and Mobile Computing **9**(2), 177–200 (2013)

Rezaei, R., Chiew, T.K., Lee, S.P.: A review on e-business interoperability frameworks. Journal of Systems and Software 93, 199–216 (2014)

Rhodes, C.J., Wilson, G.B.: Interoperability problems-prevention is better than cure. In: Internat. Conf. on Information-Decision-Action Systems in Complex Organisations, pp. 138–142 (1992)

Rosener, V., Latour, T., Dubois, E.: A model-based ontology of the software interoperability problem: Preliminary results. In: Grundspenkis, J., Kirikova, M. (eds.) CAiSE Workshops, pp. 241–252 (2004)

Salado, A.: Abandonment: A natural consequence of autonomy and belonging in systems-of-systems. In: 10th System of Systems Engineering Conf., pp. 352–357 (2015)

Saleh, M., Abel, M.-H., Mishra, A.: An architectural model for system of information systems. In: Internat. Workshop on Information Systems in Distributed Environment, vol. 9416, pp. 411–420 (2015)

Soares, D.D.S., Amaral, L.: Reflections on the concept of interoperability in information systems. Internat. Conf. on Enterprise Information Systems, 331–339 (2014)

Sobkowski, I., Freedman, R.S.: The evolution of worker connect: A case study of a system of systems. Journal of Technology in Human Services **31**(2), 129–155 (2013)

Song, F., Zacharewicz, G., Chen, D.: An architecture for interoperability of enterprise information systems based on soa and semantic web technologies. In: Internat. Conf. on Enterprise Information Systems, vol. 4, pp. 431–437 (2011)

Teixeira, G., Lopes, V.H.L., Santos, R.P., Kassab, M., Graciano Neto, V.V.: The status quo of systems-of-information systems. In: SESoS/WDES (2019)

TOUZI, J., BENABEN, F., PINGAUD, H.: Model transformation of collaborative business process into mediation information system. IFAC Proceedings Volumes **41**(2), 13857–13862 (2008)

Tripathi, R., Gupta, M., Bhattacharya, J.: Effect of organizational factors on interoperability adoption for indian portals. Transforming Government: People, Process and Policy (2013)

Ullberg, J., Chen, D., Johnson, P.: Barriers to enterprise interoperability. In: IFIP-International Workshop on Enterprise Interoperability, pp. 13–24 (2009). Springer

Ullberg, J., Johnson, P., Buschle, M.: A language for interoperability modeling and prediction. Computers in Industry **63**(8), 766–774 (2012)

Vargas, I.G., Gottardi, T., Braga, R.T.V.: An approach to integrate systems towards a directed system-of-systems. In: European Conf. onSoftware Architecture: Companion Proceedings, pp. 1–7 (2018)

Wang, W., Tolk, A., Wang, W.: The levels of conceptual interoperability model: applying systems engineering principles to M&S. arXiv preprint arXiv:0908.0191 (2009)

Wang, Y., Zhang, J., Wang, J., Chong, X.: Inter-organization collaboration management in dynamic virtual alliances. In: Internat. Conf. on E-Business and E-Government, pp. 42–45 (2010). IEEE

Weichhart, G., Guédria, W., Naudet, Y.: Supporting interoperability in complex adaptive enterprise systems: A domain specific language approach. Data & Knowledge Engineering 105, 90–106 (2016)

Whitman, L.E., Panetto, H.: The missing link: Culture and language barriers to interoperability. Annual Reviews in Control **30**(2), 233–241 (2006)

Widergren, S., Levinson, A., Mater, J., Drummond, R.: Smart grid interoperability maturity model. In: PES General Meet., pp. 1–6 (2010)

Wohlin, C.: Guidelines for snowballing in systematic literature studies and a replication in software engineering. In: Internat. Conf. on Evaluation and Assessment in Software Engineering. Association for Computing Machinery, New York, NY, USA (2014)

Yaacoubi, A.N., Pollet, Y., Ben, A.M.: Formal framework for semantic interoperability. In: Internat. Conf. on Software and Data Technologies, pp. 139–144 (2006)

Yahia, E., Bigand, M., Bourey, J.-P., Castelain, E.: Supply chain business patterns definition for process interoperability. IFAC Proceedings Volumes **42**(4), 169–174 (2009)

Zacharewicz, G., Diallo, S., Ducq, Y., Agostinho, C., Jardim-Goncalves, R., Bazoun, H., Wang, Z., Doumeingts, G.: Model-based approaches for interoperability of next generation enterprise information systems: state of the art and future challenges. Information Systems and e-Business Management **15**(2), 229–256 (2017)

Zarour, K., Zarour, N., Charrel, P.-J.: Towards enhancing interoperability in medical information systems. In: Internat. Symposium on Health Informatics and Bioinformatics, pp. 16–21 (2011). IEEE

Zdravković, M., Luis-Ferreira, F., Jardim-Goncalves, R., Trajanović, M.: On the formal definition of the systems' interoperability capability: an anthropomorphic approach. Enterprise Information Systems **11**(3), 389–413 (2017)

Zeinali, N., Asosheh, A., Setareh, S.: The conceptual model to solve the problem of interoperability in health information systems. In: Internat. Symposium on Telecommunications, pp. 684–689 (2016). IEEE

Correction to: PIS: Interoperability and Decision-Making Process—A Review

Juliana Fernandes, Lucas Oliveira, Valdemar Vicente Graciano Neto,
Rodrigo Pereira dos Santos, Rafael Angarita, Sonia Guehis,
and Yudith Cardinale

Correction to:
Chapter 7 in: M. Kirsch Pinheiro et al. (eds.),
The Evolution of Pervasive Information Systems,
https://doi.org/10.1007/978-3-031-18176-4_7

The original version of this chapter was inadvertently published with the incorrect spelling of the author as Rodrigo Pereirados Santos in the online version of this book. This has now been corrected as Dr. Rodrigo Pereira dos Santos.

The updated original version of this chapter can be found at
https://doi.org/10.1007/978-3-031-18176-4_7

Printed in the United States
by Baker & Taylor Publisher Services